Martin Luther's Recycle Bin

A Collection of Sacred Books
Missing from the Protestant Bible

Compiled and arranged by
Ann Mary O'Donnell

Holy Scripture taken from the
Douay-Rheims translation of the
Bible from the Latin Vulgate into English

NATAL PUBLISHING LLC
ARS LONGA, VITA BREVIS

Genesis
Exodus
Leviticus
Numbers
Deuteronomy
Josue (or Joshua)
Judges
Ruth
1 Kings (or 1 Samuel)
2 Kings (or 2 Samuel)
3 Kings (or 1 Kings)
4 Kings (or 2 Kings)
1 Paralipomenon (or 1 Chronicles)
2 Paralipomenon (or 2 Chronicles)
1 Esdras (or Ezra)
2 Esdras (or Nehemiah)
Tobias (or Tobit)
Judith
Esther
Job
Psalms
Proverbs
Ecclesiastes
Canticles (or Song of Solomon)
Wisdom
Ecclesiasticus (or Sirach)
Isaias (or Isaiah)
Jeremias (or Jeremiah)
Lamentations
Baruch
Ezechiel (or Ezekiel)
Daniel
Osee (or Hosea)
Joel
Amos
Abdias (or Obadiah)
Jonas (or Jonah)
Micheas (or Micah)
Nahum
Habacuc (or Habakkuk)
Sophonias (or Zephaniah)
Aggeus (or Haggai)
Zacharias (or Zechariah)
Malachias (or Malachi)
1 Machabees
2 Machabees

THE BOOK OF TOBIAS (TOBIT)

Chapter 1

1 Tobias of the tribe and city of Nephtali, (which is in the upper parts of Galilee above Naasson, beyond the way that leadeth to the west, having on the right hand the city of Sephet,) **2** When he was made captive in the days of Salmanasar king of the Assyrians, even in his captivity, forsook not the way of truth, **3** But every day gave all he could get to his brethren his fellow captives, that were of his kindred. **4** And when he was younger than any of the tribe of Nephtali, yet did he no childish thing in his work. **5** Moreover when all went to the golden calves which Jeroboam king of Israel had made, he alone fled the company of all,

6 And went to Jerusalem to the temple of the Lord, and there adored the Lord God of Israel, offering faithfully all his firstfruits, and his tithes, **7** So that in the third year he gave all his tithes to the proselytes, and strangers. **8** These and such like things did he observe when but a boy according to the law of God. **9** But when he was a man, he took to wife Anna of his own tribe, and had a son by her, whom he called after his own name, **10** And from his infancy he taught him to fear God, and to abstain from all sin.

11 And when by the captivity he with his wife and his son and all his tribe was come to the city of Ninive, **12** (When all ate of the meats of the Gentiles) he kept his soul and never was defiled with their meats. **13** And because he was mindful of the Lord with all his heart, God gave him favour in the sight of Salmanasar the king. **14** And he gave him leave to go whithersoever he would, with liberty to do whatever he had a mind. **15** He therefore went to all that were in captivity, and gave them wholesome admonitions.

16 And when he was come to Rages a city of the Medes, and had ten talents of silver of that with which he had been honoured by the king: **17** And when amongst a great multitude of his kindred, he saw Gabelus in want, who was one of his tribe, taking a note of his hand he gave him the aforesaid sum of money. **18** But after a long time, Salmanasar the king being dead, when Sennacherib his son, who reigned in his place, had a hatred for the children of Israel: **19** Tobias daily went among all his kindred, and comforted them, and distributed to every one as he was able, out of his goods: **20** He fed the hungry, and gave clothes to the naked, and was careful to bury the dead, and they that were slain.

21 And when king Sennacherib was come back, fleeing from Judea by reason of the slaughter that God had made about him for his blasphemy, and being angry slew many of the children of Israel, Tobias buried their bodies. **22** But when it was told the king, he commanded him to be slain, and took away all his substance. **23** But Tobias fleeing naked away with his son and with his wife, lay concealed, for many loved him. **24** But after forty-five days, the king was killed by his own sons. **25** And Tobias returned to his house, and all his substance was restored to him.

Chapter 2

1 But after this, when there was a festival of the Lord, and a good dinner was prepared in Tobias's house, **2** He said to his son: Go, and bring some of our tribe that fear God, to feast with us. **3** And when he had gone, returning he told him, that one of the children of Israel lay slain in the street. And he forthwith leaped up from his place at the table, and left his dinner, and came fasting to the body: **4** And taking it up carried it privately to his house, that after the sun was down, he might bury him cautiously. **5** And when he had hid the body, he ate bread with mourning and fear,

6 Remembering the word which the Lord spoke by Amos the prophet: Your festival days shall be turned into lamentation and mourning. **7** So when the sun was down, he went and buried him. **8** Now all his neighbours blamed him, saying: Once already commandment was given for thee to be slain because of this matter, and thou didst scarce escape the sentence of death, and dost thou again bury the dead? **9** But Tobias fearing God more than the king, carried off the bodies of them that were slain, and hid them in his house, and at midnight buried them. **10** Now it happened one day, that being wearied with burying, he came to his house, and cast himself down by the wall and slept,

11 And as he was sleeping, hot dung out of a swallow's nest fell upon his eyes, and he was made blind. **12** Now this trial the Lord therefore permitted to happen to him, that an example might be given to posterity of his patience, as also of holy Job. **13** For whereas he had always feared God from his infancy, and kept his commandments, he repined not against God because the evil of blindness had befallen him, **14** But continued immoveable in the fear of God, giving thanks to God all the days of his life. **15** For as the kings [territorial governors] insulted over holy Job: so his relations and kinsmen mocked at his life, saying:

16 Where is thy hope, for which thou gavest alms, and buriedst the dead? **17** But Tobias rebuked them, saying: Speak not so: **18** For we are the children of the saints, and look for that life which God will give to those that never change their faith from him. **19** Now Anna his wife went daily to weaving work, and she brought home what she could get for their living by the labour of her hands. **20** Whereby it came to pass, that she received a young kid, and brought it home:

21 And when her husband heard it bleating, he said: Take heed, lest perhaps it be stolen: restore ye it to its owners, for it is not lawful for us either to eat or to touch any thing that cometh by theft. **22** At these words his wife being angry answered: It is evident thy hope is come to nothing, and thy alms now appear. **23** And with these, and other such like words she upbraided him.

Chapter 3

1 Then Tobias sighed, and began to pray with tears, **2** Saying: Thou art just, O Lord, and all thy judgments are just, and all thy ways mercy, and truth, and judgment: **3** And now, O Lord, think of me, and take not revenge of my sins, neither remember my offenses, nor those of my parents. **4** For we have not obeyed thy commandments, therefore are we delivered to spoil and to captivity, and death, and are made a fable, and a reproach to all nations, amongst which thou hast scattered us. **5** And now, O Lord, great are thy judgments, because we have not done according to thy precepts, and have not walked sincerely before thee:

6 And now, O Lord, do with me according to thy will, and command my spirit to be received in peace: for it is better for me to die, than to live. **7** Now it happened on the same day, that Sara daughter of Raguel, in Rages a city of the Medes, received a reproach from one of her father's servant maids, **8** Because she had been given to seven husbands, and a devil named Asmodeus had killed them, at their first going in unto her. **9** So when she reproved the maid for her fault, she answered her, saying: May we never see son, or daughter of thee upon the earth, thou murderer of thy husbands. **10** Wilt thou kill me also, as thou hast already killed seven husbands? At these words she went into an upper chamber of her house: and for three days and three nights did neither eat nor drink:

11 But continuing in prayer with tears besought God, that he would deliver her from this reproach. **12** And it came to pass on the third day, when she was making an end of her prayer, blessing the Lord, **13** She said: Blessed is thy name, O God of our fathers: who when thou hast been angry, wilt shew mercy, and in the time of tribulation forgivest the sins of them that call upon thee. **14** To thee, O Lord, I turn my face, to thee I direct my eyes. **15** I beg, O Lord, that thou loose me from the bond of this reproach, or else take me away from the earth.

16 Thou knowest, O Lord, that I never coveted a husband, and have kept my soul clean from all lust. **17** Never have I joined myself with them that play: neither have I made myself partaker with them that walk in lightness. **18** But a husband I consented to take, with thy fear, not with my lust. **19** And either I was unworthy of them, or they perhaps were not worthy of me: because perhaps thou hast kept me for another man. **20** For thy counsel is not in man's power.

21 But this every one is sure of that worshippeth thee, that his life, if it be under trial, shall be crowned: and if it be under tribulation, it shall be delivered: and if it be under correction, it shall be allowed to come to thy mercy. **22** For thou art not delighted in our being lost: because after a storm thou makest a calm, and after tears and weeping thou pourest in joyfulness. **23** Be thy name, O God of Israel, blessed forever. **24** At that time the prayers of them both were heard in the sight of the glory of the most high God: **25** And the holy angel of the Lord, Raphael was sent to heal them both, whose prayers at one time were rehearsed in the sight of the Lord.

Chapter 4

1 Therefore when Tobias thought that his prayer was heard that he might die, he called to him Tobias his son, **2** And said to him: Hear, my son, the words of my mouth, and lay them as a foundation in thy heart. **3** When God shall take my soul, thou shalt bury my body: and thou shalt honour thy mother all the days of her life: **4** For thou must be mindful what and how great perils she suffered for thee in her womb. **5** And when she also shall have ended the time of her life, bury her by me.

6 And all the days of thy life have God in thy mind: and take heed thou never consent to sin, nor transgress the commandments of the Lord our God. **7** Give alms out of thy substance, and turn not away thy face from any poor person: for so it shall come to pass that the face of the Lord shall not be turned from thee. **8** According to thy ability be merciful. **9** If thou have much give abundantly: if thou have a little, take care even so to bestow willingly a little. **10** For thus thou storest up to thyself a good reward for the day of necessity.

11 For alms deliver from all sin, and from death, and will not suffer the soul to go into darkness. **12** Alms shall be a great confidence before the most high God, to all them that give it. **13** Take heed to keep thyself, my son, from all fornication, and beside thy wife never endure to know a crime. **14** Never suffer pride to reign in thy mind, or in thy words: for from it all perdition took its beginning. **15** If any man hath done any work for thee, immediately pay him his hire, and let not the wages of thy hired servant stay with thee at all.

16 See thou never do to another what thou wouldst hate to have done to thee by another. **17** Eat thy bread with the hungry and the needy, and with thy garments cover the naked. **18** Lay out thy bread, and thy wine upon the burial of a just man, and do not eat and drink thereof with the wicked. **19** Seek counsel always of a wise man. **20** Bless God at all times: and desire of him to direct thy ways, and that all thy counsels may abide in him.

21 I tell thee also, my son, that I lent ten talents of silver, while thou wast yet a child, to Gabelus, in Rages a city of the Medes, and I have a note of his hand with me: **22** Now therefore inquire how thou mayst go to him, and receive of him the foresaid sum of money, and restore to him the note of his hand. **23** Fear not, my son: we lead indeed a poor life, but we shall have many good things if we fear God, and depart from all sin, and do that which is good.

Chapter 5

1 Then Tobias answered his father, and said: I will do all things, father, which thou hast commanded me. **2** But how I shall get this money, I cannot tell; he knoweth me not, and I know not him: what token shall I give him? nor did I ever know the way which leadeth thither. **3** Then his father answered him, and said: I have a note of his hand with me, which when thou shalt shew him, he will presently pay it. **4** But go now, and seek thee out some faithful man, to go with thee for his hire: that thou mayst receive it, while I yet live. **5** Then Tobias going forth, found a beautiful young man, standing girded, and as it were ready to walk.

6 And not knowing that he was an angel of God, he saluted him, and said: From whence art thou, good young man? **7** But he answered: Of the children of Israel. And Tobias said to him: Knowest thou the way that leadeth to the country of the Medes? **8** And he answered: I know it: and I have often walked through all the ways thereof, and I have abode with Gabelus our brother, who dwelleth at Rages a city of the Medes, which is situate in the mount of Ecbatana. **9** And Tobias said to him: Stay for me, I beseech thee, till I tell these same things to my father. **10** Then Tobias going in told all these things to his father. Upon which his father being in admiration, desired that he would come in unto him.

11 So going in he saluted him, and said: Joy be to thee always. **12** And Tobias said: What manner of joy shall be to me, who sit in darkness, and see not the light of heaven? **13** And the young man said to him: Be of good courage, thy cure from God is at hand. **14** And Tobias said to him: Canst thou conduct my son to

Gabelus at Rages, a city of the Medes? and when thou shalt return, I will pay thee thy hire. **15** And the angel said to him: I will conduct him thither, and bring him back to thee.

16 And Tobias said to him: I pray thee, tell me, of what family, or what tribe art thou? **17** And Raphael the angel answered: Dost thou seek the family of him thou hirest, or the hired servant himself to go with thy son? **18** But lest I should make thee uneasy, I am *Azarias* the son of the great Ananias. [This was the name of the man whom the angel was impersonating. In Hebrew, the name signifies "help of God."] **19** And Tobias answered: Thou art of a great family. But I pray thee be not angry that I desired to know thy family. **20** And the angel said to him: I will lead thy son safe, and bring him to thee again safe.

21 And Tobias answering, said: May you have a good journey, and God be with you in your way, and his angel accompany you. **22** Then all things being ready, that were to be carried in their journey, Tobias bade his father and his mother farewell, and they set out both together. **23** And when they were departed, his mother began to weep, and to say: Thou hast taken the staff of our old age, and sent him away from us. **24** I wish the money for which thou hast sent him, had never been. **25** For poverty was sufficient for us, that we might account it as riches, that we saw our son.

26 And Tobias said to her: Weep not, our son will arrive thither safe, and will return safe to us, and thy eyes shall see him. **27** For I believe that the good angel of God doth accompany him, and doth order all things well that are done about him, so that he shall return to us with joy. **28** At these words his mother ceased weeping, and held her peace.

Chapter 6

1 And Tobias went forward, and the dog followed him, and he lodged the first night by the river of Tigris. **2** And he went out to wash his feet, and behold a monstrous fish came up to devour him. **3** And Tobias being afraid of him, cried out with a loud voice, saying: Sir, he cometh upon me. **4** And the angel said to him: Take him by the gill, and draw him to thee. And when he had done so, he drew him out upon the land, and he began to pant before his feet. **5** Then the angel said to him: Take out the entrails of the fish, and lay up his heart, and his gall, and his liver for thee: for these are necessary for useful medicines.

6 And when he had done so, he roasted the flesh thereof, and they took it with them in the way: the rest they salted as much as might serve them, till they came to Rages the city of the Medes. **7** Then Tobias asked the angel, and said to him: I beseech thee, brother Azarias, tell me what remedies are these things good for, which thou hast bid me keep of the fish? **8** And the angel, answering, said to him: If thou put a little piece of its heart [the liver] upon coals, the smoke thereof driveth away all kind of devils, either from man or from woman, so that they come no more to them. **9** And the gall is good for anointing the eyes, in which there is a white speck, and they shall be cured. **10** And Tobias said to him: Where wilt thou that we lodge?

11 And the angel answering, said: Here is one whose name is Raguel, a near kinsman of thy tribe, and he hath a daughter named Sara, but he hath no son nor any other daughter beside her. **12** All his substance is due to thee, and thou must take her to wife. **13** Ask her therefore of her father, and he will give her thee to wife. **14** Then Tobias answered, and said: I hear that she hath been given to seven husbands, and they all died: moreover I have heard, that a devil killed them. **15** Now I am afraid, lest the same thing should happen to me also: and whereas I am the only child of my parents, I should bring down their old age with sorrow to hell [limbo].

16 Then the angel Raphael said to him: Hear me, and I will shew thee who they are, over whom the devil can prevail. **17** For they who in such manner receive matrimony, as to shut out God from themselves, and from their mind, and to give themselves to their lust, as the horse and mule, which have not understanding, over them the devil hath power. **18** But thou when thou shalt take her, go into the chamber, and for three days keep thyself continent from her, and give thyself to nothing else but to prayers with her. **19** And on that night lay the liver of the fish on the fire, and the devil shall be driven away. **20** But the second night thou shalt be admitted into the society of the holy Patriarchs.

21 And the third night thou shalt obtain a blessing that sound children may be born of you. **22** And when the third night is past, thou shalt take the virgin with the fear of the Lord, moved rather for love of children than for lust, that in the seed of Abraham thou mayst obtain a blessing in children.

Chapter 7

1 And they went in to Raguel, and Raguel received them with joy. **2** And Raguel looking upon Tobias, said to Anna his wife: How like is this young man to my cousin? **3** And when he had spoken these words, he said: Whence are ye young men our brethren? **4** But they said: We are of the tribe of Nephtali, of the captivity of Ninive. **5** And Raguel said to them: Do you know Tobias my brother? And they said: We know him.

6 And when he was speaking many good things of him, the angel said to Raguel: Tobias concerning whom thou inquirest is this young man's father. **7** And Raguel went to him, and kissed him with tears, and weeping upon his neck, said: A blessing be upon thee, my son, because thou art the son of a good and most virtuous man. **8** And Anna his wife, and Sara their daughter wept. **9** And after they had spoken, Raguel commanded a sheep to be killed, and a feast to be prepared. And when he desired them to sit down to dinner, **10** Tobias said: I will not eat nor drink here this day, unless thou first grant me my petition, and promise to give me Sara thy daughter.

11 Now when Raguel heard this he was afraid, knowing what had happened to those seven husbands, that went in unto her: and he began to fear lest it might happen to him also in like manner: and as he was in suspense, and gave no answer to his petition, **12** The angel said to him: Be not afraid to give her to this man, for to him who feareth God is thy daughter due to be his wife: therefore another could not have her. **13** Then Raguel said: I doubt not but God hath regarded my prayers and tears in his sight. **14** And I believe he hath therefore made you come to me, that this maid might be married to one of her own kindred, according to the law of Moses: and now doubt not but I will give her to thee. **15** And taking the right hand of his daughter, he gave it into the right hand of Tobias, saying: The God of Abraham, and the God of Isaac, and the God of Jacob be with you, and may he join you together, and fulfill his blessing in you.

16 And taking paper they made a writing of the marriage. **17** And afterwards they made merry, blessing God. **18** And Raguel called to him Anna his wife, and bade her prepare another chamber. **19** And she brought Sara her daughter in thither, and she wept. **20** And she said to her: Be of good cheer, my daughter: the Lord of heaven give thee joy for the trouble thou hast undergone.

Chapter 8

1 And after they had supped, they brought in the young man to her. **2** And Tobias remembering the angel's word, took out of his bag part of the liver, and laid it upon burning coals. **3** Then the angel Raphael took the devil, and bound him in the desert of upper Egypt. **4** Then Tobias exhorted the virgin, and said to her: Sara, arise, and let us pray to God today, and tomorrow, and the next day: because for these three nights we are joined to God: and when the third night is over, we will be in our own wedlock. **5** For we are the children of saints, and we must not be joined together like heathens that know not God.

6 So they both arose, and prayed earnestly both together that health might be given them, **7** And Tobias said: Lord God of our father, may the heavens and the earth, and the sea, and the fountains, and the rivers, and all thy creatures that are in them, bless thee. **8** Thou madest Adam of the slime of the earth, and gavest him Eve for a helper. **9** And now, Lord, thou knowest, that not for fleshly lust do I take my sister to wife, but only for the love of posterity, in which thy name may be blessed for ever and ever. **10** Sara also said: Have mercy on us, O Lord, have mercy on us, and let us grow old both together in health.

11 And it came to pass about the cockcrowing, Raguel ordered his servants to be called for, and they went with him together to dig a grave. **12** For he said: Lest perhaps it may have happened to him, in like manner as it did to the other seven husbands, that went in unto her. **13** And when they had prepared the pit, Raguel went back to his wife, and said to her: **14** Send one of thy maids, and let her see if he be dead, that I may bury him before it be day. **15** So she sent one of her maidservants, who went into the chamber, and found them safe and sound, sleeping both together.

16 And returning she brought the good news: and Raguel and Anna his wife blessed the Lord, **17** And said: We bless thee, O Lord God of Israel, because it hath not happened as we suspected. **18** For thou hast shewn thy mercy to us, and hast shut out from us the enemy that persecuted us. **19** And thou hast taken pity upon two only children. Make them, O Lord, bless thee more fully: and to offer up to thee a sacrifice of thy praise, and of their health, that all nations may know, that thou alone art God in all the earth. **20** And immediately Raguel commanded his servants, to fill up the pit they had made, before it was day.

21 And he spoke to his wife to make ready a feast, and prepare all kind of provisions that are necessary for such as go a journey. **22** He caused also two fat kine, and four wethers to be killed, and a banquet to be prepared for all his neighbours, and all his friends. **23** And Raguel adjured Tobias, to abide with him two weeks. **24** And of all things which Raguel possessed, he gave one half to Tobias, and made him a writing, that the half that remained should after their decease come also to Tobias.

Chapter 9

1 Then Tobias called the angel to him, whom he took to be a man, and said to him: Brother Azarias, I pray thee hearken to my words: **2** If I should give myself to be thy servant I should not make a worthy return for thy care. **3** However, I beseech thee, to take with thee beasts and servants, and to go to Gabelus to Rages the city of the Medes: and to restore to him his note of hand, and receive of him the money, and desire him to come to my wedding. **4** For thou knowest that my father numbereth the days: and if I stay one day more, his soul will be afflicted. **5** And indeed thou seest how Raguel hath adjured me, whose adjuring I cannot despise.

6 Then Raphael took four of Raguel's servants, and two camels, and went to Rages the city of the Medes: and finding Gabelus, gave him his note of hand, and received of him all the money. **7** And he told him concerning Tobias the son of Tobias, all that had been done: and made him come with him to the wedding. **8** And when he was come into Raguel's house he found Tobias sitting at the table: and he leaped up, and they kissed each other: and Gabelus wept, and blessed God, **9** And said: The God of Israel bless thee, because thou art the son of a very good and just man, and that feareth God, and doth almsdeeds: **10** And may a blessing come upon thy wife and upon your parents.

11 And may you see your children, and your children's children, unto the third and fourth generation: and may your seed be blessed by the God of Israel, who reigneth for ever and ever. **12** And when all had said, Amen, they went to the feast: but the marriage feast they celebrated also with the fear of the Lord.

Chapter 10

1 But as Tobias made longer stay upon occasion of the marriage, Tobias his father was solicitous, saying: Why thinkest thou doth my son tarry, or why is he detained there? **2** Is Gabelus dead, thinkest thou, and no man will pay him the money? **3** And he began to be exceeding sad, both he and Anna his wife with him: and they began both to weep together: because their son did not return to them on the day appointed. **4** But his mother wept and was quite disconsolate, and said: Woe, woe is me, my son; why did we send thee to go to a strange country, the light of our eyes, the staff of our old age, the comfort of our life, the hope of our posterity? **5** We having all things together in thee alone, ought not to have let thee go from us.

6 And Tobias said to her: Hold thy peace, and be not troubled, our son is safe: that man with whom we sent him is very trusty. **7** But she could by no means be comforted, but daily running out looked round about, and went into all the ways by which there seemed any hope he might return, that she might if possible see him coming afar off. **8** But Raguel said to his son in law: Stay here, and I will send a messenger to Tobias thy father, that thou art in health. **9** And Tobias said to him: I know that my father and mother now count the days, and their spirit is grievously afflicted within them. **10** And when Raguel had pressed Tobias with many words, and he by no means would hearken to him, he delivered Sara unto him, and half of all his substance in menservants, and women-servants, in cattle, in camels, and in kine, and in much money, and sent him away safe and joyful from him.

11 Saying: The holy angel of the Lord be with you in your journey, and bring you through safe, and that you may find all things well about your parents, and my eyes see your children before I die. **12** And the parents taking their daughter kissed her, and let her go: **13** Admonishing her to honour her father and mother in law, to love her husband, to take care of the family, to govern the house, and to behave herself irreprehensibly.

Chapter 11

1 And as they were returning they came to Charan, which is in the midway to Ninive, the eleventh day. **2** And the angel said: Brother Tobias, thou knowest how thou didst leave thy father. **3** If it please thee therefore, let us go before, and let the family follow softly after us, together with thy wife, and with the beasts. **4** And as this their going pleased him, Raphael said to Tobias: Take with thee of the gall of the fish, for it will be necessary. So Tobias took some of that gall and departed. **5** But Anna sat beside the way daily, on the top of a hill, from whence she might see afar off.

6 And while she watched his coming from that place, she saw him afar off, and presently perceived it was her son coming: and returning she told her husband, saying: Behold thy son cometh. **7** And Raphael said to Tobias: As soon as thou shalt come into thy house, forthwith adore the Lord thy God: and giving thanks to him, go to thy father, and kiss him. **8** And immediately anoint his eyes with this gall of the fish, which thou carriest with thee. For be assured that his eyes shall be presently opened, and thy father shall see the light of heaven, and shall rejoice in the sight of thee. **9** Then the dog, which had been with them in the way, ran before, and coming as if he had brought the news, shewed his joy by his fawning and wagging his tail. **10** And his father that was blind, rising up, began to run stumbling with his feet: and giving a servant his hand, went to meet his son.

11 And receiving him kissed him, as did also his wife, and they began to weep for joy. **12** And when they had adored God, and given him thanks, they sat down together. **13** Then Tobias taking of the gall of the fish, anointed his father's eyes. **14** And he stayed about half an hour: and a white skin began to come out of his eyes, like the skin of an egg. **15** And Tobias took hold of it, and drew it from his eyes, and immediately he recovered his sight.

16 And they glorified God, both he and his wife and all that knew them. **17** And Tobias said: I bless thee, O Lord God of Israel, because thou hast chastised me, and thou hast saved me: and behold I see Tobias my son. **18** And after seven days Sara his son's wife, and all the family arrived safe, and the cattle, and the camels, and an abundance of money of his wife's: and that money also which he had received of Gabelus: **19** And he told his parents all the benefits of God, which he had done to him by the man that conducted him. **20** And Achior and Nabath the kinsmen of Tobias came, rejoicing for Tobias, and congratulating with him for all the good things that God had done for him.

21 And for seven days they feasted and rejoiced all with great joy.

Chapter 12

1 Then Tobias called to him his son, and said to him: What can we give to this holy man, that is come with thee? **2** Tobias answering, said to his father: Father, what wages shall we give him? or what can be worthy of his benefits? **3** He conducted me and brought me safe again, he received the money of Gabelus, he caused me to have my wife, and he chased from her the evil spirit, he gave joy to her parents, myself he delivered from being devoured by the fish, thee also he hath made to see the light of heaven, and we are filled with all good things through him. What can we give him sufficient for these things? **4** But I beseech thee, my father, to desire him, that he would vouchsafe to accept one half of all things that have been brought. **5** So the father and the son, calling him, took him aside: and began to desire him that he would vouchsafe to accept of half of all things that they had brought.

6 Then he said to them secretly: Bless ye the God of heaven, give glory to him in the sight of all that live, because he hath shewn his mercy to you. **7** For it is good to hide the secret of a king: but honourable to reveal and confess the works of God. **8** Prayer is good with fasting and alms more than to lay up treasures of gold: **9** For alms delivereth from death, and the same is that which purgeth away sins, and maketh to find mercy and life everlasting. **10** But they that commit sin and iniquity, are enemies to their own soul.

11 I discover then the truth unto you, and I will not hide the secret from you. **12** When thou didst pray with tears, and didst bury the dead, and didst leave thy dinner, and hide the dead by day in thy house, and bury them by night, I offered thy prayer to the Lord. **13** And because thou wast acceptable to God, it was necessary that temptation should prove thee. **14** And now the Lord hath sent me to heal thee, and to deliver Sara thy son's wife from the devil. **15** For I am the angel Raphael, one of the seven, who stand before the Lord.

16 And when they had heard these things, they were troubled, and being seized with fear they fell upon the ground on their face. **17** And the angel said to them: Peace be to you, fear not. **18** For when I was with you, I was there by the will of God: bless ye him, and sing praises to him. **19** I seemed indeed to eat and to drink with you: but I use an invisible meat and drink, which cannot be seen by men. **20** It is time therefore that I return to him that sent me: but bless ye God, and publish all his wonderful works.

21 And when he had said these things, he was taken from their sight, and they could see him no more. **22** Then they lying prostrate for three hours upon their face, blessed God: and rising up, they told all his wonderful works.

Chapter 13

1 And Tobias the elder opening his mouth, blessed the Lord, and said: Thou art great, O Lord, for ever, and thy kingdom is unto all ages: **2** For thou scourgest, and thou savest: thou leadest down to hell, and bringest up again: and there is none that can escape thy hand. **3** Give glory to the Lord, ye children of Israel, and praise him in the sight of the Gentiles: **4** Because he hath therefore scattered you among the Gentiles, who know not him, that you may declare his wonderful works, and make them know that there is no other almighty God besides him. **5** He hath chastised us for our iniquities: and he will save us for his own mercy.

6 See then what he hath done with us, and with fear and trembling give ye glory to him: and extol the eternal King of worlds in your works. **7** As for me, I will praise him in the land of my captivity: because he hath shewn his majesty toward a sinful nation. **8** Be converted therefore, ye sinners, and do justice before God, believing that he will shew his mercy to you. **9** And I and my soul will rejoice in him. **10** Bless ye the Lord, all his elect, keep days of joy, and give glory to him.

11 Jerusalem, city of God, the Lord hath chastised thee for the works of thy hands. **12** Give glory to the Lord for thy good things, and bless the God eternal, that he may rebuild his tabernacle in thee, and may call back all the captives to thee, and thou mayst rejoice for ever and ever. **13** Thou shalt shine with a glorious light: and all the ends of the earth shall worship thee. **14** Nations from afar shall come to thee: and shall bring gifts, and shall adore the Lord in thee, and shall esteem thy land as holy. **15** For they shall call upon the great name in thee.

16 They shall be cursed that shall despise thee: and they shall be condemned that shall blaspheme thee: and blessed shall they be that shall build thee up. **17** But thou shalt rejoice in thy children, because they shall all be blessed, and shall be gathered together to the Lord. **18** Blessed are all they that love thee, and that rejoice in thy peace. **19** My soul, bless thou the Lord, because the Lord our God hath delivered Jerusalem his city from all her troubles. **20** Happy shall I be if there shall remain of my seed, to see the glory of Jerusalem.

21 The gates of Jerusalem shall be built of sapphire, and of emerald, and all the walls thereof round about of precious stones. **22** All its streets shall be paved with white and clean stones: and Alleluia shall be sung in its streets. **23** Blessed be the Lord, who hath exalted it, and may he reign over it for ever and ever, Amen.

Chapter 14

1 And the words of Tobias were ended. And after Tobias was restored to his sight, he lived two and forty years, and saw the children of his grandchildren. **2** And after he had lived a hundred and two years, he was buried honourably in Ninive. **3** For he was six and fifty years old when he lost the sight of his eyes, and sixty when he recovered it again. **4** And the rest of his life was in joy, and with great increase of the fear of God he departed in peace. **5** And at the hour of his death he called unto him his son Tobias and his children, seven young men, his grandsons, and said to them:

6 The destruction of Ninive is at hand: for the word of the Lord must be fulfilled: and our brethren, that are scattered abroad from the land of Israel, shall return to it. **7** And all the land thereof that is desert shall be filled with people, and the house of God which is burnt in it, shall again be rebuilt: and all that fear God shall return thither. **8** And the Gentiles shall leave their idols, and shall come into Jerusalem, and shall dwell in it. **9** And all the kings of the earth shall rejoice in it, adoring the King of Israel. **10** Hearken therefore, my children, to your father: serve the Lord in truth, and seek to do the things that please him:

11 And command your children that they do justice and almsdeeds, and that they be mindful of God, and bless him at all times in truth, and with all their power. **12** And now, children, hear me, and do not stay here: but as soon as you shall bury your mother by me in one sepulchre, without delay direct your steps to depart hence: **13** For I see that its iniquity will bring it to destruction. **14** And it came to pass that after the death of his mother, Tobias departed out of Ninive with his wife, and children, and children's children, and returned to his father and mother in law. **15** And he found them in health in a good old age: and he took care of them, and he closed their eyes: and all the inheritance of Raguel's house came to him: and he saw his children's children to the fifth generation.

16 And after he had lived ninety-nine years in the fear of the Lord, with joy they buried him. **17** And all his kindred, and all his generation continued in good life, and in holy conversation, so that they were acceptable both to God, and to men, and to all that dwelt in the land.

THE BOOK OF JUDITH

Chapter 1

1 Now Arphaxad king of the Medes had brought many nations under his dominions, and he built a very strong city, which he called Ecbatana, **2** Of stones squared and hewed: he made the walls thereof seventy cubits broad, and thirty cubits high, and the towers thereof he made a hundred cubits high. But on the square of them, each side was extended the space of twenty feet. **3** And he made the gates thereof according to the height of the towers: **4** And he gloried as a mighty one in the force of his army and in the glory of his chariots. **5** Now in the twelfth year of his reign, Nabuchodonosor king of the Assyrians, who reigned in Ninive the great city, fought against Arphaxad and overcame him,

6 In the great plain which is called Ragua, about the Euphrates, and the Tigris, and the Jadason, in the plain of Erioch the king of the Elicians. **7** Then was the kingdom of Nabuchodonosor exalted, and his heart was elevated: and he sent to all that dwelt in Cilicia and Damascus, and Libanus, **8** And to the nations that are in Carmelus, and Cedar, and to the inhabitants of Galilee in the great plain of Asdrelon, **9** And to all that were in Samaria, and beyond the river Jordan even to Jerusalem, and all the land of Jesse till you come to the borders of Ethiopia. **10** To all these Nabuchodonosor king of the Assyrians, sent messengers:

11 But they all with one mind refused, and sent them back empty, and rejected them without honour. **12** Then king Nabuchodonosor being angry against all that land, swore by his throne and kingdom that he would revenge himself of all those countries.

Chapter 2

1 In the thirteenth year of the reign of Nabuchodonosor, the two and twentieth day of the first month, the word was given out in the house of Nabuchodonosor king of the Assyrians, that he would revenge himself. **2** And he called all the ancients, and all the governors, and his officers of war, and communicated to them the secret of his counsel: **3** And he said that his thoughts were to bring all the earth under his empire. **4** And when this saying pleased them all, Nabuchodonosor, the king, called Holofernes the general of his armies, **5** And said to him: Go out against all the kingdoms of the west, and against them especially that despised my commandment.

6 Thy eye shall not spare any kingdom, and all the strong cities thou shalt bring under my yoke. **7** Then Holofernes called the captains and officers of the power of the Assyrians: and he mustered men for the expedition, as the king commanded him, a hundred and twenty thousand fighting men on foot, and twelve thousand archers, horsemen. **8** And he made all his warlike preparations to go before with a multitude of innumerable camels, with all provisions sufficient for the armies in abundance, and herds of oxen, and flocks of sheep, without number. **9** He appointed corn to be prepared out of all Syria in his passage. **10** But gold and silver he took out of the king's house in great abundance.

11 And he went forth he and all the army, with the chariots, and horsemen, and archers, who covered the face of the earth, like locusts. **12** And when he had passed through the borders of the Assyrians, he came to the great mountains of Ange, which are on the left of Cilicia: and he went up to all their castles, and took all the strong places. **13** And he took by assault the renowned city of Melothus, and pillaged all the children of Tharsis, and the children of Ismahel, who were over against the face of the desert, and on the south of the land of Cellon. **14** And he passed over the Euphrates and came into Mesopotamia: and he forced all the stately cities that were there, from the torrent of Mambre, till one comes to the sea: **15** And he took the borders thereof from Cilicia to the coasts of Japheth, which are towards the south.

16 And he carried away all the children of Madian, and stripped them of all their riches, and all that resisted him he slew with the edge of the sword. **17** And after these things he went down into the plains of Damascus in the days of the harvest, and he set all the corn on fire, and he caused all the trees and vineyards to be cut down. **18** And the fear of them fell upon all the inhabitants of the land.

Chapter 3

1 Then the kings and the princes of all the cities and provinces, of Syria, Mesopotamia, and Syria Sobal, and Libya, and Cilicia sent their ambassadors, who coming to Holofernes, said: **2** Let thy indignation towards us cease: for it is better for us to live and serve Nabuchodonosor the great king, and be subject to thee, than to die and to perish, or suffer the miseries of slavery. **3** All our cities and our possessions, all mountains and hills, and fields, and herds of oxen, and flocks of sheep, and goats, and horses, and camels, and all our goods, and families are in thy sight: **4** Let all we have be subject

to thy law. **5** Both we and our children are thy servants.

6 Come to us a peaceable lord, and use our service as it shall please thee. **7** Then he came down from the mountains with horsemen, in great power, and made himself master of every city, and all the inhabitants of the land. **8** And from all the cities he took auxiliaries valiant men, and chosen for war. **9** And so great a fear lay upon all those provinces, that the inhabitants of all the cities, both princes and nobles, as well as the people, went out to meet him at his coming. **10** And received him with garlands, and lights, and dances, and timbrels, and flutes.

11 And though they did these things, they could not for all that mitigate the fierceness of his heart: **12** For he both destroyed their cities and cut down their groves. **13** For Nabuchodonosor the king had commanded him to destroy all the gods of the earth, that he only might be called God by those nations which could be brought under him by the power of Holofernes. **14** And when he had passed through all Syria Sobal, and all Apamea, and all Mesopotamia, he came to the Idumeans into the land of Gabaa, **15** And he took possession of their cities, and stayed there for thirty days, in which days he commanded all the troops of his army to be united.

Chapter 4

1Then the children of Israel, who dwelt in the land of Juda, hearing these things, were exceedingly afraid of him. **2** Dread and horror seized upon their minds, lest he should do the same to Jerusalem and to the temple of the Lord, that he had done to other cities and their temples. **3** And they sent into all Samaria round about, as far as Jericho, and seized upon all the tops of the mountains: **4** And they compassed their towns with walls, and gathered together corn for provision for war. **5** And Eliachim the priest wrote to all that were over against Esdrelon, which faceth the great plain near Dothain, and to all by whom there might be a passage of way, that they should take possession of the ascents of the mountains, by which there might be any way to Jerusalem, and should keep watch where the way was narrow between the mountains.

6 And the children of Israel did as the priest of the Lord Eliachim had appointed them, **7** And all the people cried to the Lord with great earnestness, and they humbled their souls in fastings, and prayers, both they and their wives. **8** And the priests put on haircloths, and they caused the little children to lie prostrate before the temple of the Lord, and the altar of the Lord they covered with haircloth. **9** And they cried to the Lord the God of Israel with one accord, that their children might not be made a prey, and their wives carried off, and their cities destroyed, and their holy things profaned, and that they might not be made a reproach to the Gentiles. **10** Then Eliachim the high priest of the Lord went about all Israel and spoke to them,

11 Saying: Know ye that the Lord will hear your prayers, if you continue with perseverance in fastings and prayers in the sight of the Lord. **12** Remember Moses the servant of the Lord, who overcame Amalec that trusted in his own strength, and in his power, and in his army, and in his shields, and in his chariots, and in his horsemen, not by fighting with the sword, but by holy prayers: **13** So shall all the enemies of Israel be, if you persevere in this work which you have begun. **14** So they being moved by this exhortation of his, prayed to the Lord, and continued in the sight of the Lord. **15** So that even they who offered the holocausts to the Lord, offered the sacrifices to the Lord girded with haircloths, and with ashes upon their head.

16 And they all begged of God with all their heart, that he would visit his people Israel.

Chapter 5

1 And it was told Holofernes the general of the army of the Assyrians, that the children of Israel prepared themselves to resist, and had shut up the ways of the mountains. **2** And he was transported with exceeding great fury and indignation, and he called all the princes of Moab and the leaders of Amman. **3** And he said to them: Tell me what is this people that besetteth the mountains: or what are their cities, and of what sort, and how great: also what is their power, or what is their multitude: or who is the king over their warfare: **4** And why they above all that dwell in the east, have despised us, and have not come out to meet us, that they might receive us with peace? **5** Then Achior captain of all the children of Ammon answering, said: If thou vouch safe, my lord, to hear, I will tell the truth in thy sight concerning this people, that dwelleth in the mountains, and there shall not a false word come out of my mouth.

6 This people is of the offspring of the Chaldeans. **7** They dwelt first in Mesopotamia, because they would not follow the gods of their fathers, who were in the land of the Chaldeans. **8** Wherefore forsaking the ceremonies of their fathers, which consisted in the worship of many gods, **9** They worshipped one God of heaven, who also commanded them to depart from thence, and to dwell in Charan. And when there was a famine over all the land, they went down into Egypt, and there for four hundred years were so multiplied, that the army of them could not be numbered. **10** And when the king of

Egypt oppressed them, and made slaves of them to labour in clay and brick, in the building of his cities, they cried to their Lord, and he struck the whole land of Egypt with divers plagues.

11 And when the Egyptians had cast them out from them, and the plague had ceased from them, and they had a mind to take them again, and bring them back to their service, **12** The God of heaven opened the sea to them in their flight, so that the waters were made to stand firm as a wall on either side, and they walked through the bottom of the sea and passed it dry foot. **13** And when an innumerable army of the Egyptians pursued after them in that place, they were so overwhelmed with the waters, that there was not one left, to tell what had happened to posterity. **14** And after they came out of the Red Sea, they abode in the deserts of mount Sina, in which never man could dwell, or son of man rested. **15** There bitter fountains were made sweet for them to drink, and for forty years they received food from heaven.

16 Wheresoever they went in without bow and arrow, and without shield and sword, their God fought for them and overcame. **17** And there was no one that triumphed over this people, but when they departed from the worship of the Lord their God. **18** But as often as beside their own God, they worshipped any other, they were given to spoil, and to the sword, and to reproach. **19** And as often as they were penitent for having revolted from the worship of their God, the God of heaven gave them power to resist. **20** So they overthrew the king of the Chanaanites, and of the Jebusites, and of the Pherezites, and of the Hethites, and of the Hevites, and of the Amorrhites, and all the mighty ones in Hesebon, and they possessed their lands, and their cities:

21 And as long as they sinned not in the sight of their God, it was well with them: for their God hateth iniquity. **22** And even some years ago when they had revolted from the way which God had given them to walk therein, they were destroyed in battles by many nations, and very many of them were led away captive into a strange land. **23** But of late returning to the Lord their God, from the different places wherein they were scattered, they are come together and are gone up into all these mountains, and possess Jerusalem again, where their holies are. **24** Now therefore, my lord, search if there be any iniquity of theirs in the sight of their God: let us go up to them, because their God will surely deliver them to thee, and they shall be brought under the yoke of thy power: **25** But if there be no offense of this people in the sight of their God, we can not resist them, because their God will defend them: and we shall be a reproach to the whole earth.

26 And it came to pass, when Achior had ceased to speak these words, all the great men of Holofernes were angry, and they had a mind to kill him, saying to each other: **27** Who is this, that saith the children of Israel can resist king Nabuchodonosor, and his armies, men unarmed, and without force, and without skill in the art of war? **28** That Achior therefore may know that he deceiveth us, let us go up into the mountains: and when the bravest of them shall be taken, then shall he with them be stabbed with the sword: **29** That every nation may know that Nabuchodonosor is god of the earth, and besides him there is no other.

Chapter 6

1 And it came to pass when they had left off speaking, that Holofernes being in a violent passion, said to Achior: **2** Because thou hast prophesied unto us, saying: That the nation of Israel is defended by their God, to shew thee that there is no God, but Nabuchodonosor: **3** When we shall slay them all as one man, then thou also shalt die with them by the sword of the Assyrians, and all Israel shall perish with thee: **4** And thou shalt find that Nabuchodonosor is lord of the whole earth: and then the sword of my soldiers shall pass through thy sides, and thou shalt be stabbed and fall among the wounded of Israel, and thou shalt breathe no more till thou be destroyed with them. **5** But if thou think thy prophecy true, let not thy countenance sink, and let the paleness that is in thy face, depart from thee, if thou imaginest these my words cannot be accomplished.

6 And that thou mayst know that thou shalt experience these things together with them, behold from this hour thou shalt be associated to their people, that when they shall receive the punishment they deserve from my sword, thou mayst fall under the same vengeance. **7** Then Holofernes commanded his servants to take Achior, and to lead him to Bethulia, and to deliver him into the hands of the children of Israel. **8** And the servants of Holofernes taking him, went through the plains: but when they came near the mountains, the slingers came out against them. **9** Then turning out of the way by the side of the mountain, they tied Achior to a tree hand and foot, and so left him bound with ropes, and returned to their master. **10** And the children of Israel coming down from Bethulia, came to him, and loosing him they brought him to Bethulia, and setting him in the midst of the people, asked him what was the matter, that the Assyrians had left him bound.

11 In those days the rulers there, were Ozias the son of Micha of the tribe of Simeon, and Charmi, called also Gothoniel. **12** And Achior related in the midst of the ancients, and in the presence of all the people, all that he had said being asked by Holofernes: and how the people of Holofernes would have killed him for this word, **13** And how Holofernes himself being angry had commanded him to be delivered for this cause to the Israelites: that when he should overcome the children of Israel, then he might command Achior also himself to be put to death by diverse torments, for having said: The God of heaven is their defender. **14** And when Achior had declared all these things, all the people fell upon their faces, adoring the Lord, and all of them together mourning and weeping poured out their prayers with one accord to the Lord, **15** Saying: O Lord God of heaven and earth, behold their pride, and look on our low condition, and have regard to the face of thy saints, and shew that thou forsakes not them that trust on thee, and that thou humblest them that presume of themselves, and glory in their own strength.

16 So when their weeping was ended, and the peoples prayer, in which they continued all the day, was concluded, they comforted Achior, **17** Saying: the God of our fathers, whose power thou hast set forth, will make this return to thee, that thou rather shalt see their destruction. **18** And when the Lord our God shall give this liberty to his servants, let God be with thee also in the midst of us: that as it shall please thee, so thou with all thine mayst converse with us. **19** Then Ozias, after the assembly was broken up, received him into his house, and made him a great supper. **20** And all the ancients were invited, and they refreshed themselves together after their fast was over.

21 And afterwards all the people were called together, and they prayed all the night long within the church, desiring help of the God of Israel.

Chapter 7

1 But Holofernes on the next day gave orders to his army, to go up against Bethulia. **2** Now there were in his troops a hundred and twenty thousand footmen, and two and twenty thousand horsemen, besides the preparations of those men who had been taken, and who had been brought away out of the provinces and cities of all the youth. **3** All these prepared themselves together to fight against the children of Israel, and they came by the hillside to the top, which looketh toward Dothain, from the place which is called Behlma, unto Chelmon, which is over against Esdrelon. **4** But the children of Israel, when they saw the multitude of them, prostrated themselves upon the ground, putting ashes upon their heads, praying with one accord, that the God of Israel would shew his mercy upon his people. **5** And taking their arms of war, they posted themselves at the places, which by a narrow pathway lead directly between the mountains, and they guarded them all day and

night.

6 Now Holofernes, in going round about, found that the fountains which supplied them with water, ran through an aqueduct without the city on the south side: and he commanded their aqueduct to be cut off. **7** Nevertheless there were springs not far from the walls, out of which they were seen secretly to draw water, to refresh themselves a little rather than to drink their fill. **8** But the children of Ammon and Moab came to Holofernes, saying: The children of Israel trust not in their spears, nor in their arrows, but the mountains are their defense, and the steep hires and precipices guard them. **9** Wherefore that thou mayst overcome them without joining battle, set guards at the springs that they may not draw water out of them, and thou shalt destroy them without sword, or at least being wearied out they will yield up their city, which they suppose, because it is situate in the mountains, to be impregnable. **10** And these words pleased Holofernes, and his officers, and he placed all round about a hundred men at every spring.

11 And when they had kept this watch for full twenty days, the cisterns, and the reserve of waters failed among all the inhabitants of Bethulia, so that there was not within the city, enough to satisfy them, no not for one day, for water was daily given out to the people by measure. **12** Then all the men and women, young men, and children, gathering themselves together to Ozias, all together with one voice, **13** Said: God be judge between us and thee, for thou hast done evil against us, in that thou wouldst not speak peaceably with the Assyrians, and for this cause God hath sold us into their hands. **14** And therefore there is no one to help us, while we are cast down before their eyes in thirst, and sad destruction. **15** And now assemble ye all that are in the city, that we may of our own accord yield ourselves all up to the people of Holofernes.

16 For it is better, that being captives we should live and bless the Lord, than that we should die, and be a reproach to all flesh, after we have seen our wives and our infants die before our eyes. **17** We call to witness this day heaven and earth, and the God of our fathers, who taketh vengeance upon us according to our sins, conjuring you to deliver now the city into the hand of the army of Holofernes, that our end may be short by the edge of the sword, which is made longer by the drought of thirst. **18** And when they had said these things, there was great weeping and lamentation of all in the assembly, and for many hours with one voice they cried to God, saying: **19** We have sinned with our fathers we have done unjustly, we have commited iniquity: **20** Have thou mercy on us, because thou art good, or punish our iniquities by chastising us thyself, and deliver not them that trust in thee to a people that knoweth not thee,

21 That they may not say among the gentiles: Where is their

God? **22** And when being wearied with these cries, and tired with these weepings, they held their peace. **23** Ozias rising up all in tears, said: Be of good courage, my brethren, and let us wait these five days for mercy from the Lord. **24** For perhaps he will put a stop to his indignation, and will give glory to his own name. **25** But if after five days be past there come no aid, we will do the things which you leave spoken.

Chapter 8

1 Now it came to pass, when Judith a widow had heard these words, who was the daughter of Merari, the son of Idox, the son of Joseph, the son of Ozias, the son of Elai, the son of Jamnor, the son of Gedeon, the son of Raphaim, the son of Achitob, the son of Melehias, the son of Enan, the son of Nathanias, the son of Salathiel, the son of Simeon, the son of Ruben: **2** And her husband was Manasses, who died in the time of the barley harvest: **3** For he was standing over them that bound sheaves in the field; and the heat came upon his head, and he died in Bethulia his own city, and was buried there with his fathers. **4** And Judith his relict was a widow now three years and six months. **5** And she made herself a private chamber in the upper part of her house, in which she abode shut up with her maids.

6 And she wore haircloth upon her loins, and fasted all the days of her life, except the sabbaths, and new moons, and the feasts of the house of Israel. **7** And she was exceedingly beautiful, and her husband left her great riches, and very many servants, and large possessions of herds of oxen, and flocks of sheep. **8** And she was greatly renowned among all, because she feared the Lord very much, neither was there any one that spoke an ill word of her. **9** When therefore she had heard that Ozias had promised that he would deliver up the city after the fifth day, she sent to the ancients Chabri and Charmi. **10** And they came to her, and she said to them: What is this word, by which Ozias hath consented to give up the city to the Assyrians, if within five days there come no aid to us?

11 And who are you that tempt the Lord? **12** This is not a word that may draw down mercy, but rather that may stir up wrath, and enkindle indignation. **13** You have set a time for the mercy of the Lord, and you have appointed him a day, according to your pleasure. **14** But forasmuch as the Lord is patient, let us be penitent for this same thing, and with many tears let us beg his pardon: **15** For God will not threaten like man, nor be inflamed to anger like the son of man.

16 And therefore let us humble our souls before him, and continuing in an humble spirit, in his service: **17** Let us ask the Lord with tears, that according to his will so he would shew his mercy to us: that as our heart is troubled by their pride, so also we may glorify in our humility. **18** For we have not followed the sins of our fathers, who forsook their God, and worshipped strange gods. **19** For which crime they were given up to their enemies, to the sword, and to pillage, and to confusion: but we know no other God but him. **20** Let us humbly wait for his consolation, and the Lord our God will require our blood of the afflictions of our enemies, and he will humble all the nations that shall rise up against us, and bring them to disgrace.

21 And now, brethren, as you are the ancients among the people of God, and their very soul resteth upon you: comfort their hearts by your speech, that they may be mindful how our fathers were tempted that they might be proved, whether they worshipped their God truly. **22** They must remember how our father Abraham was tempted, and being proved by many tribulations, was made the friend of God. **23** So Isaac, so Jacob, so Moses, and all that have pleased God, passed through many tribulations, remaining faithful. **24** But they that did not receive the trials with the fear of the Lord, but uttered their impatience and the reproach of their murmuring against the Lord, **25** Were destroyed by the destroyer, and perished by serpents.

26 As for us therefore let us not revenge ourselves for these things which we suffer. **27** But esteeming these very punishments to be less than our sins deserve, let us believe that these scourges of the Lord, with which like servants we are chastised, have happened for our amendment, and not for our destruction. **28** And Ozias and the ancients said to her: All things which thou hast spoken are true, and there is nothing to be reprehended in thy words. **29** Now therefore pray for us, for thou art a holy woman, and one fearing God. **30** And Judith said to them: As you know that what I have been able to say is of God:

31 So that which I intend to do prove ye if it be of God, and pray that God may strengthen my design. **32** You shall stand at the gate this night, and I will go out with my maidservant: and pray ye, that as you have said, in five days the Lord may look down upon his people Israel. **33** But I desire that you search not into what I am doing, and till I bring you word let nothing else be done but to pray for me to the Lord our God. **34** And Ozias the prince of Juda said to her: Go in peace, and the Lord be with thee to take revenge of our enemies. So returning they departed.

Chapter 9

1 And when they were gone, Judith went into her oratory: and

putting on haircloth, laid ashes on her head: and falling down prostrate before the Lord, she cried to the Lord, saying: **2** O Lord God of my father Simeon, who *gavest him a sword* to execute vengeance against strangers, who had defiled by their uncleanness, and uncovered the virgin unto confusion: **3** And who gavest their wives to be made a prey, and their daughters into captivity: and all their spoils to be divided to thy servants, who were zealous with thy zeal: assist, I beseech thee, O Lord God, me a widow. **4** For thou hast done the things of old, and hast devised one thing after another: and what thou hast designed hath been done. **5** For all thy ways are prepared, and in thy providence thou hast placed thy judgments.

6 Look upon the camp of the Assyrians now, as thou wast pleased to look upon the camp of the Egyptians, when they pursued armed after thy servants, trusting in their chariots, and in their horsemen, and in a multitude of warriors. **7** But thou lookedst over their camp, and darkness wearied them. **8** The deep held their feet, and the waters overwhelmed them. **9** So may it be with these also, O Lord, who trust in their multitude, and in their chariots, and in their pikes, and in their shields, and in their arrows, and glory in their spears, **10** And know not that thou art our God, who destroyest wars from the beginning, and the Lord is thy name.

11 Lift up thy arm as from the beginning, and crush their power with thy power: let their power fall in their wrath, who promise themselves to violate thy sanctuary, and defile the dwelling place of thy name, and to beat down with their sword the horn of thy altar. **12** Bring to pass, O Lord, that his pride may be cut off with his own sword. **13** Let him be caught in the net of his own eyes in my regard, and do thou strike him by the graces of the words of my lips. **14** Give me constancy in my mind, that I may despise him: and fortitude that I may overthrow him. **15** For this will be a glorious monument for thy name, when he shall fall by the hand of a woman.

16 For thy power, O Lord, is not in a multitude, nor is thy pleasure in the strength of horses, nor from the beginning have the proud been acceptable to thee: but the prayer of the humble and the meek hath always pleased thee. **17** O God of the heavens, creator of the waters, and Lord of the whole creation, hear me a poor wretch, making supplication to thee, and presuming of thy mercy. **18** Remember, O Lord, thy covenant, and put thou words in my mouth, and strengthen the resolution in my heart, that thy house may continue in thy holiness: **19** And all nations may acknowledge that thou art God, and there is no other besides thee.

Chapter 10

1 And it came to pass, when she had ceased to cry to the Lord,

that she rose from the place wherein she lay prostrate before the Lord. **2** And she called her maid, and going down into her house she took off her haircloth, and put away the garments of her widowhood, **3** And she washed her body, and anointed herself with the best ointment, and plaited the hair of her head, and put a bonnet upon her head, and clothed herself with the garments of her gladness, and put sandals on her feet, and took her bracelets, and lilies, and earlets, and rings, and adorned herself with all her ornaments. **4** And the Lord also gave her more beauty: because all this dressing up did not proceed from sensuality, but from virtue: and therefore the Lord increased this her beauty, so that she appeared to all men's eyes incomparably lovely. **5** And she gave to her maid a bottle of wine to carry, and a vessel of oil, and parched corn, and dry figs, and bread and cheese, and went out.

6 And when they came to the gate of the city, they found Ozias, and the ancients of the city waiting. **7** And when they saw her they were astonished, and admired her beauty exceedingly. **8** But they asked her no question, only they let her pass, saying: The God of our fathers give thee grace, and may he strengthen all the counsel of thy heart with his power, that Jerusalem may glory in thee, and thy name may be in the number of the holy and just. **9** And they that were there said, all with one voice: So be it, so be it. **10** But Judith praying to the Lord, passed through the gates, she and her maid.

11 And it came to pass, when she went down the hill, about break of day, that the watchmen of the Assyrians met her and stopped her, saying: Whence comest thou? or whither goest thou? **12** And she answered: I am a daughter of the Hebrews, and I am fled from them, because I knew they would be made a prey to you, because they despised you, and would not of their own accord yield themselves, that they might find mercy in your sight. **13** For this reason I thought with myself, saying: I will go to the presence of the prince Holofernes, that I may tell him their secrets, and shew him by what way he may take them, without the loss of one man of his army. **14** And when the men had heard her words, they beheld her face, and their eyes were amazed, for they wondered exceedingly at her beauty. **15** And they said to her: Thou hast saved thy life by taking this resolution, to come down to our lord.

16 And be assured of this, that when thou shalt stand before him, he will treat thee well, and thou wilt be most acceptable to his heart. And they brought her to the tent of Holofernes, telling him of her. **17** And when she was come into his presence, forthwith Holofernes was caught by his eyes. **18** And his officers said to him: Who can despise the people of the Hebrews who have such beautiful women, that we should not think it worth our while for their sakes to fight against them? **19** And Judith seeing Holofernes sitting under a canopy, which was woven of purple and gold, with emeralds and precious stones: **20** After she had looked on his face bowed down to him, prostrating herself to the ground. And the servants of Holofernes lifted her up, by the command of their master.

Chapter 11

1 Then Holofernes said to her: Be of good comfort, and fear not in thy heart: for I have never hurt a man that was willing to serve Nabuchodonosor the king. **2** And if thy people had not despised me, I would never have lifted up my spear against them. **3** But now tell me, for what cause hast thou left them, and why it hath pleased thee to come to us? **4** And Judith said to him: Receive the words of thy handmaid, for if thou wilt follow the words of thy handmaid, the Lord will do with thee a perfect thing. **5** For as Nabuchodonosor the king of the earth liveth, and his power liveth which is in thee for chastising of all straying souls: not only men serve him through thee, but also the beasts of the field obey him.

6 For the industry of thy mind is spoken of among all nations, and it is told through the whole world, that thou only art excellent, and mighty in all his kingdom, and thy discipline is cried up in all provinces. **7** It is known also what Achior said, nor are we ignorant of what thou hast commanded to be done to him. **8** For it is certain that our God is so offended with sins, that he hath sent word by his prophets to the people, that he will deliver them up for their sins. **9** And because the children of Israel know they have offended their God, thy dread is upon them. **10** Moreover also a famine hath come upon them, and for drought of water they are already to be counted among the dead.

11 And they have a design even to kill their cattle, and to drink the blood of them. **12** And the consecrated things of the Lord their God which God forbade them to touch, in corn, wine, and oil, these have they purposed to make use of, and they design to consume the things which they ought not to touch with their hands: therefore because they do these things, it is certain they will be given up to destruction. **13** And I thy handmaid knowing this, am fled from them, and the Lord hath sent me to tell thee these very things. **14** For I thy handmaid worship God even now that I am with thee, and thy handmaid will go out, and I will pray to God, **15** And he will tell me when he will repay them for their sins, and I will come and tell thee, so that I may bring thee through the midst of Jerusalem, and thou shalt have all the people of Israel, as sheep that have no shepherd, and there shall not so much as one dog bark against thee:

16 Because these things are told me by the providence of

God. **17** And because God is angry with them, I am sent to tell these very things to thee. **18** And all these words pleased Holofernes, and his servants, and they admired her wisdom, and they said one to another: **19** There is not such another woman upon earth in look, in beauty, and in sense of words. **20** And Holofernes said to her: God hath done well who sent thee before the people, that thou mightest give them into our hands:

21 And because thy promise is good, if thy God shall do this for me, he shall also be my God, and thou shalt be great in the house of Nabuchodonosor, and thy name shall be renowned through all the earth.

Chapter 12

1 Then he ordered that she should go in where his treasures were laid up, and bade her tarry there, and he appointed what should be given her from his own table. **2** And Judith answered him and said: Now I cannot eat of these things which thou commandest to be given me, lest sin come upon me: but I will eat of the things which I have brought. **3** And Holofernes said to her: If these things which thou hast brought with thee fail thee, what shall we do for thee? **4** And Judith said: As thy soul liveth, my lord, thy handmaid shall not spend all these things till God do by my hand that which I have purposed. And his servants brought her into the tent which he had commanded. **5** And when she was going in, she desired that she might have liberty to go out at night and before day to prayer, and to beseech the Lord.

6 And he commanded his chamberlains, that she might go out and in, to adore her God as she pleased, for three days. **7** And she went out in the nights into the valley of Bethulia, and washed herself in a fountain of water. **8** And as she came up, she prayed to the Lord the God of Israel, that he would direct her way to the deliverance of his people. **9** And going in, she remained pure in the tent, until she took her own meat in the evening. **10** And it came to pass on the fourth day, that Holofernes made a supper for his servants, and said to Vagao his eunuch: Go, and persuade that Hebrew woman, to consent of her own accord to dwell with me.

11 For it is looked upon as shameful among the Assyrians, if a woman mock a man, by doing so as to pass free from him. **12** Then Vagao went in to Judith, and said: Let not my good maid be afraid to go in to my lord, that she may be honoured before his face, that she may eat with him and drink wine and be merry. **13** And Judith answered him: Who am I, that I should gainsay my lord? **14** All that shall be good and best before his eyes, I will do. And whatsoever shall please him, that shall be best to me all the days of my life. **15** And she arose and dressed herself out with her garments, and going in she stood before his face.

16 And the heart of Holofernes was smitten, for he was burning with the desire of her. **17** And Holofernes said to her: Drink now, and sit down and be merry for thou hast found favour before me. **18** And Judith said: I will drink my lord, because my life is magnified this day above all my days. **19** And she took and ate and drank before him what her maid had prepared for her. **20** And Holofernes was made merry on her occasion, and drank exceeding much wine, so much as he had never drunk in his life.

Chapter 13

1 And when it was grown late, his servants made haste to their lodgings, and Vagao shut the chamber doors, and went his way. **2** And they were all overcharged with wine. **3** And Judith was alone in the chamber. **4** But Holofernes lay on his bed, fast asleep, being exceedingly drunk. **5** And Judith spoke to her maid to stand without before the chamber, and to watch:

6 And Judith stood before the bed praying with tears, and the motion of her lips in silence, **7** Saying: Strengthen me, O Lord God of Israel, and in this hour look on the works of my hands, that as thou hast promised, thou mayst raise up Jerusalem thy city: and that I may bring to pass that which I have purposed, having a belief that it might be done by thee. **8** And when she had said this, she went to the pillar that was at his bed's head, and loosed his sword that hung tied upon it. **9** And when she had drawn it out, she took him by the hair of his head, and said: Strengthen me, O Lord God, at this hour. **10** And she struck twice upon his neck, and cut off his head, and took off his canopy from the pillars, and rolled away his headless body.

11 And after a while she went out, and delivered the head of Holofernes to her maid, and bade her put it into her wallet. **12** And they two went out according to their custom, as it were to prayer, and they passed the camp, and having compassed the valley, they came to the gate of the city. **13** And Judith from afar off cried to the watchmen upon the walls: Open the gates for God is with us, who hath shewn his power in Israel. **14** And it came to pass, when the men had heard her voice, that they called the ancients of the city. **15** And all ran to meet her from the least to the greatest: for they now had no hopes that she would come.

16 And lighting up lights they all gathered round about her: and she went up to a higher place, and commanded silence to be made. And when all had held their peace, **17** Judith said: Praise ye the Lord our God, who hath not forsaken them that hope in him. **18** And by me his handmaid he hath fulfilled his mercy, which he promised to the house of Israel: and he hath killed the enemy of his people by my hand this night. **19** Then she brought forth the head of Holofernes out of the wallet, and shewed it them, saying: Behold the head of Holofernes the general of the army of the Assyrians, and behold his canopy, wherein he lay in his drunkenness, where the Lord our God slew him by the hand of a woman. **20** But as the same Lord liveth, his angel hath been my keeper both going hence, and abiding there, and returning from thence hither: and the Lord hath not suffered me his handmaid to be defiled, but hath brought me back to you without pollution of sin, rejoicing for his victory, for my escape, and for your deliverance.

21 Give all of you glory to him, because he is good, because his mercy endureth for ever. **22** And they all adored the Lord, and said to her: The Lord hath blessed thee by his power, because by thee he hath brought our enemies to nought. **23** And Ozias the prince of the people of Israel, said to her: Blessed art thou, O daughter, by the Lord the most high God, above all women upon the earth. **24** Blessed be the Lord who made heaven and earth, who hath directed thee to the cutting off the head of the prince of our enemies. **25** Because he hath so magnified thy name this day, that thy praise shall not depart out of the mouth of men who shall be mindful of the power of the Lord for ever, for that thou hast not spared thy life, by reason of the distress and tribulation of thy people, but hast prevented our ruin in the presence of our God.

26 And all the people said: So be it, so be it. **27** And Achior being called for came, and Judith said to him: The God of Israel, to whom thou gavest testimony, that he revengeth himself of his enemies, he hath cut off the head of all the unbelievers this night by my hand. **28** And that thou mayst find that it is so, behold the head of Holofernes, who in the contempt of his pride despised the God of Israel: and threatened thee with death, saying: When the people of Israel shall be taken, I will command thy sides to be pierced with a sword. **29** Then Achior seeing the head of Holofernes, being seized with a great fear he fell on his face upon the earth, and his soul swooned away. **30** But after he had recovered his spirits he fell down at her feet, and reverenced her and said:

31 Blessed art thou by thy God in every tabernacle of Jacob, for in every nation which shall hear thy name, the God of Israel shall be magnified on occasion of thee.

Chapter 14

1 And Judith said to all the people: Hear me, my brethren, hang ye up this head upon our walls. **2** And as soon as the sun shall rise,

let every man take his arms, and rush ye out, not as going down beneath, but as making an assault. **3** Then the watchmen must needs run to awake their prince for the battle. **4** And when the captains of them shall run to the tent of Holofernes, and shall find him without his head wallowing in his blood, fear shall fall upon them. **5** And when you shall know that they are fleeing, go after them securely, for the Lord will destroy them under your feet.

6 Then Achior seeing the power that the God of Israel had wrought, leaving the religion of the gentiles, he believed God, and circumcised the flesh of his foreskin, and was joined to the people of Israel, with all the succession of his kindred until this present day. **7** And immediately at break of day, they hung up the head of Holofernes upon the walls, and every man took his arms, and they sent out with a great noise and shouting. **8** And the watchmen seeing this, ran to the tent of Holofernes. **9** And they that were in the tent came, and made a noise before the door of the chamber to awake him, endeavouring by art to break his rest, that Holofernes might awake, not by their calling him, but by their noise. **10** For no man durst knock, or open and go into the chamber of the general of the Assyrians.

11 But when his captains and tribunes were come, and all the chiefs of the army of the king of the Assyrians, they said to the chamberlains: **12** Go in, and awake him, for the mice coming out of their holes, have presumed to challenge us to fight. **13** Then Vagao going into his chamber, stood before the curtain, and made a clapping with his hands: for he thought that he was sleeping with Judith. **14** But when with hearkening, he perceived no motion of one lying, he came near to the curtain, and lifting it up, and seeing the body of Holofernes, lying upon the ground, without the head, sweltering in his blood, he cried out with a loud voice, with weeping, and rent his garments. **15** And he went into the tent of Judith, and not finding her, he ran out to the people,

16 And said: One Hebrew woman hath made confusion in the house of king Nabuchodonosor: for behold Holofernes lieth upon the ground, and his head is not upon him. **17** Now when the chiefs of the army of the Assyrians had heard this, they all rent their garments, and an intolerable fear and dread fell upon them, and their minds were troubled exceedingly. **18** And there was a very great cry in the midst of their camp.

Chapter 15

1 And when all the army heard that Holofernes was beheaded, courage and counsel fled from them, and being seized with trembling and fear they thought only to save themselves by

flight: **2** So that no one spoke to his neighbour, but hanging down the head, leaving all things behind, they made haste to escape from the Hebrews, who, as they heard, were coming armed upon them, and fled by the ways of the fields, and the paths of the hills. **3** So the children of Israel seeing them fleeing, followed after them. And they went down sounding with trumpets and shouting after them. **4** And because the Assyrians were not united together, they went without order in their flight; but the children of Israel pursuing in one body, defeated all that they could find. **5** And Ozias sent messengers through all the cities and countries of Israel.

6 And every country, and every city, sent their chosen young men armed after them, and they pursued them with the edge of the sword until they came to the extremities of their confines. **7** And the rest that were in Bethulia went into the camp of the Assyrians, and took away the spoils, which the Assyrians in their flight had left behind them, and they were laden exceedingly. **8** But they that returned conquerors to Bethulia, brought with them all things that were theirs, so that there was no numbering of their cattle, and beasts, and all their moveables, insomuch that from the least to the greatest all were made rich by their spoils. **9** And Joachim the high priest came from Jerusalem to Bethulia with all his ancients to see Judith. **10** And when she was come out to him, they all blessed her with one voice, saying: Thou art the glory of Jerusalem, thou art the joy of Israel, thou art the honour of our people:

11 For thou hast done manfully, and thy heart has been strengthened, because thou hast loved chastity, and after thy husband hast not known any other: therefore also the hand of the Lord hath strengthened thee, and therefore thou shalt be blessed for ever. **12** And all the people said: So be it, so be it. **13** And thirty days were scarce sufficient for the people of Israel to gather up the spoils of the Assyrians. **14** But all those things that were proved to be the peculiar goods of Holofernes, they gave to Judith in gold, and silver, and garments and precious stones, and all household stuff, and they all were delivered to her by the people. **15** And all the people rejoiced, with the women, and virgins, and young men, playing on instruments and harps.

Chapter 16

1 Then Judith sung this canticle to the Lord, saying: **2** Begin ye to the Lord with timbrels, sing ye to the Lord with cymbals, tune unto him a new psalm, extol and call upon his name. **3** The Lord putteth an end to wars, the Lord is his name. **4** He hath set his camp in the midst of his people, to deliver us from the hand of all our enemies. **5** The Assyrians came out of the mountains from the north

in the multitude of his strength: his multitude stopped up the torrents, and their horses covered the valleys.

6 He bragged that he would set my borders on fire, and kill my young men with the sword, to make my infants a prey, and my virgins captives. **7** But the almighty Lord hath struck him, and hath delivered him into the hands of a woman, and hath slain him. **8** For their mighty one did not fall by young men, neither did the sons of Titan strike him, nor tall giants oppose themselves to him, but Judith the daughter of Merari weakened him with the beauty of her face. **9** For she put off her the garments of widowhood, and put on her the garments of joy, to give joy to the children of Israel. **10** She anointed her face with ointment, and bound up her locks with a crown, she took a new robe to deceive him.

11 Her sandals ravished his eyes, her beauty made his soul her captive, with a sword she cut off his head. **12** The Persians quaked at her constancy, and the Medes at her boldness. **13** Then the camp of the Assyrians howled, when my lowly ones appeared, parched with thirst. **14** The sons of the damsels have pierced them through, and they have killed them like children fleeing away: they perished in battle before the face of the Lord my God. **15** Let us sing a hymn to the Lord, let us sing a new hymn to our God.

16 O Adonai, Lord, great art thou, and glorious in thy power, and no one can overcome thee. **17** Let all thy creatures serve thee: because thou hast spoken, and they were made: thou didst send forth thy spirit, and they were created, and there is no one that can resist thy voice. **18** The mountains shall be moved from the foundations with the waters: the rocks shall melt as wax before thy face. **19** But they that fear thee, shall be great with thee in all things. **20** Woe be to the nation that riseth up against my people: for the Lord almighty will take revenge on them, in the day of judgment he will visit them.

21 For he will give fire, and worms into their flesh, that they may burn, and may feel for ever. **22** And it came to pass after these things, that all the people, after the victory, came to Jerusalem to adore the Lord: and as soon as they were purified, they all offered holocausts, and vows, and their promises. **23** And Judith offered for an anathema of oblivion all the arms of Holofernes, which the people gave her, and the canopy that she had taken away out of his chamber. **24** And the people were joyful in the sight of the sanctuary, and for three months the joy of this victory was celebrated with Judith. **25** And after those days every man returned to his house, and Judith was made great in Bethulia, and she was most renowned in all the land of Israel.

26 And chastity was joined to her virtue, so that she knew no man all the days of her life, after the death of Manasses her husband. **27** And on festival days she came forth with great glory. **28** And she abode in her husband's house a hundred and five years, and made her handmaid free, and she died, and was buried with her husband in Bethulia. **29** And all the people mourned for seven days. **30** And all the time of her life there was none that troubled Israel, nor many years after her death.

31 But the day of the festivity of this victory is received by the Hebrews in the number of holy days, and is religiously observed by the Jews from that time until this day.

THE BOOK OF WISDOM

Chapter 1

1 Love justice, you that are the judges of the earth. Think of the Lord in goodness, and seek him in simplicity of heart. **2** For he is found by them that tempt him not: and he sheweth himself to them that have faith in him. **3** For perverse thoughts separate from God: and his power, when it is tried, reproveth the unwise: **4** For wisdom will not enter into a malicious soul, nor dwell in a body subject to sins. **5** For the Holy Spirit of discipline will flee from the deceitful, and will withdraw himself from thoughts that are without understanding, and he shall not abide when iniquity cometh in.

6 For the spirit of wisdom is benevolent, and will not acquit the evil speaker from his lips: for God is witness of his reins, and he is a true searcher of his heart, and a hearer of his tongue. **7** For the spirit of the Lord hath filled the whole world: and that, which containeth all things, hath knowledge of the voice. **8** Therefore he that speaketh unjust things cannot be hid, neither shall the chastising judgment pass him by. **9** For inquisition shall be made into the thoughts of the ungodly: and the hearing of his words shall come to God, to the chastising of his iniquities. **10** For the ear of jealousy heareth all things, and the tumult of murmuring shall not be hid.

11 Keep yourselves therefore from murmuring, which profiteth nothing, and refrain your tongue from detraction, for an obscure speech shall not go for nought: and the mouth that belieth, killeth the soul. **12** Seek not death in the error of your life, neither procure ye destruction by the works of your hands. **13** For God made not death, neither hath he pleasure in the destruction of the living. **14** For he created all things that they might be: and he made the nations of the earth for health: and there is no poison of destruction in them, nor kingdom of hell upon the earth. **15** For justice is perpetual and immortal.

16 But the wicked with works and words have called it to them: and esteeming it a friend have fallen away, and have made a covenant with it: because they are worthy to be of the part thereof.

Chapter 2

1 For they have said, reasoning with themselves, but not right: The time of our life is short and tedious, and in the end of a man there is no remedy, and no man hath been known to have returned

from hell: **2** For we are born of nothing, and after this we shall be as if we had not been: for the breath in our nostrils is smoke: and speech a spark to move our heart, **3** Which being put out, our body shall be ashes, and our spirit shall be poured abroad as soft air, and our life shall pass away as the trace of a cloud, and shall be dispersed as a mist, which is driven away by the beams of the sun, and overpowered with the heat thereof: **4** And our name in time shall be forgotten, and no man shall have any remembrance of our works. **5** For our time is as the passing of a shadow, and there is no going back of our end: for it is fast sealed, and no man returneth.

6 Come therefore, and let us enjoy the good things that are present, and let us speedily use the creatures as in youth. **7** Let us fill ourselves with costly wine, and ointments: and let not the flower of the time pass by us. **8** Let us crown ourselves with roses, before they be withered: let no meadow escape our riot. **9** Let none of us go without his part in luxury: let us everywhere leave tokens of joy: for this is our portion, and this our lot. **10** Let us oppress the poor just man, and not spare the widow, nor honour the ancient grey hairs of the aged.

11 But let our strength be the law of justice: for that which is feeble, is found to be nothing worth. **12** Let us therefore lie in wait for the just, because he is not for our turn, and he is contrary to our doings, and upbraideth us with transgressions of the law, and divulgeth against us the sins of our way of life. **13** He boasteth that he hath the knowledge of God, and calleth himself the son of God. **14** He is become a censurer of our thoughts. **15** He is grievous unto us, even to behold: for his life is not like other men's, and his ways are very different.

16 We are esteemed by him as triflers, and he abstaineth from our ways as from filthiness, and he preferreth the latter end of the just, and glorieth that he hath God for his father. **17** Let us see then if his words be true, and let us prove what shall happen to him, and we shall know what his end shall be. **18** For if he be the true son of God, he will defend him, and will deliver him from the hands of his enemies. **19** Let us examine him by outrages and tortures, that we may know his meekness and try his patience. **20** Let us condemn him to a most shameful death: for there shall be respect had unto him by his words.

21 These things they thought, and were deceived: for their own malice blinded them. **22** And they knew not the secrets of God, nor hoped for the wages of justice, nor esteemed the honour of holy souls. **23** For God created man incorruptible, and to the image of his own likeness he made him. **24** But by the envy of the devil, death came into the world: **25** And they follow him that are of his side.

Chapter 3

1 But the souls of the just are in the hand of God, and the torment of death shall not touch them. **2** In the sight of the unwise they seemed to die: and their departure was taken for misery: **3** And their going away from us, for utter destruction: but they are in peace. **4** And though in the sight of men they suffered torments, their hope is full of immortality. **5** Afflicted in few things, in many they shall be well rewarded: because God hath tried them, and found them worthy of himself.

6 As gold in the furnace he hath proved them, and as a victim of a holocaust he hath received them, and in time there shall be respect had to them. **7** The just shall shine, and shall run to and fro like sparks among the reeds. **8** They shall judge nations, and rule over people, and their Lord shall reign for ever. **9** They that trust in him, shall understand the truth: and they that are faithful in love shall rest in him: for grace and peace is to his elect. **10** But the wicked shall be punished according to their own devices: who have neglected the just, and have revolted from the Lord.

11 For he that rejecteth wisdom, and discipline, is unhappy: and their hope is vain, and their labours without fruit, and their works unprofitable. **12** Their wives are foolish, and their children wicked. **13** Their offspring is cursed: for happy is the barren: and the undefiled, that hath not known bed in sin: she shall have fruit in the visitation of holy souls. **14** And the eunuch, that hath not wrought iniquity with his hands, nor thought wicked things against God: for the precious gift of faith shall be given to him, and a most acceptable lot in the temple of God. **15** For the fruit of good labours is glorious, and the root of wisdom never faileth.

16 But the children of adulterers shall not come to perfection, and the seed of the unlawful bed shall be rooted out. **17** And if they live long, they shall be nothing regarded, and their last old age shall be without honour. **18** And if they die quickly, they shall have no hope, nor speech of comfort in the day of trial. **19** For dreadful are the ends of a wicked race.

Chapter 4

1 O how beautiful is the chaste generation with glory: for the memory thereof is immortal: because it is known both with God and with men. **2** When it is present, they imitate it: and they desire it when it hath withdrawn itself, and it triumpheth crowned for ever, winning the reward of undefiled conflicts. **3** But the multiplied brood of the wicked shall not thrive, and bastard slips shall not take

deep root, nor any fast foundation. **4** And if they flourish in branches for a time, yet standing not fast, they shall be shaken with the wind, and through the force of winds they shall be rooted out. **5** For the branches not being perfect, shall be broken, and their fruits shall be unprofitable, and sour to eat, and fit for nothing.

6 For the children that are born of unlawful beds, are witnesses of wickedness against their parents in their trial. **7** But the just man, if he be prevented with death, shall be in rest. **8** For venerable old age is not that of long time, nor counted by the number of years: but the understanding of a man is grey hairs. **9** And a spotless life is old age. **10** He pleased God and was beloved, and living among sinners he was translated.

11 He was taken away lest wickedness should alter his understanding, or deceit beguile his soul. **12** For the bewitching of vanity obscureth good things, and the wandering of concupiscence overturneth the innocent mind. **13** Being made perfect in a short space, he fulfilled a long time: **14** For his soul pleased God: therefore he hastened to bring him out of the midst of iniquities: but the people see this, and understand not, nor lay up such things in their hearts: **15** That the grace of God, and his mercy is with his saints, and that he hath respect to his chosen.

16 But the just that is dead, condemneth the wicked that are living, and youth soon ended, the long life of the unjust. **17** For they shall see the end of the wise man, and shall not understand what God hath designed for him, and why the Lord hath set him in safety. **18** They shall see him, and shall despise him: but the Lord shall laugh them to scorn. **19** And they shall fall after this without honour, and be a reproach among the dead for ever: for he shall burst them puffed up and speechless, and shall shake them from the foundations, and they shall be utterly laid waste: they shall be in sorrow, and their memory shall perish. **20** They shall come with fear at the thought of their sins, and their iniquities shall stand against them to convict them.

Chapter 5

1 Then shall the just stand with great constancy against those that have afflicted them, and taken away their labours. **2** These seeing it, shall be troubled with terrible fear, and shall be amazed at the suddenness of their unexpected salvation. **3** Saying within themselves, repenting, and groaning for anguish of spirit: These are they, whom we had some time in derision, and for a parable of reproach. **4** We fools esteemed their life madness, and their end without honour. **5** Behold how they are numbered among the children of God, and their lot is among the saints.

6 Therefore we have erred from the way of truth, and the light of justice hath not shined unto us, and the sun of understanding hath not risen upon us. **7** We wearied ourselves in the way of iniquity and destruction, and have walked through hard ways, but the way of the Lord we have not known. **8** What hath pride profited us? or what advantage hath the boasting of riches brought us? **9** All those things are passed away like a shadow, and like a post that runneth on, **10** And as a ship that passeth through the waves: whereof when it is gone by, the trace cannot be found, nor the path of its keel in the waters:

11 Or as when a bird flieth through the air, of the passage of which no mark can be found, but only the sound of the wings beating the light air, and parting it by the force of her flight; she moved her wings, and hath flown through, and there is no mark found afterwards of her way: **12** Or as when an arrow is shot at a mark, the divided air presently cometh together again, so that the passage thereof is not known: **13** So we also being born, forthwith ceased to be: and have been able to shew no mark of virtue: but are consumed in our wickedness. **14** Such things as these the sinners said in hell: **15** For the hope of the wicked is as dust, which is blown away with the wind, and as a thin froth which is dispersed by the storm: and a smoke that is scattered abroad by the wind: and as the remembrance of a guest of one day that passeth by.

16 But the just shall live for evermore: and their reward is with the Lord, and the care of them with the most High. **17** Therefore shall they receive a kingdom of glory, and a crown of beauty at the hand of the Lord: for with his right hand he will cover them, and with his holy arm he will defend them. **18** And his zeal will take armour, and he will arm the creature for the revenge of his enemies. **19** He will put on justice as a breastplate, and will take true judgment instead of a helmet. **20** He will take equity for an invincible shield:

21 And he will sharpen his severe wrath for a spear, and the whole world shall fight with him against the unwise. **22** Then shafts of lightning shall go directly from the clouds, as from a bow well bent, they shall be shot out, and shall fly to the mark. **23** And thick hail shall be cast upon them from the stone casting wrath: the water of the sea shall rage against them, and the rivers shall run together in a terrible manner. **24** A mighty wind shall stand up against them, and as a whirlwind shall divide them: and their iniquity shall bring all the earth to a desert, and wickedness shall overthrow the thrones of the mighty.

Chapter 6

1 Wisdom is better than strength, and a wise man is better than a strong man. **2** Hear therefore, ye kings, and understand: learn, ye that are judges of the ends of the earth. **3** Give ear, you that rule the people, and that please yourselves in multitudes of nations: **4** For power is given you by the Lord, and strength by the most High, who will examine your works, and search out your thoughts: **5** Because being ministers of his kingdom, you have not judged rightly, nor kept the law of justice, nor walked according to the will of God.

6 Horribly and speedily will he appear to you: for a most severe judgment shall be for them that bear rule. **7** For to him that is little, mercy is granted: but the mighty shall be mightily tormented. **8** For God will not except any man's person, neither will he stand in awe of any man's greatness: for he made the little and the great, and he hath equally care of all. **9** But a greater punishment is ready for the more mighty. **10** To you, therefore, O kings, are these my words, that you may learn wisdom, and not fall from it.

11 For they that have kept just things justly, shall be justified: and they that have learned these things, shall find what to answer. **12** Covet ye therefore my words, and love them, and you shall have instruction. **13** Wisdom is glorious, and never fadeth away, and is easily seen by them that love her, and is found by them that seek her. **14** She preventeth them that covet her, so that she first sheweth herself unto them. **15** He that awaketh early to seek her, shall not labour: for he shall find her sitting at his door.

16 To think therefore upon her, is perfect understanding: and he that watcheth for her, shall quickly be secure. **17** For she goeth about seeking such as are worthy of her, and she sheweth herself to them cheerfully in the ways, and meeteth them with all providence. **18** For the beginning of her is the most true desire of discipline. **19** And the care of discipline is love: and love is the keeping of her laws: and the keeping of her laws is the firm foundation of incorruption: **20** And incorruption bringeth near to God.

21 Therefore the desire of wisdom bringeth to the everlasting kingdom. **22** If then your delight be in thrones, and sceptres, O ye kings of the people, love wisdom, that you may reign for ever. **23** Love the light of wisdom, all ye that bear rule over peoples. **24** Now what wisdom is, and what was her origin, I will declare: and I will not hide from you the mysteries of God, but will seek her out from the beginning of her birth, and bring the knowledge of her to light, and will not pass over the truth: **25** Neither will I go with consuming envy: for such a man shall not be partaker of wisdom.

26 Now the multitude of the wise is the welfare of the whole world: and a wise king is the upholding of the people. **27** Receive therefore instruction by my words, and it shall be profitable to you.

Chapter 7

1 I myself also am a mortal man, like all others, and of the race of him, that was first made of the earth, and in the womb of my mother I was fashioned to be flesh. **2** In the time of ten months I was compacted in blood, of the seed of man, and the pleasure of sleep concurring. **3** And being born I drew in the common air, and fell upon the earth, that is made alike, and the first voice which I uttered was crying, as all others do. **4** I was nursed in swaddling clothes, and with great cares. **5** For none of the kings had any other beginning of birth.

6 For all men have one entrance into life, and the like going out. **7** Wherefore I wished, and understanding was given me: and I called upon God, and the spirit of wisdom came upon me: **8** And I preferred her before kingdoms and thrones, and esteemed riches nothing in comparison of her. **9** Neither did I compare unto her any precious stone: for all gold in comparison of her, is as a little sand, and silver in respect to her shall be counted as clay. **10** I loved her above health and beauty, and chose to have her instead of light: for her light cannot be put out.

11 Now all good things came to me together with her, and innumerable riches through her hands, **12** And I rejoiced in all these: for this wisdom went before me, and I knew not that she was the mother of them all. **13** Which I have learned without guile, and communicate without envy, and her riches I hide not. **14** For she is an infinite treasure to men! which they that use, become the friends of God, being commended for the gift of discipline. **15** And God hath given to me to speak as I would, and to conceive thoughts worthy of those things that are given me: because he is the guide of wisdom, and the director of the wise:

16 For in his hand are both we, and our words, and all wisdom, and the knowledge and skill of works. **17** For he hath given me the true knowledge of the things that are: to know the disposition of the whole world, and the virtues of the elements, **18** The beginning, and ending, and midst of the times, the alterations of their courses, and the changes of seasons, **19** The revolutions of the year, and the dispositions of the stars, **20** The natures of living creatures, and rage of wild beasts, the force of winds, and reasonings of men, the diversities of plants, and the virtues of roots,

21 And all such things as are hid and not foreseen, I have learned: for wisdom, which is the worker of all things, taught me. **22** For in her is the spirit of understanding: holy, one, manifold, subtile, eloquent, active, undefiled, sure, sweet, loving that which is good, quick, which nothing hindereth, beneficent, **23** Gentle, kind, steadfast, assured, secure, having all power, overseeing all things, and containing all spirits, intelligible, pure, subtile. **24** For wisdom is more active than all active things: and reacheth everywhere by reason of her purity. **25** For she is a vapour of the power of God, and a certain pure emanation of the glory of the almighty God: and therefore no defiled thing cometh into her.

26 For she is the brightness of eternal light, and the unspotted mirror of God's majesty, and the image of his goodness. **27** And being but one, she can do all things: and remaining in herself the same, she reneweth all things, and through nations conveyeth herself into holy souls, she maketh the friends of God and prophets. **28** For God loveth none but him that dwelleth with wisdom. **29** For she is more beautiful than the sun, and above all the order of the stars: being compared with the light, she is found before it. **30** For after this cometh night, but no evil can overcome wisdom.

Chapter 8

1 She reacheth therefore from end to end mightily, and ordereth all things sweetly. **2** Her have I loved, and have sought her out from my youth, and have desired to take her for my spouse, and I became a lover of her beauty. **3** She glorifieth her nobility by being conversant with God: yea and the Lord of all things hath loved her. **4** For it is she that teacheth the knowledge of God, and is the chooser of his works. **5** And if riches be desired in life, what is richer than wisdom, which maketh all things?

6 And if sense do work: who is a more artful worker than she of those things that are? **7** And if a man love justice: her labours have great virtues; for she teacheth temperance, and prudence, and justice, and fortitude, which are such things as men can have nothing more profitable in life. **8** And if a man desire much knowledge: she knoweth things past, and judgeth of things to come: she knoweth the subtilties of speeches, and the solutions of arguments: she knoweth signs and wonders before they be done, and the events of times and ages. **9** I purposed therefore to take her to me to live with me: knowing that she will communicate to me of her good things, and will be a comfort in my cares and grief. **10** For her sake I shall have glory among the multitude, and honour with the ancients, though I be young:

11 And I shall be found of a quick conceit in judgment, and shall be admired in the sight of the mighty, and the faces of princes shall wonder at me. **12** They shall wait for me when I hold my peace, and they shall look upon me when I speak, and if I talk much they shall lay their hands on their mouths. **13** Moreover by the means of her I shall have immortality: and shall leave behind me an everlasting memory to them that come after me. **14** I shall set the people in order: and nations shall be subject to me. **15** Terrible kings hearing shall be afraid of me: among the multitude I shall be found good, and valiant in war.

16 When I go into my house, I shall repose myself with her: for her conversation hath no bitterness, nor her company any tediousness, but joy and gladness. **17** Thinking these things with myself, and pondering them in my heart, that to be allied to wisdom is immortality, **18** And that there is great delight in her friendship, and inexhaustible riches in the works of her hands, and in the exercise of conference with her, wisdom, and glory in the communication of her words: I went about seeking, that I might take her to myself. **19** And I was a witty child and had received a good soul. **20** And whereas I was more good, I came to a body undefiled.

21 And as I knew that I could not otherwise be continent, except God gave it, and this also was a point of wisdom, to know whose gift it was: I went to the Lord, and besought him, and said with my whole heart:

Chapter 9

1 God of my fathers, and Lord of mercy, who hast made all things with thy word, **2** And by thy wisdom hast appointed man, that he should have dominion over the creature that was made by thee, **3** That he should order the world according to equity and justice, and execute justice with an upright heart: **4** Give me wisdom, that sitteth by thy throne, and cast me not off from among thy children: **5** For I am thy servant, and the son of thy handmaid, a weak man, and of short time, and falling short of the understanding of judgment and laws.

6 For if one be perfect among the children of men, yet if thy wisdom be not with him, he shall be nothing regarded. **7** Thou hast chosen me to be king of thy people, and a judge of thy sons and daughters. **8** And hast commanded me to build a temple on thy holy mount, and an altar in the city of thy dwelling place, a resemblance of thy holy tabernacle, which thou hast prepared from the beginning: **9** And thy wisdom with thee, which knoweth thy works, which then also was present when thou madest the world, and knew what was agreeable to thy eyes, and what was right in thy commandments. **10** Send her out of thy holy heaven, and from the throne of thy majesty, that she may be with me, and may labour with me, that I may know what is acceptable with thee:

11 For she knoweth and understandeth all things, and shall lead me soberly in my works, and shall preserve me by her power. **12** So shall my works be acceptable, and I shall govern thy people justly, and shall be worthy of the throne of my father. **13** For who among men is he that can know the counsel of God? or who can think what the will of God is? **14** For the thoughts of mortal men are fearful, and our counsels uncertain. **15** For the corruptible body is a load upon the soul, and the earthly habitation presseth down the mind that museth upon many things.

16 And hardly do we guess aright at things that are upon earth: and with labour do we find the things that are before us. But the things that are in heaven, who shall search out? **17** And who shall know thy thought, except thou give wisdom, and send thy Holy Spirit from above: **18** And so the ways of them that are upon earth may be corrected, and men may learn the things that please thee? **19** For by wisdom they were healed, whosoever have pleased thee, O Lord, from the beginning.

Chapter 10

1 She preserved him, that was first formed by God the father of the world, when he was created alone, **2** And she brought him out of his sin, and gave him power to govern all things. **3** But when the unjust went away from her in his anger, he perished by the fury wherewith he murdered his brother. **4** For whose cause, when water destroyed the earth, wisdom healed it again, directing the course of the just by contemptible wood. **5** Moreover when the nations had conspired together to consent to wickedness, she knew the just, and preserved him without blame to God, and kept him strong against the compassion for his son.

6 She delivered the just man who fled from the wicked that were perishing, when the fire came down upon Pentapolis: **7** Whose land for a testimony of their wickedness is desolate, and smoketh to this day, and the trees bear fruits that ripen not, and a standing pillar of salt is a monument of an incredulous soul. **8** For regarding not wisdom, they did not only slip in this, that they were ignorant of good things, but they left also unto men a memorial of their folly, so that in the things in which they sinned, they could not so much as lie hid. **9** But wisdom hath delivered from sorrow them that attend upon her. **10** She conducted the just, when he fled from his brother's wrath, through the right ways, and shewed him the kingdom of God, and gave him the knowledge of the holy things, made him honourable in his labours, and accomplished his labours.

11 In the deceit of them that overreached him, she stood by him, and made him honourable. **12** She kept him safe from his enemies, and she defended him from seducers, and gave him a strong conflict, that he might overcome, and know that wisdom is mightier than all. **13** She forsook not the just when he was sold, but delivered him from sinners: she went down with him into the pit. **14** And in bands she left him not, till she brought him the sceptre of the kingdom, and power against those that oppressed him: and shewed them to be liars that had accused him, and gave him everlasting glory. **15** She delivered the just people, and blameless seed from the nations that oppressed them.

16 She entered into the soul of the servant of God, and stood against dreadful kings in wonders and signs. **17** And she rendered to the just the wages of their labours, and conducted them in a wonderful way: and she was to them for a covert by day, and for the light of stars by night: **18** And she brought them through the Red Sea, and carried them over through a great water. **19** But their enemies she drowned in the sea, and from the depth of hell she brought them out. Therefore the just took the spoils of the wicked. **20** And they sung to thy holy name, O Lord, and they praised with one accord thy victorious hand.

21 For wisdom opened the mouth of the dumb, and made the tongues of infants eloquent.

Chapter 11

1 She prospered their works in the hands of the holy prophet. **2** They went through wildernesses that were not inhabited, and in desert places they pitched their tents. **3** They stood against their enemies, and revenged themselves of their adversaries. **4** They were thirsty, and they called upon thee, and water was given them out of the high rock, and a refreshment of their thirst out of the hard stone. **5** For by what things their enemies were punished, when their drink failed them, while the children of Israel abounded therewith and rejoiced:

6 By the same things they in their need were benefited. **7** For instead of a fountain of an ever running river, thou gavest human blood to the unjust. **8** And whilst they were diminished for a manifest reproof of their murdering the infants, thou gavest to thine abundant water unlooked for: **9** shewing by the thirst that was then, how thou didst exalt thine, and didst kill their adversaries. **10** For when they were tried, and chastised with mercy, they knew how the wicked were judged with wrath and tormented.

11 For thou didst admonish and try them as a father: but the others, as a severe king, thou didst examine and condemn. **12** For whether absent or present, they were tormented alike. **13** For a double affliction came upon them, and a groaning for the remembrance of things past. **14** For when they heard that by their punishments the others were benefited, they remembered the Lord, wondering at the end of what was come to pass. **15** For whom they scorned before, when he was thrown out at the time of his being wickedly exposed to perish, him they admired in the end, when they saw the event: their thirsting being unlike to that of the just.

16 But for the foolish devices of their iniquity, because some being deceived worshipped dumb serpents and worthless beasts, thou didst send upon them a multitude of dumb beasts for vengeance. **17** That they might know that by what things a man sinneth, by the same also he is tormented. **18** For thy almighty hand, which made the world of matter without form, was not unable to send upon them a multitude of bears, or fierce lions, **19** Or unknown beasts of a new kind, full of rage: either breathing out a fiery vapour, or sending forth a stinking smoke, or shooting horrible sparks out of their eyes: **20** Whereof not only the hurt might be able to destroy them, but also the very sight might kill them through fear.

21 Yea and without these, they might have been slain with one blast, persecuted by their own deeds, and scattered by the breath of thy power: but thou hast ordered all things in measure, and number, and weight. **22** For great power always belonged to thee alone: and who shall resist the strength of thy arm? **23** For the whole world before thee is as the least grain of the balance, and as a drop of the morning dew, that falleth down upon the earth: **24** But thou hast mercy upon all, because thou canst do all things, and overlookest the sins of men for the sake of repentance. **25** For thou lovest all things that are, and hatest none of the things which thou hast made: for thou didst not appoint, or make any thing hating it.

26 And how could any thing endure, if thou wouldst not? or be preserved, if not called by thee. **27** But thou sparest all: because they are thine, O Lord, who lovest souls.

Chapter 12

1 O how good and sweet is thy spirit, O Lord, in all things! **2** And therefore thou chastisest them that err, by little and little: and admonishest them, and speakest to them, concerning the things wherein they offend: that leaving their wickedness, they may believe in thee, O Lord. **3** For those ancient inhabitants of thy holy land, whom thou didst abhor, **4** Because they did works hateful to thee by their sorceries, and wicked sacrifices, **5** And those merciless murderers of their own children, and eaters of men's bowels, and devourers of blood from the midst of thy consecration,

6 And those parents sacrificing with their own hands helpless souls, it was thy will to destroy by the hands of our parents, **7** That the land which of all is most dear to thee might receive a worthy colony of the children of God. **8** Yet even those thou sparedst as men, and didst send wasps, forerunners of thy host, to destroy them by little and little. **9** Not that thou wast unable to bring the wicked under the just by war, or by cruel beasts, or with one rough word to destroy them at once: **10** But executing thy judgments by degrees thou gavest them place of repentance, not being ignorant that they were a wicked generation, and their malice natural, and that their thought could never be changed.

11 For it was a cursed seed from the beginning: neither didst thou for fear of any one give pardon to their sins. **12** For who shall say to thee: What hast thou done? or who shall withstand thy judgment? or who shall come before thee to be a revenger of wicked men? or who shall accuse thee, if the nations perish, which thou hast made? **13** For there is no other God but thou, who hast care of all, that thou shouldst shew that thou dost not give judgment unjustly. **14** Neither shall king, nor tyrant in thy sight inquire about them whom thou hast destroyed. **15** For so much then as thou art just, thou orderest all things justly: thinking it not agreeable to thy power, to condemn him who deserveth not to be punished.

16 For thy power is the beginning of justice: and because thou art Lord of all, thou makest thyself gracious to all. **17** For thou shewest thy power, when men will not believe thee to be absolute in power, and thou convincest the boldness of them that know thee not. **18** But thou being master of power, judgest with tranquillity; and with great favour disposest of us: for thy power is at hand when thou wilt. **19** But thou hast taught thy people by such works, that they must be just and humane, and hast made thy children to be of a good hope: because in judging thou givest place for repentance for sins. **20** For if thou didst punish the enemies of thy servants, and that deserved to die, with so great deliberation, giving them time and place whereby they might be changed from their wickedness:

21 With what circumspection hast thou judged thy own children, to whose parents thou hast sworn and made covenants of good promises? **22** Therefore whereas thou chastisest us, thou scourgest our enemies very many ways, to the end that when we judge we may think on thy goodness: and when we are judged, we may hope for thy mercy. **23** Wherefore thou hast also greatly tormented them who in their life have lived foolishly and unjustly, by the same things which they worshipped. **24** For they went astray for a long time in the ways of error, holding those things for gods which are the most worthless among beasts, living after the manner of children without understanding. **25** Therefore thou hast sent a judgment upon them as senseless children to mock them.

26 But they that were not amended by mockeries and

reprehensions, experienced the worthy judgment of God. **27** For seeing with indignation that they suffered by those very things which they took for gods, when they were destroyed by the same, they acknowledged him the true God, whom in time past they denied that they knew: for which cause the end also of their condemnation came upon them.

Chapter 13

1 But all men are vain, in whom there is not the knowledge of God: and who by these good things that are seen, could not understand him that is, neither by attending to the works have acknowledged who was the workman: **2** But have imagined either the fire, or the wind, or the swift air, or the circle of the stars, or the great water, or the sun and moon, to be the gods that rule the world. **3** With whose beauty, if they, being delighted, took them to be gods: let them know how much the Lord of them is more beautiful than they: for the first author of beauty made all those things. **4** Or if they admired their power and their effects, let them understand by them, that he that made them, is mightier than they: **5** For by the greatness of the beauty, and of the creature, the creator of them may be seen, so as to be known thereby.

6 But yet as to these they are less to be blamed. For they perhaps err, seeking God, and desirous to find him. **7** For being conversant among his works, they search: and they are persuaded that the things are good which are seen. **8** But then again they are not to be pardoned. **9** For if they were able to know so much as to make a judgment of the world: how did they not more easily find out the Lord thereof? **10** But unhappy are they, and their hope is among the dead, who have called gods the works of the hands of men, gold and silver, the inventions of art, and the resemblances of beasts, or an unprofitable stone the work of an ancient hand.

11 Or if an artist, a carpenter, hath cut down a tree proper for his use in the wood, and skillfully taken off all the bark thereof, and with his art, diligently formeth a vessel profitable for the common uses of life, **12** And useth the chips of his work to dress his meat: **13** And taking what was left thereof, which is good for nothing, being a crooked piece of wood, and full of knots, carveth it diligently when he hath nothing else to do, and by the skill of his art fashioneth it and maketh it like the image of a man: **14** Or the resemblance of some beast, laying it over with vermilion, and painting it red, and covering every spot that is in it: **15** And maketh a convenient dwelling place for it, and setting it in a wall, and fastening it with iron,

16 Providing for it, lest it should fall, knowing that it is unable to help itself: for it is an image, and hath need of help. **17** And then maketh prayer to it, inquiring concerning his substance, and his children, or his marriage. And he is not ashamed to speak to that which hath no life: **18** And for health he maketh supplication to the weak, and for life prayeth to that which is dead, and for help calleth upon that which is unprofitable: **19** And for a good journey he petitioneth him that cannot walk: and for getting, and for working, and for the event of all things he asketh him that is unable to do any thing.

Chapter 14

1 Again, another designing to sail, and beginning to make his voyage through the raging waves, calleth upon a piece of wood more frail than the wood that carrieth him. **2** For this the desire of gain devised, and the workman built it by his skill. **3** But thy providence, O Father, governeth it: for thou hast made a way even in the sea, and a most sure path among the waves, **4** shewing that thou art able to save out of all things, yea though a man went to sea without art. **5** But that the works of thy wisdom might not be idle: therefore men also trust their lives even to a little wood, and passing over the sea by ship are saved.

6 And from the beginning also when the proud giants perished, the hope of the world fleeing to a vessel, which was governed by thy hand, left to the world seed of generation. **7** For blessed is the wood, by which justice cometh. **8** But the idol that is made by hands, is cursed, as well it, as he that made it: he because he made it; and it because being frail it is called a god. **9** But to God the wicked and his wickedness are hateful alike. **10** For that which is made, together with him that made it, shall suffer torments.

11 Therefore there shall be no respect had even to the idols of the Gentiles: because the creatures of God are turned to an abomination, and a temptation to the souls of men, and a snare to the feet of the unwise. **12** For the beginning of fornication is the devising of idols: and the invention of them is the corruption of life. **13** For neither were they from the beginning, neither shall they be for ever. **14** For by the vanity of men they came into the world: and therefore they shall be found to come shortly to an end. **15** For a father being afflicted with bitter grief, made to himself the image of his son who was quickly taken away: and him who then had died as a man, he began now to worship as a god, and appointed him rites and sacrifices among his servants.

16 Then in process of time, wicked custom prevailing, this error was kept as a law, and statues were worshipped by the commandment of tyrants. **17** And those whom men could not honour in presence, because they dwelt far off, they brought their resemblance from afar, and made an express image of the king whom they had a mind to honour: that by this their diligence, they might honour as present, him that was absent. **18** And to worshipping of these, the singular diligence also of the artificer helped to set forward the ignorant. **19** For he being willing to please him that employed him, laboured with all his art to make the resemblance in the best manner. **20** And the multitude of men, carried away by the beauty of the work, took him now for a god that a little before was but honoured as a man.

21 And this was the occasion of deceiving human life: for men serving either their affection, or their kings, gave the incommunicable name to stones and wood. **22** And it was not enough for them to err about the knowledge of God, but whereas they lived in a great war of ignorance, they call so many and so great evils peace. **23** For either they sacrifice their own children, or use hidden sacrifices, or keep watches full of madness, **24** So that now they neither keep life, nor marriage undefiled, but one killeth another through envy, or grieveth him by adultery: **25** And all things are mingled together, blood, murder, theft and dissimulation, corruption and unfaithfulness, tumults and perjury, disquieting of the good,

26 Forgetfulness of God, defiling of souls, changing of nature, disorder in marriage, and the irregularity of adultery and uncleanness. **27** For the worship of abominable idols is the cause, and the beginning and end of all evil. **28** For either they are mad when they are merry: or they prophesy lies, or they live unjustly, or easily forswear themselves. **29** For whilst they trust in idols, which are without life, though they swear amiss, they look not to be hurt. **30** But for two things they shall be justly punished, because they have thought not well of God, giving heed to idols, and have sworn unjustly, in guile despising justice.

31 For it is not the power of them, by whom they swear, but the just vengeance of sinners always punisheth the transgression of the unjust.

Chapter 15

1 But thou, our God, art gracious and true, patient, and ordering all things in mercy. **2** For if we sin, we are thine, knowing thy greatness: and if we sin not, we know that we are counted with thee. **3** For to know thee is perfect justice: and to know thy justice, and thy power, is the root of immortality. **4** For the invention of mischievous men hath not deceived us, nor the shadow of a picture, a fruitless labour, a graven figure with divers colours, **5** The sight

whereof enticeth the fool to lust after it, and he loveth the lifeless figure of a dead image.

6 The lovers of evil things deserve to have no better things to trust in, both they that make them, and they that love them, and they that worship them. **7** The potter also tempering soft earth, with labour fashioneth every vessel for our service, and of the same clay he maketh both vessels that are for clean uses, and likewise such as serve to the contrary: but what is the use of these vessels, the potter is the judge. **8** And of the same clay by a vain labour he maketh a god: he who a little before was made of earth himself, and a little after returneth to the same out of which he was taken, when his life which was lent him shall be called for again. **9** But his care is, not that he shall labour, nor that his life is short, but he striveth with the goldsmiths and silversmiths: and he endeavoureth to do like the workers in brass, and counteth it a glory to make vain things. **10** For his heart is ashes, and his hope vain earth, and his life more base than clay:

11 Forasmuch as he knew not his maker and him that inspired into him the soul that worketh, and that breathed into him a living spirit. **12** Yea and they have counted our life a pastime, and the business of life to be gain, and that we must be getting every way, even out of evil. **13** For that man knoweth that he offendeth above all others, who of earthly matter maketh brittle vessels, and graven gods. **14** But all the enemies of thy people that hold them in subjection, are foolish, and unhappy, and proud beyond measure: **15** For they have esteemed all the idols of the heathens for gods, which neither have the use of eyes to see, nor noses to draw breath, nor ears to hear, nor fingers of hands to handle, and as for their feet, they are slow to walk.

16 For man made them: and he that borroweth his own breath, fashioned them. For no man can make a god like to himself. **17** For being mortal himself, he formeth a dead thing with his wicked hands. For he is better than they whom he worshippeth, because he indeed hath lived, though he were mortal, but they never. **18** Moreover they worship also the vilest creatures: but things without sense compared to these, are worse than they. **19** Yea, neither by sight can any man see good of these beasts. But they have fled from the praise of God, and from his blessing.

Chapter 16

1 For these things, and by the like things to these, they were worthily punished, and were destroyed by a multitude of beasts. **2** Instead of which punishment, dealing well with thy people, thou gavest them their desire of delicious food, of a new

taste, preparing for them quails for their meat: **3** To the end that they indeed desiring food, by means of those things that were shewn and sent among them, might loathe even that which was necessary to satisfy their desire. But these, after suffering want for a short time, tasted a new meat. **4** For it was requisite that inevitable destruction should come upon them that exercised tyranny: but to these it should only be shewn how their enemies were destroyed. **5** For when the fierce rage of beasts came upon these, they were destroyed with the bitings of crooked serpents.

6 But thy wrath endured not for ever, but they were troubled for a short time for their correction, having a sign of salvation to put them in remembrance of the commandment of thy law. **7** For he that turned to it, was not healed by that which he saw, but by thee the Saviour of all. **8** And in this thou didst shew to our enemies, that thou art he who deliverest from all evil. **9** For the bitings of locusts, and of flies killed them, and there was found no remedy for their life: because they were worthy to be destroyed by such things. **10** But not even the teeth of venomous serpents overcame thy children: for thy mercy came and healed them.

11 For they were examined for the remembrance of thy words, and were quickly healed, lest falling into deep forgetfulness, they might not be able to use thy help. **12** For it was neither herb, nor mollifying plaster that healed them, but thy word, O Lord, which healeth all things. **13** For it is thou, O Lord, that hast power of life and death, and leadest down to the gates of death, and bringest back again: **14** A man indeed killeth through malice, and when the spirit is gone forth, it shall not return, neither shall he call back the soul that is received: **15** But it is impossible to escape thy hand.

16 For the wicked that denied to know thee, were scourged by the strength of thy arm, being persecuted by strange waters, and hail, and rain, and consumed by fire. **17** And which was wonderful, in water, which extinguisheth all things, the fire had more force: for the world fighteth for the just. **18** For at one time, the fire was mitigated, that the beasts which were sent against the wicked might not be burned, but that they might see and perceive that they were persecuted by the judgment of God. **19** And at another time the fire, above its own power, burned in the midst of water, to destroy the fruits of a wicked land. **20** Instead of which things thou didst feed thy people with the food of angels, and gavest them bread from heaven prepared without labour; having in it all that is delicious, and the sweetness of every taste.

21 For thy sustenance shewed thy sweetness to thy children, and serving every man's will, it was turned to what every man liked. **22** But snow and ice endured the force of fire, and melted not: that they might know that fire burning in the hail and flashing in the rain destroyed the fruits of the enemies. **23** But this same again, that the just might be nourished, did even forget its own strength. **24** For the creature serving thee the Creator, is made fierce against the unjust for their punishment; and abateth its strength for the benefit of them that trust in thee. **25** Therefore even then it was transformed into all things, and was obedient to thy grace that nourisheth all, according to the will of them that desired it of thee.

26 That thy children, O Lord, whom thou lovedst, might know that it is not the growing of fruits that nourisheth men, but thy word preserveth them that believe in thee: **27** For that which could not be destroyed by fire, being warmed with a little sunbeam presently melted away: **28** That it might be known to all, that we ought to prevent the sun to bless thee, and adore thee at the dawning of the light. **29** For the hope of the unthankful shall melt away as the winter's ice, and shall run off as unprofitable water.

Chapter 17

1 For thy judgments, O Lord, are great, and thy words cannot be expressed: therefore undisciplined souls have erred. **2** For while the wicked thought to be able to have dominion over the holy nation, they themselves being fettered with the bonds of darkness, and a long night, shut up in their houses, lay there exiled from the eternal providence. **3** And while they thought to lie hid in their obscure sins, they were scattered under a dark veil of forgetfulness, being horribly afraid and troubled with exceeding great astonishment. **4** For neither did the den that held them, keep them from fear: for noises coming down troubled them, and sad visions appearing to them, affrighted them. **5** And no power of fire could give them light, neither could the bright flames of the stars enlighten that horrible night.

6 But there appeared to them a sudden fire, very dreadful: and being struck with the fear of that face, which was not seen, they thought the things which they saw to be worse: **7** And the delusions of their magic art were put down, and their boasting of wisdom was reproachfully rebuked. **8** For they who promised to drive away fears and troubles from a sick soul, were sick themselves of a fear worthy to be laughed at. **9** For though no terrible thing disturbed them: yet being scared with the passing by of beasts, and hissing of serpents, they died for fear: and denying that they saw the air, which could by no means be avoided. **10** For whereas wickedness is fearful, it beareth witness of its condemnation: for a troubled conscience always forecasteth grievous things.

11 For fear is nothing else but a yielding up of the succours from thought. **12** And while there is less expectation from within, the greater doth it count the ignorance of that cause which bringeth the torment. **13** But they that during that night, in which nothing could be done, and which came upon them from the lowest and deepest hell, slept the same sleep. **14** Were sometimes molested with the fear of monsters, sometimes fainted away, their soul failing them: for a sudden and unlooked for fear was come upon them. **15** Moreover if any of them had fallen down, he was kept shut up in prison without irons.

16 For if any one were a husbandman, or a shepherd, or a labourer in the field, and was suddenly overtaken, he endured a necessity from which he could not fly. **17** For they were all bound together with one chain of darkness. Whether it were a whistling wind, or the melodious voice of birds, among the spreading branches of trees, or a fall of water running down with violence, **18** Or the mighty noise of stones tumbling down, or the running that could not be seen of beasts playing together, or the roaring voice of wild beasts, or a rebounding echo from the highest mountains: these things made them to swoon for fear. **19** For the whole world was enlightened with a clear light, and none were hindered in their labours. **20** But over them only was spread a heavy night, an image of that darkness which was to come upon them. But they were to themselves more grievous than the darkness.

Chapter 18

1 But thy saints had a very great light, and they heard their voice indeed, but did not see their shape. And because they also did not suffer the same things, they glorified thee: **2** And they that before had been wronged, gave thanks, because they were not hurt now: and asked this gift, that there might be a difference. **3** Therefore they received a burning pillar of fire for a guide of the way which they knew not, and thou gavest them a harmless sun of a good entertainment. **4** The others indeed were worthy to be deprived of light, and imprisoned in darkness, who kept thy children shut up, by whom the pure light of the law was to be given to the world. **5** And whereas they thought to kill the babes of the just, one child being cast forth, and saved, to reprove them, thou tookest away a multitude of their children, and destroyedst them all together in a mighty water.

6 For that night was known before by our fathers, that assuredly knowing what oaths they had trusted to, they might be of better courage. **7** So thy people received the salvation of the just, and destruction of the unjust. **8** For as thou didst punish the adversaries: so thou didst also encourage and glorify us. **9** For the just children of good men were offering sacrifice secretly, and they unanimously ordered a law of justice: that the just should receive both good and evil alike, singing now the praises of the fathers. **10** But on the other side there sounded an ill according cry of the enemies, and a lamentable mourning was heard for the children that were bewailed.

11 And the servant suffered the same punishment as the master, and a common man suffered in like manner as the king. **12** So all alike had innumerable dead, with one kind of death. Neither were the living sufficient to bury them; for in one moment the noblest offspring of them was destroyed. **13** For whereas they would not believe any thing before by reason of the enchantments, then first upon the destruction of the firstborn, they acknowledged the people to be of God. **14** For while all things were in quiet silence, and the night was in the midst of her course, **15** Thy almighty word leapt down from heaven from thy royal throne, as a fierce conqueror into the midst of the land of destruction.

16 With a sharp sword carrying thy unfeigned commandment, and he stood and filled all things with death, and standing on the earth reached even to heaven. **17** Then suddenly visions of evil dreams troubled them, and fears unlooked for came upon them. **18** And one thrown here, another there, half dead, shewed the cause of his death. **19** For the visions that troubled them foreshewed these things, lest they should perish and not know why they suffered these evils. **20** But the just also were afterwards touched by an assault of death, and there was a disturbance of the multitude in the wilderness: but thy wrath did not long continue.

21 For a blameless man made haste to pray for the people, bringing forth the shield of his ministry, prayer, and by incense making supplication, withstood the wrath, and put an end to the calamity, shewing that he was thy servant. **22** And he overcame the disturbance, not by strength of body nor with force of arms, but with a word he subdued him that punished them, alleging the oaths and covenant made with the fathers. **23** For when they were now fallen down dead by heaps one upon another, he stood between and stayed the assault, and cut off the way to the living. **24** For in the priestly robe which he wore, was the whole world: and in the four rows of the stones the glory of the fathers was graven, and thy majesty was written upon the diadem of his head. **25** And to these the destroyer gave place, and was afraid of them: for the proof only of wrath was enough.

Chapter 19

1 But as to the wicked, even to the end there came upon them wrath without mercy. For he knew before also what they would

do: **2** For when they had given them leave to depart, and had sent them away with great care, they repented, and pursued after them. **3** For whilst they were yet mourning, and lamenting at the graves of the dead, they took up another foolish device: and pursued them as fugitives whom they had pressed to be gone: **4** For a necessity, of which they were worthy, brought them to this end: and they lost the remembrance of those things which had happened, that their punishment might fill up what was wanting to their torments: **5** And that thy people might wonderfully pass through, but they might find a new death.

6 For every creature according to its kind was fashioned again as from the beginning, obeying thy commandments, that thy children might be kept without hurt. **7** For a cloud overshadowed their camp, and where water was before, dry land appeared, and in the Red Sea a way without hinderance, and out of the great deep a springing field: **8** Through which all the nation passed which was protected with thy hand, seeing thy miracles and wonders. **9** For they fed on their food like horses, and they skipped like lambs, praising thee, O Lord, who hadst delivered them. **10** For they were yet mindful of those things which had been done in the time of their sojourning, how the ground brought forth flies instead of cattle, and how the river cast up a multitude of frogs instead of fishes.

11 And at length they saw a new generation of birds, when being led by their appetite they asked for delicate meats. **12** For to satisfy their desire, the quail came up to them from the sea: and punishments came upon the sinners, not without foregoing signs by the force of thunders: for they suffered justly according to their own wickedness. **13** For they exercised a more detestable inhospitality than any: others indeed received not strangers unknown to them, but these brought their guests into bondage that had deserved well of them. **14** And not only so, but in another respect also they were worse: for the others against their will received the strangers. **15** But these grievously afflicted them whom they had received with joy, and who lived under the same laws.

16 But they were struck with blindness: as those others were at the doors of the just man, when they were covered with sudden darkness, and every one sought the passage of his own door. **17** For while the elements are changed in themselves, as in an instrument the sound of the quality is changed, yet all keep their sound: which may clearly be perceived by the very sight. **18** For the things of the land were turned into things of the water: and the things before swam in the water passed upon the land. **19** The fire had power in water above its own virtue, and the water forgot its quenching nature. **20** On the other side, the flames wasted not the flesh of corruptible animals walking therein, neither did they melt that good food, which was apt to melt as ice. For in all things thou didst magnify thy people, O Lord, and didst honour them, and didst not despise them, but didst assist them at all times, and in every place.

THE BOOK OF ECCLESIASTICUS (SIRACH)

Chapter 1

1 All wisdom is from the Lord God, and hath been always with him, and is before all time. **2** Who hath numbered the sand of the sea, and the drops of rain, and the days of the world? Who hath measured the height of heaven, and the breadth of the earth, and the depth of the abyss? **3** Who hath searched out the wisdom of God that goeth before all things? **4** Wisdom hath been created before all things, and the understanding of prudence from everlasting. **5** The word of God on high is the fountain of wisdom, and her ways are everlasting commandments.

6 To whom hath the root of wisdom been revealed, and who hath known her wise counsels? **7** To whom hath the discipline of wisdom been revealed and made manifest? and who hath understood the multiplicity of her steps? **8** There is one most high Creator Almighty, and a powerful king, and greatly to be feared, who sitteth upon his throne, and is the God of dominion. **9** He created her in the Holy Ghost, and saw her, and numbered her, and measured her. **10** And he poured her out upon all his works, and upon all flesh according to his gift, and hath given her to them that love him.

11 The fear of the Lord is honour, and glory, and gladness, and a crown of joy. **12** The fear of the Lord shall delight the heart, and shall give joy, and gladness, and length of days. **13** With him that feareth the Lord, it shall go well in the latter end, and in the day of his death he shall be blessed. **14** The love of God is honourable wisdom. **15** And they to whom she shall shew herself love her by the sight, and by the knowledge of her great works.

16 The fear of the Lord is the beginning of wisdom, and was created with the faithful in the womb, it walketh with chosen women, and is known with the just and faithful. **17** The fear of the Lord is the religiousness of knowledge. **18** Religiousness shall keep and justify the heart, it shall give joy and gladness. **19** It shall go well with him that feareth the Lord, and in the days of his end he shall be blessed. **20** To fear God is the fulness of wisdom, and fulness is from the fruits thereof.

21 She shall fill all her house with her increase, and the storehouses with her treasures. **22** The fear of the Lord is a crown of wisdom, filling up peace and the fruit of salvation: **23** And it hath seen, and numbered her: but both are the gifts of God. **24** Wisdom shall distribute knowledge, and understanding of prudence: and exalteth the glory of them that hold her. **25** The root of wisdom is to fear the Lord: and the branches thereof are longlived.

26 In the treasures of wisdom is understanding, and religiousness of knowledge: but to sinners wisdom is an abomination. **27** The fear of the Lord driveth out sin: **28** For he that is without fear, cannot be justified: for the wrath of his high spirits is his ruin. **29** A patient man shall bear for a time, and afterwards joy shall be restored to him. **30** A good understanding will hide his words for a time, and the lips of many shall declare his wisdom.

31 In the treasures of wisdom is the signification of discipline: **32** But the worship of God is an abomination to a sinner. **33** Son, if thou desire wisdom, keep justice, and God will give her to thee. **34** For the fear of the Lord is wisdom and discipline: and that which is agreeable to him, **35** Is faith, and meekness: and he will fill up his treasures.

36 Be not incredulous to the fear of the Lord: and come not to him with a double heart. **37** Be not a hypocrite in the sight of men, and let not thy lips be a stumblingblock to thee. **38** Watch over them, lest thou fall, and bring dishonour upon thy soul, **39** And God discover thy secrets, and cast thee down in the midst of the congregation. **40** Because thou camest to the Lord wickedly, and thy heart is full of guile and deceit.

Chapter 2

1 Son, when thou comest to the service of God, stand in justice and in fear, and prepare thy soul for temptation. **2** Humble thy heart, and endure: incline thy ear, and receive the words of understanding: and make not haste in the time of clouds. **3** Wait on God with patience: join thyself to God, and endure, that thy life may be increased in the latter end. **4** Take all that shall be brought upon thee: and in thy sorrow endure, and in thy humiliation keep patience. **5** For gold and silver are tried in the fire, but acceptable men in the furnace of humiliation.

6 Believe God, and he will recover thee: and direct thy way, and trust in him. Keep his fear, and grow old therein. **7** Ye that fear the Lord, wait for his mercy: and go not aside from him, lest ye fall. **8** Ye that fear the Lord, believe him: and your reward shall not be made void. **9** Ye that fear the Lord, hope in him: and mercy shall come to you for your delight. **10** Ye that fear the Lord, love him, and your hearts shall be enlightened.

11 My children behold the generations of men: and know ye that no one hath hoped in the Lord, and hath been confounded. **12** For who hath continued in his commandment, and hath been forsaken? or who hath called upon him, and he despised him? **13** For God is compassionate and merciful, and will forgive sins in the day of tribulation: and he is a protector to all that seek him in truth. **14** Woe to them that are of a double heart and to wicked lips, and to the hands that do evil, and to the sinner that goeth on the earth two ways. **15** Woe to them that are fainthearted, who believe not God: and therefore they shall not be protected by him.

16 Woe to them that have lost patience, and that have forsaken the right ways, and have gone aside into crooked ways. **17** And what will they do, when the Lord shall begin to examine? **18** They that fear the Lord, will not be incredulous to his word: and they that love him, will keep his way. **19** They that fear the Lord, will seek after the things that are well pleasing to him: and they that love him, shall be filled with his law. **20** They that fear the Lord, will prepare their hearts, and in his sight will sanctify their souls.

21 They that fear the Lord, keep his Commandments, and will have patience even until his visitation, **22** Saying: If we do not penance, we shall fall into the hands of the Lord, and not into the hands of men. **23** For according to his greatness, so also is his mercy with him.

Chapter 3

1 The sons of wisdom are the church of the just: and their generation, obedience and love. **2** Children, hear the judgment of your father, and so do that you may be saved. **3** For God hath made the father honourable to the children: and seeking the judgment of the mothers, hath confirmed it upon the children. **4** He that loveth God, shall obtain pardon for his sins by prayer, and shall refrain himself from them, and shall be heard in the prayer of days. **5** And he that honoureth his mother is as one that layeth up a treasure.

6 He that honoureth his father shall have joy in his own children, and in the day of his prayer he shall be heard. **7** He that honoureth his father shall enjoy a long life: and he that obeyeth the father, shall be a comfort to his mother. **8** He that feareth the Lord, honoureth his parents, and will serve them as his masters that brought him into the world. **9** Honour thy father, in work and word, and all patience, **10** That a blessing may come upon thee from him, and his blessing may remain in the latter end.

11 The father's blessing establisheth the houses of the children: but the mother's curse rooteth up the foundation. **12** Glory not in the dishonour of thy father: for his shame is no glory to thee. **13** For the glory of a man is from the honour of his father, and a father without honour is the disgrace of the son. **14** Son, support the old age of thy father, and grieve him not in his life; **15** And if his understanding fail, have patience with him, and despise him not when thou art in thy strength: for the relieving of the father shall not be forgotten.

16 For good shall be repaid to thee for the sin of thy mother. **17** And in justice thou shalt be built up, and in the day of affliction thou shalt be remembered: and thy sins shall melt away as the ice in the fair warm weather. **18** Of what an evil fame is he that forsaketh his father: and he is cursed of God that angereth his mother. **19** My son, do thy works in meekness, and thou shalt be beloved above the glory of men. **20** The greater thou art, the more humble thyself in all things, and thou shalt find grace before God:

21 For great is the power of God alone, and he is honoured by the humble. **22** Seek not the things that are too high for thee, and search not into things above thy ability: but the things that God hath commanded thee, think on them always, and in many of his works be not curious. **23** For it is not necessary for thee to see with thy eyes those things that are hid. **24** In unnecessary matters be not over curious, and in many of his works thou shalt not be inquisitive. **25** For many things are shewn to thee above the understanding of men.

26 And the suspicion of them hath deceived many, and hath detained their minds in vanity. **27** A hard heart shall fear evil at the last: and he that loveth danger shall perish in it. **28** A heart that goeth two ways shall not have success, and the perverse of heart shall be scandalized therein. **29** A wicked heart shall be laden with sorrows, and the sinner will add sin to sin. **30** The congregation of the proud shall not be healed: for the plant of wickedness shall take root in them, and it shall not be perceived.

31 The heart of the wise is understood in wisdom, and a good ear will hear wisdom with all desire. **32** A wise heart, and which hath understanding, will abstain from sins, and in the works of justice shall have success. **33** Water quencheth a flaming fire, and alms resisteth sins: **34** And God provideth for him that sheweth favour: he remembereth him afterwards, and in the time of his fall he shall find a sure stay.

Chapter 4

1 Son, defraud not the poor of alms, and turn not away thy eyes from the poor. **2** Despise not the hungry soul: and provoke not the poor in his want. **3** Afflict not the heart of the needy, and defer not to give to him that is in distress. **4** Reject not the petition of the afflicted: and turn not away thy face from the needy. **5** Turn not away thy eyes from the poor for fear of anger: and leave not to them that ask of thee to curse thee behind thy back.

6 For the prayer of him that curseth thee in the bitterness of his soul, shall be heard, for he that made him will hear him. **7** Make thyself affable to the congregation of the poor, and humble thy soul to the ancient, and bow thy head to a great man. **8** Bow down thy ear cheerfully to the poor, and pay what thou owest, and answer him peaceable words with mildness. **9** Deliver him that suffereth wrong out of the hand of the proud: and be not fainthearted in thy soul. **10** In judging be merciful to the fatherless as a father, and as a husband to their mother.

11 And thou shalt be as the obedient son of the most High, and he will have mercy on thee more than a mother. **12** Wisdom inspireth life into her children, and protecteth them that seek after her, and will go before them in the way of justice. **13** And he that loveth her, loveth life: and they that watch for her, shall embrace her sweetness. **14** They that hold her fast, shall inherit life: and whithersoever she entereth, God will give a blessing. **15** They that serve her, shall be servants to the holy one: and God loveth them that love her.

16 He that hearkeneth to her, shall judge nations: and he that looketh upon her, shall remain secure. **17** If he trust to her, he shall inherit her, and his generation shall be in assurance. **18** For she walketh with him in temptation, and at the first she chooseth him. **19** She will bring upon him fear and dread and trial: and she will scourge him with the affliction of her discipline, till she try him by her laws, and trust his soul. **20** Then she will strengthen him, and make a straight way to him, and give him joy,

21 And will disclose her secrets to him, and will heap upon him treasures of knowledge and understanding of justice. **22** But if he go astray, she will forsake him, and deliver him into the hands of his enemy. **23** Son, observe the time, and fly from evil. **24** For thy soul be not ashamed to say the truth. **25** For there is a shame that bringeth sin, and there is a shame that bringeth glory and grace.

26 Accept no person against thy own person, nor against thy soul a lie. **27** Reverence not thy neighbour in his fall: **28** And refrain not to speak in the time of salvation. Hide not thy wisdom in her beauty. **29** For by the tongue wisdom is discerned: and understanding, and knowledge, and learning by the word of the wise, and steadfastness in the works of justice. **30** In nowise speak against the truth, but be ashamed of the lie of thy ignorance.

31 Be not ashamed to confess thy sins, but submit not thyself to every man for sin. **32** Resist not against the face of the mighty, and do not strive against the stream of the river. **33** Strive for justice for thy soul, and even unto death fight for justice, and God will overthrow thy enemies for thee. **34** Be not hasty in thy tongue: and slack and remiss in thy works. **35** Be not as a lion in thy house, terrifying them of thy household, and oppressing them that are under thee.

36 Let not thy hand be stretched out to receive, and shut when thou shouldst give.

Chapter 5

1 Set not thy heart upon unjust possessions, and say not: I have enough to live on: for it shall be of no service in the time of vengeance and darkness. **2** Follow not in thy strength the desires of thy heart: **3** And say not: How mighty am I? and who shall bring me under for my deeds? for God will surely take revenge. **4** Say not: I have sinned, and what harm hath befallen me? for the most High is a patient rewarder. **5** Be not without fear about sin forgiven, and add not sin upon sin:

6 And say not: The mercy of the Lord is great, he will have mercy on the multitude of my sins. **7** For mercy and wrath quickly come from him, and his wrath looketh upon sinners. **8** Delay not to be converted to the Lord, and defer it not from day to day. **9** For his wrath shall come on a sudden, and in the time of vengeance he will destroy thee. **10** Be not anxious for goods unjustly gotten: for they shall not profit thee in the day of calamity and revenge.

11 Winnow not with every wind, and go not into every way: for so is every sinner proved by a double tongue. **12** Be steadfast in the way of the Lord, and in the truth of thy judgment, and in knowledge, and let the word of peace and justice keep with thee. **13** Be meek to hear the word, that thou mayst understand: and return a true answer with wisdom. **14** If thou have understanding, answer thy neighbour: but if not, let thy hand be upon thy mouth, lest thou be surprised in an unskillful word, and be confounded. **15** Honour and glory is in the word of the wise, but the tongue of the fool is his ruin.

16 Be not called a whisperer, and be not taken in thy tongue, and confounded. **17** For confusion and repentance is upon a thief, and an evil mark of disgrace upon the double tongued, but to the whisperer hatred, and enmity, and reproach. **18** Justify alike the small and the great.

Chapter 6

1 Instead of a friend become not an enemy to thy neighbour: for an evil man shall inherit reproach and shame, so shall every sinner that is envious and double tongued. **2** Extol not thyself in the thoughts of thy soul like a bull: lest thy strength be quashed by folly, **3** And it eat up thy leaves, and destroy thy fruit: and thou be left as a dry tree in the wilderness. **4** For a wicked soul shall destroy him that hath it, and maketh him to be a joy to his enemies, and shall lead him into the lot of the wicked. **5** A sweet word multiplieth friends, and appeaseth enemies, and a gracious tongue in a good man aboundeth.

6 Be in peace with many, but let one of a thousand be thy counsellor. **7** If thou wouldst get a friend, try him before thou takest him, and do not credit him easily. **8** For there is a friend for his own occasion, and he will not abide in the day of thy trouble. **9** And there is a friend that turneth to enmity; and there is a friend that will disclose hatred and strife and reproaches. **10** And there is a friend a companion at the table, and he will not abide in the day of distress.

11 A friend if he continue steadfast, shall be to thee as thyself, and shall act with confidence among them of thy household. **12** If he humble himself before thee, and hide himself from thy face, thou shalt have unanimous friendship for good. **13** Separate thyself from thy enemies, and take heed of thy friends. **14** A faithful friend is a strong defence: and he that hath found him, hath found a treasure. **15** Nothing can be compared to a faithful friend, and no weight of gold and silver is able to countervail the goodness of his fidelity.

16 A faithful friend is the medicine of life and immortality: and they that fear the Lord, shall find him. **17** He that feareth God, shall likewise have good friendship: because according to him shall his friend be. **18** My son, from thy youth up receive instruction, and even to thy grey hairs thou shalt find wisdom. **19** Come to her as one that plougheth, and soweth, and wait for her good fruits: **20** For in working about her thou shalt labour a little, and shalt quickly eat of her fruits.

21 How very unpleasant is wisdom to the unlearned, and the unwise will not continue with her. **22** She shall be to them as a mighty stone of trial, and they will cast her from them before it be long. **23** For the wisdom of doctrine is according to her name, and she is not manifest unto many, but with them to whom she is known, she continueth even to the sight of God. **24** Give ear, my son, and take wise counsel, and cast not away my advice. **25** Put thy feet into her fetters, and thy neck into her chains:

26 Bow down thy shoulder, and bear her, and be not grieved with her bands. **27** Come to her with all thy mind, and keep her ways with all thy power. **28** Search for her, and she shall be made known to thee, and when thou hast gotten her, let her not go: **29** For in the latter end thou shalt find rest in her, and she shall be turned to thy joy. **30** Then shall her fetters be a strong defence for thee, and a firm foundation, and her chain a robe of glory:

31 For in her is the beauty of life, and her bands are a healthful binding. **32** Thou shalt put her on as a robe of glory, and thou shalt set her upon thee as a crown of joy. **33** My son, if thou wilt attend to me, thou shalt learn: and if thou wilt apply thy mind, thou shalt be wise. **34** If thou wilt incline thy ear, thou shalt receive instruction: and if thou love to hear, thou shalt be wise. **35** Stand in the multitude of ancients that are wise, and join thyself from thy heart to their wisdom, that thou mayst hear every discourse of God, and the sayings of praise may not escape thee.

36 And if thou see a man of understanding, go to him early in the morning, and let thy foot wear the steps of his doors. **37** Let thy thoughts be upon the precepts of God, and meditate continually on his commandments: and he will give thee a heart, and the desire of wisdom shall be given to thee.

Chapter 7

1 Do no evils, and no evils shall lay hold of thee. **2** Depart from the unjust, and evils shall depart from thee. **3** My son, sow not evils in the furrows of injustice, and thou shalt not reap them sevenfold. **4** Seek not of the Lord a pre-eminence, nor of the king the seat of honour. **5** Justify not thyself before God, for he knoweth the heart: and desire not to appear wise before the king.

6 Seek not to be made a judge, unless thou have strength enough to extirpate iniquities: lest thou fear the person of the powerful, and lay a stumblingblock for thy integrity. **7** Offend not against the multitude of a city, neither cast thyself in upon the people, **8** Nor bind sin to sin: for even in one thou shalt not be unpunished. **9** Be not fainthearted in thy mind: **10** Neglect not to pray, and to give alms.

11 Say not: God will have respect to the multitude of my gifts, and when I offer to the most high God, he will accept my offerings. **12** Laugh no man to scorn in the bitterness of his soul: for there is one that humbleth and exalteth, God who seeth all. **13** Devise not a lie against thy brother: neither do the like against thy friend. **14** Be not willing to make any manner of lie: for the custom thereof is not good. **15** Be not full of words in a multitude of ancients, and repeat not the word in thy prayer.

16 Hate not laborious works, nor husbandry ordained by the most High. **17** Number not thyself among the multitude of the disorderly. **18** Remember wrath, for it will not tarry long. **19** Humble thy spirit very much: for the vengeance on the flesh of the ungodly is fire and worms. **20** Do not transgress against thy friend deferring money, nor despise thy dear brother for the sake of gold.

21 Depart not from a wise and good wife, whom thou hast gotten in the fear of the Lord: for the grace of her modesty is above gold. **22** Hurt not the servant that worketh faithfully, nor the hired man that giveth thee his life. **23** Let a wise servant be dear to thee as thy own soul, defraud him not of liberty, nor leave him needy. **24** Hast thou cattle? have an eye to them: and if they be for thy profit, keep them with thee. **25** Hast thou children? instruct them, and bow down their neck from their childhood.

26 Hast thou daughters? have a care of their body, and shew not thy countenance gay towards them. **27** Marry thy daughter well, and thou shalt do a great work, and give her to a wise man. **28** If thou hast a wife according to thy soul, cast her not off: and to her that is hateful, trust not thyself. With thy whole heart, **29** Honour thy father, and forget not the groanings of thy mother: **30** Remember that thou hadst not been born but through them: and make a return to them as they have done for thee.

31 With all thy soul fear the Lord, and reverence his priests. **32** With all thy strength love him that made thee: and forsake not his ministers. **33** Honour God with all thy soul, and give honour to the priests, and purify thyself with thy arms. **34** Give them their portion, as it is commanded thee, of the firstfruits and of purifications: and for thy negligences purify thyself with a few. **35** Offer to the Lord the gift of thy shoulders, and the sacrifice of sanctification, and the firstfruits of the holy things:

36 And stretch out thy hand to the poor, that thy expiation and thy blessing may be perfected. **37** A gift hath grace in the sight of all the living, and restrain not grace from the dead. **38** Be not wanting in comforting them that weep, and walk with them that mourn. **39** Be not slow to visit the sick: for by these things thou shalt be confirmed in love. **40** In all thy works remember thy last end, and thou shalt never sin.

Chapter 8

1 Strive not with a powerful man, lest thou fall into his hands. **2** Contend not with a rich man, lest he bring an action against thee. **3** For gold and silver hath destroyed many, and hath reached even to the heart of kings, and perverted them. **4** Strive not with a man that is full of tongue, and heap not wood upon his fire. **5** Communicate not with an ignorant man, lest he speak ill of thy family.

6 Despise not a man that turneth away from sin, nor reproach him therewith: remember that we are all worthy of reproof. **7** Despise not a man in his old age; for we also shall become old. **8** Rejoice not at the death of thy enemy; knowing that we all die, and are not willing that others should rejoice at our death. **9** Despise not the discourse of them that are ancient and wise, but acquaint thyself with their proverbs. **10** For of them thou shalt learn wisdom, and instruction of understanding, and to serve great men without blame.

11 Let not the discourse of the ancients escape thee, for they have learned of their fathers: **12** For of them thou shalt learn understanding, and to give an answer in time of need. **13** Kindle not the coals of sinners by rebuking them, lest thou be burnt with the flame of the fire of their sins. **14** Stand not against the face of an injurious person, lest he sit as a spy to entrap thee in thy words. **15** Lend not to a man that is mightier than thyself: and if thou lendest, count it as lost.

16 Be not surety above thy power: and if thou be surety, think as if thou wert to pay it. **17** Judge not against a judge: for he judgeth according to that which is just. **18** Go not on the way with a bold man, lest he burden thee with his evils: for he goeth according to his own will, and thou shalt perish together with his folly. **19** Quarrel not with a passionate man, and go not into the desert with a bold man: for blood is as nothing in his sight, and where there is no help he will overthrow thee. **20** Advise not with fools, for they cannot love but such things as please them.

21 Before a stranger do no matter of counsel: for thou knowest not what he will bring forth. **22** Open not thy heart to every man: lest he repay thee with an evil turn, and speak reproachfully to thee.

Chapter 9

1 Be not jealous over the wife of thy bosom, lest she shew in thy regard the malice of a wicked lesson. **2** Give not the power of thy soul to a woman, lest she enter upon thy strength, and thou be confounded. **3** Look not upon a woman that hath a mind for many: lest thou fall into her snares. **4** Use not much the company of her that is a dancer, and hearken not to her, lest thou perish by the force of her charms. **5** Gaze not upon a maiden, lest her beauty be a stumblingblock to thee.

6 Give not thy soul to harlots in any point: lest thou destroy thyself and thy inheritance. **7** Look not round about thee in the ways of the city, nor wander up and down in the streets thereof. **8** Turn away thy face from a woman dressed up, and gaze not about upon another's beauty. **9** For many have perished by the beauty of a woman, and hereby lust is enkindled as a fire. **10** Every woman that is a harlot, shall be trodden upon as dung in the way.

11 Many by admiring the beauty of another man's wife, have become reprobate, for her conversation burneth as fire. **12** Sit not at all with another man's wife, nor repose upon the bed with her: **13** And strive not with her over wine, lest thy heart decline towards her, and by thy blood thou fall into destruction. **14** Forsake not an old friend, for the new will not be like to him. **15** A new friend is as new wine: it shall grow old, and thou shalt drink it with pleasure.

16 Envy not the glory and riches of a sinner: for thou knowest not what his ruin shall be. **17** Be not pleased with the wrong done by the unjust, knowing that even to hell the wicked shall not please. **18** Keep thee far from the man that hath power to kill, so thou shalt not suspect the fear of death. **19** And if thou come to him, commit no fault, lest he take away thy life. **20** Know it to be a communication with death: for thou art going in the midst of snares, and walking upon the arms of them that are grieved:

21 According to thy power beware of thy neighbour, and treat with the wise and prudent. **22** Let just men be thy guests, and let thy glory be in the fear of God. **23** And let the thought of God be in thy mind, and all thy discourse on the commandments of the Highest. **24** Works shall be praised for the hand of the artificers, and the prince of the people for the wisdom of his speech, but the word of the ancients for the sense. **25** A man full of tongue is terrible in his city, and he that is rash in his word shall be hateful.

Chapter 10

1 A wise judge shall judge his people, and the government of a prudent man shall be steady. **2** As the judge of the people is himself, so also are his ministers: and what manner of man the ruler of a city is, such also are they that dwell therein. **3** An unwise king shall be the ruin of his people: and cities shall be inhabited through the prudence of the rulers. **4** The power of the earth is in the hand of God, and in his time he will raise up a profitable ruler over it. **5** The prosperity of man is in the hand of God, and upon the person of the scribe he shall lay his honour.

6 Remember not any injury done thee by thy neighbour, and do thou nothing by deeds of injury. **7** Pride is hateful before God and men: and all iniquity of nations is execrable. **8** A kingdom is translated from one people to another, because of injustices, and wrongs, and injuries, and divers deceits. **9** But nothing is more wicked than the covetous man. Why is earth and ashes proud? **10** There is not a more wicked thing than to love money: for such a one setteth even his own soul to sale: because while he liveth he hath cast away his bowels.

11 All power is of short life. A long sickness is troublesome to the physician. **12** The physician cutteth off a short sickness: so also a king is today, and tomorrow he shall die. **13** For when a man shall die, he shall inherit serpents, and beasts, and worms. **14** The beginning of the pride of man, is to fall off from God: **15** Because his heart is departed from him that made him: for pride is the beginning of all sin: he that holdeth it, shall be filled with maledictions, and it shall ruin him in the end.

16 Therefore hath the Lord disgraced the assemblies of the wicked, and hath utterly destroyed them. **17** God hath overturned the thrones of proud princes, and hath set up the meek in their stead. **18** God hath made the roots of proud nations to wither, and hath planted the humble of these nations. **19** The Lord hath overthrown the lands of the Gentiles, and hath destroyed them even to the foundation. **20** He hath made some of them to wither away, and hath destroyed them, and hath made the memory of them to cease from the earth.

21 God hath abolished the memory of the proud, and hath preserved the memory of them that are humble in mind. **22** Pride was not made for men: nor wrath for the race of women. **23** That seed of men shall be honoured, which feareth God: but that seed shall be dishonoured, which transgresseth the commandments of the Lord. **24** In the midst of brethren their chief is honourable: so shall they that fear the Lord, be in his eyes. **25** The fear of God is the glory of the rich, and of the honourable, and of the poor:

26 Despise not a just man that is poor, and do not magnify a sinful man that is rich. **27** The great man, and the judge, and the mighty is in honour: and there is none greater than he that feareth God. **28** They that are free shall serve a servant that is wise: and a man that is prudent and well instructed will not murmur when he is reproved; and he that is ignorant, shall not be honoured. **29** Extol not thyself in doing thy work, and linger not in the time of distress: **30** Better is he that laboureth, and aboundeth in all things, than he that boasteth himself and wanteth bread.

31 My son, keep thy soul in meekness, and give it honour according to its desert. **32** Who will justify him that sinneth against his own soul? and who will honour him that dishonoureth his own soul? **33** The poor man is glorified by his discipline and fear: and there is a man that is honoured for his wealth. **34** But he that is glorified in poverty, how much more in wealth? and he that is glorified in wealth, let him fear poverty.

Chapter 11

1 The wisdom of the humble shall exalt his head, and shall make him sit in the midst of great men. **2** Praise not a man for his beauty, neither despise a man for his look. **3** The bee is small among flying things, but her fruit hath the chiefest sweetness. **4** Glory not in apparel at any time, and be not exalted in the day of thy honour: for the works of the Highest only are wonderful, and his works are glorious, and secret, and hidden. **5** Many tyrants have sat on the throne, and he whom no man would think on, hath worn the crown.

6 Many mighty men have been greatly brought down, and the glorious have been delivered into the hand of others. **7** Before thou inquire, blame no man: and when thou hast inquired, reprove justly. **8** Before thou hear, answer not a word: and interrupt not others in the midst of their discourse. **9** Strive not in a matter which doth not concern thee, and sit not in judgment with sinners. **10** My son, meddle not with many matters: and if thou be rich, thou shalt not be free from sin: for if thou pursue after thou shalt not overtake: and if thou run before thou shalt not escape.

11 There is an ungodly man that laboureth, and maketh haste, and is in sorrow, and is so much the more in want. **12** Again, there is an inactive man that wanteth help, is very weak in ability, and full of poverty: **13** Yet the eye of God hath looked upon him for good, and hath lifted him up from his low estate, and hath exalted his head: and many have wondered at him, and have glorified God. **14** Good things and evil, life and death, poverty and riches, are from God. **15** Wisdom and discipline, and the knowledge of the law are with God. Love and the ways of good things are with him.

16 Error and darkness are created with sinners: and they that glory in evil things, grow old in evil. **17** The gift of God abideth with the just, and his advancement shall have success for ever. **18** There is one that is enriched by living sparingly, and this is the portion of his reward. **19** In that he saith: I have found me rest, and now I will eat of my goods alone: **20** And he knoweth not what time shall pass, and that death approacheth, and that he must leave all to others, and shall die.

21 Be steadfast in thy covenant, and be conversant therein, and grow old in the work of thy commandments. **22** Abide not in the works of sinners. But trust in God, and stay in thy place. **23** For it is easy in the eyes of God on a sudden to make the poor man rich. **24** The blessing of God maketh haste to reward the just, and in a swift hour his blessing beareth fruit. **25** Say not: What need I, and what good shall I have by this?

26 Say not: I am sufficient for myself: and what shall I be made worse by this? **27** In the day of good things be not unmindful of evils: and in the day of evils be not unmindful of good things: **28** For it is easy before God in the day of death to reward every one according to his ways. **29** The affliction of an hour maketh one forget great delights, and in the end of a man is the disclosing of his works. **30** Praise not any man before death, for a man is known by his children.

31 Bring not every man into thy house: for many are the snares of the deceitful. **32** For as corrupted bowels send forth stinking breath, and as the partridge is brought into the cage, and as the roe into the snare: so also is the heart of the proud, and as a spy that looketh on the fall of his neighbour. **33** For he lieth in wait and turneth good into evil, and on the elect he will lay a blot. **34** Of one spark cometh a great fire, and of one deceitful man much blood: and a sinful man lieth in wait for blood. **35** Take heed to thyself of a mischievous man, for he worketh evils: lest he bring upon thee reproach for ever.

36 Receive a stranger in, and he shall overthrow thee with a whirlwind, and shall turn thee out of thy own.

Chapter 12

1 If thou do good, know to whom thou dost it, and there shall be much thanks for thy good deeds. **2** Do good to the just, and thou shalt find great recompense: and if not of him, assuredly of the Lord. **3** For there is no good for him that is always occupied in evil, and that giveth no alms: for the Highest hateth sinners, and hath mercy on the penitent. **4** Give to the merciful and uphold not the sinner: God will repay vengeance to the ungodly and to sinners, and keep them against the day of vengeance. **5** Give to the good, and receive not a sinner.

6 Do good to the humble, and give not to the ungodly: hold back thy bread, and give it not to him, lest thereby he overmaster thee. **7** For thou shalt receive twice as much evil for all the good thou shalt have done to him: for the Highest also hateth sinners, and will repay vengeance to the ungodly. **8** A friend shall not be known in prosperity, and an enemy shall not be hidden in adversity. **9** In the prosperity of a man, his enemies are grieved: and a friend is known in his adversity. **10** Never trust thy enemy: for as a brass pot his wickedness rusteth:

11 Though he humble himself and go crouching, yet take good heed and beware of him. **12** Set him not by thee, neither let him sit on thy right hand, lest he turn into thy place, and seek to take thy seat: and at the last thou acknowledge my words, and be pricked with my sayings. **13** Who will pity an enchanter struck by a serpent, or any that come near wild beasts? so is it with him that keepeth company with a wicked man, and is involved in his sins. **14** For an hour he will abide with thee: but if thou begin to decline, he will not endure it. **15** An enemy speaketh sweetly with his lips, but in his heart he lieth in wait, to throw thee into a pit.

16 An enemy weepeth with his eyes: but if he find an opportunity he will not be satisfied with blood: **17** And if evils come upon thee, thou shalt find him there first. **18** An enemy hath tears in his eyes, and while he pretendeth to help thee, will undermine thy feet. **19** He will shake his head, and clap his hands, and whisper much, and change his countenance.

Chapter 13

1 He that toucheth pitch, shall be defiled with it: and he that hath fellowship with the proud, shall put on pride. **2** He shall take a burden upon him that hath fellowship with one more honourable than himself. And have no fellowship with one that is richer than thyself. **3** What agreement shall the earthen pot have with the kettle? for if they knock one against the other, it shall be broken. **4** The rich man hath done wrong, and yet he will fume: but the poor is wronged and must hold his peace. **5** If thou give, he will make use of thee: and if thou have nothing, he will forsake thee.

6 If thou have any thing, he will live with thee, and will make thee bare, and he will not be sorry for thee. **7** If he have need of thee he will deceive thee, and smiling upon thee will put thee in hope; he will speak thee fair, and will say: What wantest thou? **8** And he will shame thee by his meats, till he have drawn thee dry twice or thrice, and at last he will laugh at thee: and afterward when he seeth thee, he will forsake thee, and shake his head at thee. **9** Humble thyself to God, and wait for his hands. **10** Beware that thou be not deceived into folly, and be humbled.

11 Be not lowly in thy wisdom, lest being humbled thou be deceived into folly. **12** If thou be invited by one that is mightier, withdraw thyself: for so he will invite thee the more. **13** Be not troublesome to him, lest thou be put back: and keep not far from him, lest thou be forgotten. **14** Affect not to speak with him as an equal: and believe not his many words: for by much talk he will sift thee, and smiling will examine thee concerning thy secrets. **15** His cruel mind will lay up thy words: and he will not spare to do thee hurt, and to cast thee into prison.

16 Take heed to thyself, and attend diligently to what thou hearest: for thou walkest in danger of thy ruin. **17** When thou hearest those things, see as it were in sleep, and thou shalt awake. **18** Love God all thy life, and call upon him for thy salvation. **19** Every beast loveth its like: so also every man him that is nearest to himself. **20** All flesh shall consort with the like to itself, and every man shall associate himself to his like.

21 If the wolf shall at any time have fellowship with the lamb, so the sinner with the just. **22** What fellowship hath a holy man with a dog, or what part hath the rich with the poor? **23** The wild ass is the lion's prey in the desert: so also the poor are devoured by the rich. **24** And as humility is an abomination to the proud: so also the rich man abhorreth the poor. **25** When a rich man is shaken, he is kept up by his friends: but when a poor man is fallen down, he is thrust away even by his acquaintance.

26 When a rich man hath been deceived, he hath many helpers: he hath spoken proud things, and they have justified him. **27** The poor man was deceived, and he is rebuked also: he hath spoken wisely, and could have no place. **28** The rich man spoke, and all held their peace, and what he said they extol even to the clouds. **29** The poor man spoke, and they say: Who is this? and if he stumble, they will overthrow him. **30** Riches are good to him that hath no sin in his conscience: and poverty is very wicked in the mouth of the ungodly.

31 The heart of a man changeth his countenance, either for good, or for evil. **32** The token of a good heart, and a good countenance thou shalt hardly find, and with labour.

Chapter 14

1 Blessed is the man that hath not slipped by a word out of his mouth, and is not pricked with the remorse of sin. **2** Happy is he that hath had no sadness of his mind, and who is not fallen from his hope. **3** Riches are not comely for a covetous man and a niggard, and what should an envious man do with gold? **4** He that gathereth together by wronging his own soul, gathereth for others, and another will squander away his goods in rioting. **5** He that is evil to himself, to whom will he be good? and he shall not take pleasure in his goods.

6 There is none worse than he that envieth himself, and this is the reward of his wickedness: **7** And if he do good, he doth it ignorantly, and unwillingly: and at the last he discovereth his wickedness. **8** The eye of the envious is wicked: and he turneth away his face, and despiseth his own soul. **9** The eye of the covetous man is insatiable in his portion of iniquity: he will not be satisfied till he consume his own soul, drying it up. **10** An evil eye is towards evil things: and he shall not have his fill of bread, but shall be needy and pensive at his own table.

11 My son, if thou have any thing, do good to thyself, and offer to God worthy offerings. **12** Remember that death is not slow, and that the covenant of hell hath been shewn to thee: for the covenant of this world shall surely die. **13** Do good to thy friend before thou die, and according to thy ability, stretching out thy hand give to the poor. **14** Defraud not thyself of the good day, and let not the part of a good gift overpass thee. **15** Shalt thou not leave to others to divide by lot thy sorrows and labours?

16 Give and take, and justify thy soul. **17** Before thy death work justice: for in hell there is no finding food. **18** All flesh shall fade as grass, and as the leaf that springeth out on a green tree. **19** Some grow, and some fall off: so is the generation of flesh and blood, one cometh to an end, and another is born. **20** Every work that is corruptible shall fail in the end: and the worker thereof shall go with it.

21 And every excellent work shall be justified: and the worker thereof shall be honoured therein. **22** Blessed is the man that shall continue in wisdom, and that shall meditate in his justice, and in his mind shall think of the all seeing eye of God. **23** He that considereth her ways in his heart, and hath understanding in her secrets, who goeth after her as one that traceth, and stayeth in her ways: **24** He who looketh in at her windows, and hearkeneth at her door: **25** He that lodgeth near her house, and fastening a pin in her walls shall set up his tent nigh unto her, where good things shall rest in his lodging for ever.

26 He shall set his children under her shelter, and shall lodge under her branches: **27** He shall be protected under her covering from the heat, and shall rest in her glory.

Chapter 15

1 He that feareth God, will do good: and he that possesseth justice, shall lay hold on her, **2** And she will meet him as an honourable mother, and will receive him as a wife married of a virgin. **3** With the bread of life and understanding, she shall feed him, and give him the water of wholesome wisdom to drink: and she shall be made strong in him, and he shall not be moved: **4** And she shall hold him fast, and he shall not be confounded: and she shall exalt him among his neighbours. **5** And in the midst of the church she shall open his mouth, and shall fill him with the spirit of wisdom and understanding, and shall clothe him with a robe of glory.

6 She shall heap upon him a treasure of joy and gladness, and shall cause him to inherit an everlasting name. **7** But foolish men shall not obtain her, and wise men shall meet her, foolish men shall not see her: for she is far from pride and deceit. **8** Lying men shall not be mindful of her: but men that speak truth shall be found with her, and shall advance, even till they come to the sight of God. **9** Praise is not seemly in the mouth of a sinner: **10** For wisdom came forth from God: for praise shall be with the wisdom of God, and shall abound in a faithful mouth, and the sovereign Lord will give praise unto it.

11 Say not: It is through God, that she is not with me: for do not thou the things that he hateth. **12** Say not: He hath caused me to err: for he hath no need of wicked men. **13** The Lord hateth all abomination of error, and they that fear him shall not love it. **14** God made man from the beginning, and left him in the hand of his own counsel. **15** He added his commandments and precepts.

16 If thou wilt keep the commandments and perform acceptable fidelity for ever, they shall preserve thee. **17** He hath set water and fire before thee: stretch forth thy hand to which thou wilt. **18** Before man is life and death, good and evil, that which he shall choose shall be given him: **19** For the wisdom of God is great, and he is strong in power, seeing all men without ceasing. **20** The eyes of the Lord are towards them that fear him, and he knoweth all the work of man.

21 He hath commanded no man to do wickedly, and he hath given no man license to sin: **22** For he desireth not a multitude of faithless and unprofitable children.

Chapter 16

1 Rejoice not in ungodly children, if they be multiplied: neither be delighted in them, if the fear of God be not with them. **2** Trust not to their life, and respect not their labours. **3** For better is one that feareth God, than a thousand ungodly children. **4** And it is better to die without children, than to leave ungodly children. **5** By one that is wise a country shall be inhabited, the tribe of the ungodly shall become desolate.

6 Many such things hath my eyes seen, and greater things than these my ear hath heard. **7** In the congregation of sinners a fire shall be kindled, and in an unbelieving nation wrath shall flame out. **8** The ancient giants did not obtain pardon for their sins, who were destroyed trusting to their own strength: **9** And he spared not the place where Lot sojourned, but abhorred them for the pride of their word. **10** He had not pity on them, destroying the whole nation that extolled themselves in their sins.

11 So did he with the six hundred thousand footmen, who were gathered together in the hardness of their heart: and if one had been stiffnecked, it is a wonder if he had escaped unpunished: **12** For mercy and wrath are with him. He is mighty to forgive, and to pour out indignation: **13** According as his mercy is, so his correction judgeth a man according to his works. **14** The sinner shall not escape in his rapines, and the patience of him that sheweth mercy shall not be put off. **15** All mercy shall make a place for every man according to the merit of his works, and according to the wisdom of his sojournment.

16 Say not: I shall be hidden from God, and who shall remember me from on high? **17** In such a multitude I shall not be known: for what is my soul in such an immense creation? **18** Behold the heaven, and the heavens of heavens, the deep, and all the earth, and the things that are in them, shall be moved in his sight, **19** The mountains also, and the hills, and the foundations of the earth: when God shall look upon them, they shall be shaken with trembling. **20** And in all these things the heart is senseless: and every heart is understood by him:

21 And his ways who shall understand, and the storm, which no eye of man see? **22** For many of his works are hidden: but the works of his justice who shall declare? or who shall endure? for the testament is far from some, and the examination of all is in the end. **23** He that wanteth understanding thinketh vain things: and the foolish, and erring man, thinketh foolish things. **24** Hearken to me, my son, and learn the discipline of understanding, and attend to my words in thy heart. **25** And I will shew forth good doctrine in equity, and will seek to declare wisdom: and attend to my words in thy heart, whilst with equity of spirit I tell thee the virtues that God hath put upon his works from the beginning, and I shew forth in truth his knowledge.

26 The works of God are done in judgment from the beginning, and from the making of them he distinguished their parts, and their beginnings in their generations. **27** He beautified their works for ever, they have neither hungered, nor laboured, and they have not ceased from their works. **28** Nor shall any of them straiten his neighbour at any time. **29** Be not thou incredulous to his word. **30** After this God looked upon the earth, and filled it with his goods.

31 The soul of every living thing hath shewn forth before the face thereof, and into it they return again.

Chapter 17

1 God created man of the earth, and made him after his own image. **2** And he turned him into it again, and clothed him with strength according to himself. **3** He gave him the number of his days and time, and gave him power over all things that are upon the earth. **4** He put the fear of him upon all flesh, and he had dominion over beasts and fowls. **5** He created of him a helpmate like to himself: he gave them counsel, and a tongue, and eyes, and ears, and a heart to devise: and he filled them with the knowledge of understanding.

6 He created in them the science of the spirit, he filled their heart with wisdom, and shewed them both good and evil. **7** He set his eye upon their hearts to shew them the greatness of his works: **8** That they might praise the name which he hath sanctified: and glory in his wondrous acts, that they might declare the glorious things of his works. **9** Moreover he gave them instructions, and the law of life for an inheritance. **10** He made an everlasting covenant with them, and he shewed them his justice and judgments.

11 And their eye saw the majesty of his glory. and their ears heard his glorious voice, and he said to them: Beware of all iniquity. **12** And he gave to every one of them commandment concerning his neighbour. **13** Their ways are always before him, they are not hidden from his eyes. **14** Over every nation he set a ruler. **15** And Israel was made the manifest portion of God.

16 And all their works are as the sun in the sight of God: and his eyes are continually upon their ways. **17** Their covenants were not hid by their iniquity, and all their iniquities are in the sight of God. **18** The alms of a man is as a signet with him, and shall preserve the grace of a man as the apple of the eye: **19** And afterward he shall rise up, and shall render them their reward, to every one upon their own head, and shall turn them down into the bowels of the earth. **20** But to the penitent he hath given the way of justice, and he hath strengthened them that were fainting in patience, and hath appointed to them the lot of truth.

21 Turn to the Lord, and forsake thy sins: **22** Make thy prayer before the face of the Lord, and offend less. **23** Return to the Lord, and turn away from thy injustice, and greatly hate abomination. **24** And know the justices and judgments of God, and stand firm in the lot set before thee, and in prayer to the most high God. **25** Go to the side of the holy age, with them that live and give praise to God.

26 Tarry not in the error of the ungodly, give glory before death. Praise perisheth from the dead as nothing. **27** Give thanks whilst thou art living, whilst thou art alive and in health thou shalt give thanks, and shalt praise God, and shalt glory in his mercies. **28** How great is the mercy of the Lord, and his forgiveness to them that turn to him! **29** For all things cannot be in men, because the son of man is not immortal, and they are delighted with the vanity of evil. **30** What is brighter than the sun; yet it shall be eclipsed. Or what is more wicked than that which flesh and blood hath invented? and this shall be reproved.

31 He beholdeth the power of the height of heaven: and all men are earth and ashes.

Chapter 18

1 He that liveth for ever created all things together. God only shall be justified, and he remaineth an invincible king for ever. **2** Who is able to declare his works? **3** For who shall search out his glorious acts? **4** And who shall shew forth the power of his majesty? or who shall be able to declare his mercy? **5** Nothing may be taken away, nor added, neither is it possible to find out the glorious works of God:

6 When a man hath done, then shall he begin: and when he leaveth off, he shall be at a loss. **7** What is man, and what is his grace? and what is his good, or what is his evil? **8** The number of the days of men at the most are a hundred years: as a drop of water of the sea are they esteemed: and as a pebble of the sand, so are a few years compared to eternity. **9** Therefore God is patient in them, and poureth forth his mercy upon them. **10** He hath seen the presumption of their heart that it is wicked, and hath known their end that it is evil.

11 Therefore hath he filled up his mercy in their favour, and hath shewn them the way of justice. **12** The compassion of man is toward his neighbour: but the mercy of God is upon all flesh. **13** He hath mercy, and teacheth, and correcteth, as a shepherd doth his flock. **14** He hath mercy on him that receiveth the discipline of mercy, and that maketh haste in his judgments. **15** My son, in thy good deeds, make no complaint, and when thou givest any thing, add not grief by an evil word.

16 Shall not the dew assuage the heat? so also the good word is better than the gift. **17** Lo, is not a word better than a gift? but both are with a justified man. **18** A fool will upbraid bitterly: and a gift of one ill taught consumeth the eyes. **19** Before judgment prepare thee justice, and learn before thou speak. **20** Before sickness take a medicine, and before judgment examine thyself, and thou shalt find mercy in the sight of God.

21 Humble thyself before thou art sick, and in the time of sickness shew thy conversation. **22** Let nothing hinder thee from praying always, and be not afraid to be justified even to death: for the reward of God continueth for ever. **23** Before prayer prepare thy soul: and be not as a man that tempteth God. **24** Remember the wrath that shall be at the last day, and the time of repaying when he shall turn away his face. **25** Remember poverty in the time of abundance, and the necessities of poverty in the day of riches.

26 From the morning until the evening the time shall be changed, and all these are swift in the eyes of God. **27** A wise man will fear in every thing, and in the days of sins will beware of sloth. **28** Every man of understanding knoweth wisdom, and will give praise to him that findeth her. **29** They that were of good understanding in words, have also done wisely themselves: and have understood truth and justice, and have poured forth proverbs and judgments. **30** Go not after thy lusts, but turn away from thy own will.

31 If thou give to thy soul her desires, she will make thee a joy to thy enemies. **32** Take no pleasure in riotous assemblies, be they ever so small: for their concertation is continual. **33** Make not thyself poor by borrowing to contribute to feasts when thou hast nothing in thy purse: for thou shalt be an enemy to thy own life.

Chapter 19

1 A workman that is a drunkard shall not be rich: and he that contemneth small things, shall fall by little and little. **2** Wine and women make wise men fall off, and shall rebuke the prudent. **3** And he that joineth himself to harlots, will be wicked. Rottenness and worms shall inherit him, and he shall be lifted up for a greater example, and his soul shall be taken away out of the number. **4** He that is hasty to give credit, is light of heart, and shall be lessened: and he that sinneth against his own soul, shall be despised. **5** He that rejoiceth in iniquity, shall be censured, and he that hateth chastisement, shall have less life: and he that hateth babbling, extinguisheth evil.

6 He that sinneth against his own soul, shall repent: and he that is delighted with wickedness, shall be condemned. **7** Rehearse not again a wicked and harsh word, and thou shalt not fare the worse. **8** Tell not thy mind to friend or foe: and if there be a sin with thee, disclose it not. **9** For he will hearken to thee, and will watch thee, and as it were defending thy sin he will hate thee, and so will he be with thee always. **10** Hast thou heard a word against thy neighbour? let it die within thee, trusting that it will not burst thee.

11 At the hearing of a word the fool is in travail, as a woman groaning in the bringing forth a child. **12** As an arrow that sticketh in a man's thigh: so is a word in the heart of a fool. **13** Reprove a friend, lest he may not have understood, and say: I did it not: or if he did it, that he may do it no more. **14** Reprove thy neighbour, for it may be he hath not said it: and if he hath said it, that he may not say it again. **15** Admonish thy friend: for there is often a fault committed.

16 And believe not every word. There is one, that slippeth with the tongue, but not from his heart. **17** For who is there that hath not offended with his tongue? Admonish thy neighbour before thou threaten him. **18** And give place to the fear of the most High: for the fear of God is all wisdom, and therein is to fear God, and the disposition of the law is in all wisdom. **19** But the learning of wickedness is not wisdom: and the device of sinners is not prudence. **20** There is a subtle wickedness, and the same is detestable: and there is a man that is foolish, wanting in wisdom.

21 Better is a man that hath less wisdom, and wanteth understanding, with the fear of God, than he that aboundeth in understanding, and transgresseth the law of the most

High. **22** There is an exquisite subtilty, and the same is unjust. **23** And there is one that uttereth an exact word telling the truth. There is one that humbleth himself wickedly, and his interior is full of deceit: **24** And there is one that submitteth himself exceedingly with a great lowliness: and there is one that casteth down his countenance, and maketh as if he did not see that which is unknown: **25** And if he be hindered from sinning for want of power, if he shall find opportunity to do evil, he will do it.

26 A man is known by his look, and a wise man, when thou meetest him, is known by his countenance. **27** The attire of the body, and the laughter of the teeth, and the gait of the man, shew what he is. **28** There is a lying rebuke in the anger of an injurious man: and there is a judgment that is not allowed to be good: and there is one that holdeth his peace, he is wise.

Chapter 20

1 How much better is it to reprove, than to be angry, and not to hinder him that confesseth in prayer. **2** The lust of an eunuch shall devour a young maiden: **3** So is he that by violence executeth unjust judgment. **4** How good is it, when thou art reproved, to shew repentance! for so thou shalt escape wilful sin. **5** There is one that holdeth his peace, that is found wise: and there is another that is hateful, that is bold in speech.

6 There is one that holdeth his peace, because he knoweth not what to say: and there is another that holdeth his peace, knowing the proper time. **7** A wise man will hold his peace till he see opportunity: but a babbler, and a fool, will regard no time. **8** He that useth many words shall hurt his own soul: and he that taketh authority to himself unjustly shall be hated. **9** There is success in evil things to a man without discipline, and there is a finding that turneth to loss. **10** There is a gift that is not profitable: and there is a gift, the recompense of which is double.

11 There is an abasement because of glory: and there is one that shall lift up his head from a low estate. **12** There is that buyeth much for a small price, and restoreth the same sevenfold. **13** A man wise in words shall make himself beloved: but the graces of fools shall be poured out. **14** The gift of the fool shall do thee no good: for his eyes are sevenfold. **15** He will give a few things, and upbraid much: and the opening of his mouth is the kindling of a fire.

16 Today a man lendeth, and tomorrow he asketh it again: such a man as this is hateful. **17** A fool shall have no friend, and there shall be no thanks for his good deeds. **18** For they that eat his bread, are of a false tongue. How often, and how many will laugh him to scorn! **19** For he doth not distribute with right understanding that which was to be had: in like manner also that which was not to be had. **20** The slipping of a false tongue is as one that falleth on the pavement: so the fall of the wicked shall come speedily.

21 A man without grace is as a vain fable, it shall be continually in the mouth of the unwise. **22** A parable coming out of a fool's mouth shall be rejected: for he doth not speak it in due season. **23** There is that is hindered from sinning through want, and in his rest he shall be pricked. **24** There is that will destroy his own soul through shamefacedness, and by occasion of an unwise person he will destroy it: and by respect of person he will destroy himself. **25** There is that for bashfulness promiseth to his friend, and maketh him his enemy for nothing.

26 A lie is a foul blot in a man, and yet it will be continually in the mouth of men without discipline. **27** A thief is better than a man that is always lying: but both of them shall inherit destruction. **28** The manners of lying men are without honour: and their confusion is with them without ceasing. **29** A wise man shall advance himself with his words, and a prudent man shall please the great ones. **30** He that tilleth his land shall make a high heap of corn: and he that worketh justice shall be exalted: and he that pleaseth great men shall escape iniquity.

31 Presents and gifts blind the eyes of judges, and make them dumb in the mouth, so that they cannot correct. **32** Wisdom that is hid, and treasure that is not seen: what profit is there in them both? **33** Better is he that hideth his folly, than the man that hideth his wisdom.

Chapter 21

1 My son, hast thou sinned? do so no more: but for thy former sins also pray that they may be forgiven thee. **2** Flee from sins as from the face of a serpent: for if thou comest near them, they will take hold of thee. **3** The teeth thereof are the teeth of a lion, killing the souls of men. **4** All iniquity is like a two-edged sword, there is no remedy for the wound thereof. **5** Injuries and wrongs will waste riches: and the house that is very rich shall be brought to nothing by pride: so the substance of the proud shall be rooted out.

6 The prayer out of the mouth of the poor shall reach the ears of God, and judgment shall come for him speedily. **7** He that hateth to be reproved walketh in the trace of a sinner: and he that feareth God will turn to his own heart. **8** He that is mighty by a bold tongue is known afar off, but a wise man knoweth to slip by him. **9** He that buildeth his house at other men's charges, is as he that gathereth himself stones to build in the winter. **10** The congregation of sinners is like tow heaped together, and the end of them is a flame of fire.

11 The way of sinners is made plain with stones, and in their end is hell, and darkness, and pains. **12** He that keepeth justice shall get the understanding thereof. **13** The perfection of the fear of God is wisdom and understanding. **14** He that is not wise in good, will not be taught. **15** But there is a wisdom that aboundeth in evil: and there is no understanding where there is bitterness.

16 The knowledge of a wise man shall abound like a flood, and his counsel continueth like a fountain of life. **17** The heart of a fool is like a broken vessel, and no wisdom at all shall it hold. **18** A man of sense will praise every wise word he shall hear, and will apply it to himself: the luxurious man hath heard it, and it shall displease him, and he will cast it behind his back. **19** The talking of a fool is like a burden in the way: but in the lips of the wise, grace shall be found. **20** The mouth of the prudent is sought after in the church, and they will think upon his words in their hearts.

21 As a house that is destroyed, so is wisdom to a fool: and the knowledge of the unwise is as words without sense. **22** Doctrine to a fool is as fetters on the feet, and like manacles on the right hand. **23** A fool lifteth up his voice in laughter: but a wise man will scarce laugh low to himself. **24** Learning to the prudent is as an ornament of gold, and like a bracelet upon his right arm. **25** The foot of a fool is soon in his neighbour's house: but a man of experience will be abashed at the person of the mighty.

26 A fool will peep through the window into the house: but he that is well taught will stand without. **27** It is the folly of a man to hearken at the door: and a wise man will be grieved with the disgrace. **28** The lips of the unwise will be telling foolish things but the words of the wise shall be weighed in a balance. **29** The heart of fools is in their mouth: and the mouth of wise men is in their heart. **30** While the ungodly curseth the devil, he curseth his own soul.

1 The talebearer shall defile his own soul, and shall be hated by all: and he that shall abide with him shall be hateful: the silent and wise man shall be honoured.

Chapter 22

1 The sluggard is pelted with a dirty stone, and all men will speak of his disgrace. **2** The sluggard is pelted with the dung of oxen: and every one that toucheth him will shake his hands. **3** A son ill taught is the confusion of the father: and a foolish daughter shall be to his loss. **4** A wise daughter shall bring an inheritance to her husband: but she that confoundeth, becometh a disgrace to her father. **5** She that is bold shameth both her father and husband, and will not be inferior to the ungodly: and shall be disgraced by them both.

6 A tale out of time is like music in mourning: but the stripes and instruction of wisdom are never out of time. **7** He that teacheth a fool, is like one that glueth a potsherd together. **8** He that telleth a word to him that heareth not, is like one that waketh a man out of a deep sleep. **9** He speaketh with one that is asleep, who uttereth wisdom to a fool: and in the end of the discourse he saith: Who is this? **10** Weep for the dead, for his light hath failed: and weep for the fool, for his understanding faileth.

11 Weep but a little for the dead, for he is at rest. **12** For the wicked life of a wicked fool is worse than death. **13** The mourning for the dead is seven days: but for a fool and an ungodly man all the days of their life. **14** Talk not much with a fool, and go not with him that hath no sense. **15** Keep thyself from him, that thou mayst not have trouble, and thou shalt not be defiled with his sin.

16 Turn away from him, and thou shalt find rest, and shalt not be wearied out with his folly. **17** What is heavier than lead? and what other name hath he but fool? **18** Sand and salt, and a mass of iron is easier to bear, than a man without sense, that is both foolish and wicked. **19** A frame of wood bound together in the foundation of a building, shall not be loosed: so neither shall the heart that is established by advised counsel. **20** The thought of him that is wise at all times, shall not be depraved by fear.

21 As pales set in high places, and plasterings made without cost, will not stand against the face of the wind: **22** So also a fearful heart in the imagination of a fool shall not resist against the violence of fear. **23** As a fearful heart in the thought of a fool at all times will not fear, so neither shall he that continueth always in the commandments of God. **24** He that pricketh the eye, bringeth out tears: and he that pricketh the heart, bringeth forth resentment. **25** He that flingeth a stone at birds, shall drive them away: so he that upbraideth his friend, breaketh friendship.

26 Although thou hast drawn a sword at a friend, despair not: for there may be a returning. To a friend, **27** If thou hast opened a sad mouth, fear not, for there may be a reconciliation: except upbraiding, and reproach, and pride, and disclosing of secrets, or a treacherous wound: for in all these cases a friend will flee away. **28** Keep fidelity with a friend in his poverty, that in his prosperity also thou mayst rejoice. **29** In the time of his trouble continue faithful to him, that thou mayst also be heir with him in his inheritance. **30** As the vapour of a chimney, and the smoke of the fire goeth up before the fire: so also injurious words, and reproaches, and threats, before blood.

31 I will not be ashamed to salute a friend, neither will I hide myself from his face: and if any evil happen to me by him, I will bear it. **32** But every one that shall hear it, will beware of him. **33** Who will set a guard before my mouth, and a sure seal upon my lips, that I fall not by them, and that my tongue destroy me not?

Chapter 23

1 O Lord, father, and sovereign ruler of my life, leave me not to their counsel: nor suffer me to fall by them. **2** Who will set scourges over my thoughts, and the discipline of wisdom over my heart, that they spare me not in their ignorances, and that their sins may not appear: **3** Lest my ignorance increase, and my offences be multiplied, and my sins abound, and I fall before my adversaries, and my enemy rejoice over me? **4** O Lord, father, and God of my life, leave me not to their devices. **5** Give me not haughtiness of my eyes, and turn away from me all coveting.

6 Take from me the greediness of the belly, and let not the lusts of the flesh take hold of me, and give me not over to a shameless and foolish mind. **7** Hear, O ye children, the discipline of the mouth: and he that will keep it shall not perish by his lips, nor be brought to fall into most wicked works. **8** A sinner is caught in his own vanity, and the proud and the evil speakers shall fall thereby. **9** Let not thy mouth be accustomed to swearing: for in it there are many falls. **10** And let not the naming of God be usual in thy mouth, and meddle not with the names of saints, for thou shalt not escape free from them.

11 For as a slave daily put to the question, is never without a blue mark: so every one that sweareth, and nameth, shall not be wholly pure from sin. **12** A man that sweareth much, shall be filled with iniquity, and a scourge shall not depart from his house. **13** And if he make it void, his sin shall be upon him: and if he dissemble it, he offendeth double: **14** And if he swear in vain, he shall not be justified: for his house shall be filled with his punishment. **15** There is also another speech opposite to death, let it not be found in the inheritance of Jacob.

16 For from the merciful all these things shall be taken away, and they shall not wallow in sins. **17** Let not thy mouth be accustomed to indiscreet speech: for therein is the word of sin. **18** Remember thy father and thy mother, for thou sittest in the midst of great men: **19** Lest God forget thee in their sight, and thou, by thy daily custom, be infatuated and suffer reproach: and wish that thou hadst not been born, and curse the day of thy nativity. **20** The man that is accustomed to opprobrious words, will never be corrected all the days of his life.

21 Two sorts of men multiply sins, and the third bringeth wrath and destruction. **22** A hot soul is a burning fire, it will never be quenched, till it devour some thing. **23** And a man that is wicked in the mouth of his flesh, will not leave off till he hath kindled a fire. **24** To a man that is a fornicator all bread is sweet, he will not be weary of sinning unto the end. **25** Every man that passeth beyond his own bed, despising his own soul, and saying: Who seeth me?

26 Darkness compasseth me about, and the walls cover me, and no man seeth me: whom do I fear? the most High will not remember my sins. **27** And he understandeth not that his eye seeth all things, for such a man's fear driveth from him the fear of God, and the eyes of men fearing him: **28** And he knoweth not that the eyes of the Lord are far brighter than the sun, beholding round about all the ways of men, and the bottom of the deep, and looking into the hearts of men, into the most hidden parts. **29** For all things were known to the Lord God, before they were created: so also after they were perfected he beholdeth all things. **30** This man shall be punished in the streets of the city, and he shall be chased as a colt: and where he suspected not, he shall be taken.

31 And he shall be in disgrace with all men, because he understood not the fear of the Lord. **32** So every woman also that leaveth her husband, and bringeth in an heir by another: **33** For first she hath been unfaithful to the law of the most High: and secondly, she hath offended against her husband: thirdly, she hath fornicated in adultery, and hath gotten her children of another man. **34** This woman shall be brought into the assembly, and inquisition shall be made of her children. **35** Her children shall not take root, and her branches shall bring forth no fruit.

36 She shall leave her memory to be cursed, and her infamy shall not be blotted out. **37** And they that remain shall know. that there is nothing better than the fear of God: and that there is nothing sweeter than to have regard to the commandments of the Lord. **38** It is great glory to follow the Lord for length of days shall be received from him.

Chapter 24

1 Wisdom shall praise her own self, and shall be honoured in God, and shall glory in the midst of her people, **2** And shall open her mouth in the churches of the most High, and shall glorify herself in the sight of his power, **3** And in the midst of her own people she shall be exalted, and shall be admired in the holy assembly. **4** And in the multitude of the elect she shall have praise, and among the blessed she shall be blessed, saying: **5** I came out of the mouth of the most High, the firstborn before all creatures:

6 I made that in the heavens there should rise light that never faileth, and as a cloud I covered all the earth: **7** I dwelt in the highest places, and my throne is in a pillar of a cloud. **8** I alone have compassed the circuit of heaven, and have penetrated into the bottom of the deep, and have walked in the waves of the sea, **9** And have stood in all the earth: and in every people, **10** And in every nation I have had the chief rule:

11 And by my power I have trodden under my feet the hearts of all the high and low: and in all these I sought rest, and I shall abide in the inheritance of the Lord. **12** Then the creator of all things commanded, and said to me: and he that made me, rested in my tabernacle, **13** And he said to me: Let thy dwelling be in Jacob, and thy inheritance in Israel, and take root in my elect. **14** From the beginning, and before the world, was I created, and unto the world to come I shall not cease to be, and in the holy dwelling place I have ministered before him. **15** And so was I established in Sion, and in the holy city likewise I rested, and my power was in Jerusalem.

16 And I took root in an honourable people, and in the portion of my God his inheritance, and my abode is in the full assembly of saints. **17** I was exalted like a cedar in Libanus, and as a cypress tree on mount Sion. **18** I was exalted like a palm tree in Cades, and as a rose plant in Jericho: **19** As a fair olive tree in the plains, and as a plane tree by the water in the streets, was I exalted. **20** I gave a sweet smell like cinnamon. and aromatical balm: I yielded a sweet odour like the best myrrh:

21 And I perfumed my dwelling as storax, and galbanum, and onyx, and aloes, and as the frankincense not cut, and my odour is as the purest balm. **22** I have stretched out my branches as the turpentine tree, and my branches are of honour and grace. **23** As the vine I have brought forth a pleasant odour: and my flowers are the fruit of honour and riches. **24** I am the mother of fair love, and of fear, and of knowledge, and of holy hope. **25** In me is all grace of the way and of the truth, in me is all hope of life and of virtue.

26 Come over to me, all ye that desire me, and be filled with my fruits. **27** For my spirit is sweet above honey, and my inheritance above honey and the honeycomb. **28** My memory is unto everlasting generations. **29** They that eat me, shall yet hunger: and they that drink me, shall yet thirst. **30** He that hearkeneth to me, shall not be confounded: and they that work by me, shall not sin.

31 They that explain me shall have life everlasting. **32** All these things are the book of life, and the covenant of the most High, and the knowledge of truth. **33** Moses commanded a law in the precepts of justices, and an inheritance to the house of Jacob, and the promises to Israel. **34** He appointed to David his servant to raise up of him a most mighty king, and sitting on the throne of glory for ever. **35** Who filleth up wisdom as the Phison, and as the Tigris in the days of the new fruits.

36 Who maketh understanding to abound as the Euphrates, who multiplieth it as the Jordan in the time of harvest. **37** Who sendeth knowledge as the light, and riseth up as Gehon in the time of the vintage. **38** Who first hath perfect knowledge of her, and a weaker shall not search her out. **39** For her thoughts are more vast than the sea, and her counsels more deep than the great ocean. **40** I, wisdom, have poured out rivers.

41 I, like a brook out of a river of a mighty water; I, like a channel of a river. and like an aqueduct, came out of paradise. **42** I said: I will water my garden of plants, and I will water abundantly the fruits of my meadow. **43** And behold my brook became a great river, and my river came near to a sea: **44** For I make doctrine to shine forth to all as the morning light, and I will declare it afar off. **45** I will penetrate to all the lower parts of the earth, and will behold all that sleep, and will enlighten all that hope in the Lord.

46 I will yet pour out doctrine as prophecy, and will leave it to them that seek wisdom, and will not cease to instruct their offspring even to the holy age. **47** See ye that I have not laboured for myself only, but for all that seek out the truth.

Chapter 25

1 With three things my spirit is pleased, which are approved before God and men: **2** The concord of brethren, and the love of neighbours, and man and wife that agree well together. **3** Three sorts my soul hateth, and I am greatly grieved at their life: **4** A poor man that is proud: a rich man that is a liar: an old man that is a fool, and doting. **5** The things that thou hast not gathered in thy youth, how shalt thou find them in thy old age?

6 O how comely is judgment for a grey head, and for ancients to know counsel! **7** O how comely is wisdom for the aged, and understanding and counsel to men of honour! **8** Much experience is the crown of old men, and the fear of God is their glory. **9** Nine things that are not to be imagined by the heart have I magnified, and the tenth I will utter to men with my tongue. **10** A man that hath joy of his children: and he that liveth and seeth the fall of his enemies.

11 Blessed is he that dwelleth with a wise woman, and that hath not slipped with his tongue, and that hath not served such as are unworthy of him. **12** Blessed is he that findeth a true friend, and that declareth justice to an ear that heareth. **13** How great is he that findeth wisdom and knowledge! but there is none above him that feareth the Lord. **14** The fear of God hath set itself above all things: **15** Blessed is the man, to whom it is given to have the fear of God: he that holdeth it, to whom shall he be likened?

16 The fear of God is the beginning of his love: and the beginning of faith is to be fast joined unto it. **17** The sadness of the heart is every plague: and the wickedness of a woman is all evil. **18** And a man will choose any plague, but the plague of the heart: **19** And any wickedness, but the wickedness of a woman: **20** And any affliction, but the affliction from them that hate him:

21 And any revenge, but the revenge of enemies. **22** There is no head worse than the head of a serpent: **23** And there is no anger above the anger of a woman. It will be more agreeable to abide with a lion and a dragon, than to dwell with a wicked woman. **24** The wickedness of a woman changeth her face: and she darkeneth her countenance as a bear: and sheweth it like sackcloth. In the midst of her neighbours, **25** Her husband groaned, and hearing he sighed a little.

26 All malice is short to the malice of a woman, let the lot of sinners fall upon her. **27** As the climbing of a sandy way is to the feet of the aged, so is a wife full of tongue to a quiet man. **28** Look not upon a woman's beauty, and desire not a woman for beauty. **29** A woman's anger, and impudence, and confusion is great. **30** A woman, if she have superiority, is contrary to her husband.

31 A wicked woman abateth the courage, and maketh a heavy countenance, and a wounded heart. **32** Feeble hands, and disjointed knees, a woman that doth not make her husband happy. **33** From the woman came the beginning of sin, and by her we all die. **34** Give no issue to thy water, no, not a little: nor to a wicked woman liberty to gad abroad. **35** If she walk not at thy hand, she will confound thee in the sight of thy enemies.

36 Cut her off from thy flesh, lest she always abuse thee.

Chapter 26

1 Happy is the husband of a good wife: for the number of his years is double. **2** A virtuous woman rejoiceth her husband: and shall fulfill the years of his life in peace. **3** A good wife is a good portion, she shall be given in the portion of them that fear God, to a man for his good deeds. **4** Rich or poor, if his heart is good, his countenance shall be cheerful at all times. **5** Of three things my heart hath been afraid, and at the fourth my face hath trembled:

6 The accusation of a city, and the gathering together of the people: **7** And a false calumny, all are more grievous than death. **8** A jealous woman is the grief and mourning of the heart. **9** With a jealous woman is a scourge of the tongue which communicateth with all. **10** As a yoke of oxen that is moved to and fro, so also is a wicked woman: he that hath hold of her, is as he that taketh hold of a scorpion.

11 A drunken woman is a great wrath: and her reproach and shame shall not be hid. **12** The fornication of a woman shall be known by the haughtiness of her eyes, and by her eyelids. **13** On a daughter that turneth not away herself, set a strict watch: lest finding an opportunity she abuse herself. **14** Take heed of the impudence of her eyes, and wonder not if she slight thee. **15** She will open her mouth as a thirsty traveller to the fountain, and will drink of every water near her, and will sit down by every hedge, and open her quiver against every arrow, until she fail.

16 The grace of a diligent woman shall delight her husband, and shall fat his bones. **17** Her discipline is the gift of God. **18** Such is a wise and silent woman, and there is nothing so much worth as a well instructed soul. **19** A holy and shamefaced woman is grace upon grace. **20** And no price is worthy of a continent soul.

21 As the sun when it riseth to the world in the high places of God, so is the beauty of a good wife for the ornament of her house. **22** As the lamp shining upon the holy candlestick, so is the beauty of the face in a ripe age. **23** As golden pillars upon bases of silver, so are the firm feet upon the soles of a steady woman. **24** As everlasting foundations upon a solid rock, so the commandments of God In the heart of a holy woman. **25** At two things my heart is grieved, and the third bringeth anger upon me:

26 A man of war fainting through poverty: and a man of sense despised: **27** And he that passeth over from justice to sin, God hath prepared such an one for the sword. **28** Two sorts of callings have appeared to me hard and dangerous: a merchant is hardly free from negligence: and a huckster shall not be justified from the sins of the lips.

Chapter 27

1 Through poverty many have sinned: and he that seeketh to be enriched, turneth away his eye. **2** As a stake sticketh fast in the midst of the joining of stones, so also in the midst of selling and buying, sin shall stick fast. **3** Sin shall be destroyed with the sinner. **4** Unless thou hold thyself diligently in the fear of the Lord, thy house shall quickly be overthrown. **5** As when one sifteth with a sieve, the dust will remain: so will the perplexity of a man in his thoughts.

6 The furnace trieth the potter's vessels, and the trial of affliction just men. **7** As the dressing of a tree sheweth the fruit thereof, so a word out of the thought of the heart of man. **8** Praise not a man before he speaketh, for this is the trial of men. **9** If thou followest justice, thou shalt obtain her: and shalt put her on as a long robe of honour, and thou shalt dwell with her: and she shall protect thee for ever, and in the day of acknowledgment thou shalt find a strong foundation. **10** Birds resort unto their like: so truth will return to them that practise her.

11 The lion always lieth in wait for prey: so do sins for them that work iniquities. **12** A holy man continueth in wisdom as the sun: but a fool is changed as the moon. **13** In the midst of the unwise keep in the word till its time: but be continually among men that think. **14** The discourse of sinners is hateful, and their laughter is at the pleasures of sin. **15** The speech that sweareth much shall make the hair of the head stand upright: and its irreverence shall make one stop his ears.

16 In the quarrels of the proud is the shedding of blood: and their cursing is a grievous hearing. **17** He that discloseth the secret of a friend loseth his credit, and shall never find a friend to his mind. **18** Love thy neighbour, and be joined to him with fidelity. **19** But if thou discover his secrets, follow no more after him. **20** For as a man that destroyeth his friend, so also is he that destroyeth the friendship of his neighbour.

21 And as one that letteth a bird go out of his hand, so hast thou let thy neighbour go, and thou shalt not get him again. **22** Follow after him no more, for he is gone afar off, he is fled, as a roe escaped out of the snare: because his soul is wounded. **23** Thou canst no more bind him up. And of a curse there is reconciliation: **24** But to disclose the secrets of a friend, leaveth no hope to an unhappy soul. **25** He that winketh with the eye forgeth wicked things, and no man will cast him off:

26 In the sight of thy eyes he will sweeten his mouth, and will admire thy words: but at the last he will writhe his mouth, and on thy words he will lay a stumblingblock. **27** I have hated many things, but not like him, and the Lord will hate him. **28** If one cast a stone on high, it will fall upon his own head: and the deceitful stroke will wound the deceitful. **29** He that diggeth a pit, shall fall into it: and he that setteth a stone for his neighbour, shall stumble upon it: and he that layeth a snare for another, shall perish in it. **30** A mischievous counsel shall be rolled back upon the author, and he shall not know from whence it cometh to him.

31 Mockery and reproach are of the proud, and vengeance as a lion shall lie in wait for him. **32** They shall perish in a snare that are delighted with the fall of the just: and sorrow shall consume them before they die. **33** Anger and fury are both of them abominable, and the sinful man shall be subject to them.

Chapter 28

1 He that seeketh to revenge himself, shall find vengeance from the Lord, and he will surely keep his sins in remembrance. **2** Forgive thy neighbour if he hath hurt thee: and then shall thy sins be forgiven to thee when thou prayest. **3** Man to man reserveth anger, and doth he seek remedy of God? **4** He hath no mercy on a man like himself, and doth he entreat for his own sins? **5** He that is but flesh, nourisheth anger, and doth he ask forgiveness of God? who shall obtain pardon for his sins?

6 Remember thy last things, and let enmity cease: **7** For corruption and death hang over in his commandments. **8** Remember the fear of God, and be not angry with thy neighbour. **9** Remember the covenant of the most High, and overlook the ignorance of thy neighbour. **10** Refrain from strife, and thou shalt diminish thy sins:

11 For a passionate man kindleth strife, and a sinful man will trouble his friends, and bring in debate in the midst of them that are at peace. **12** For as the wood of the forest is, so the fire burneth: and as a man's strength is, so shall his anger be, and according to his riches he shall increase his anger. **13** A hasty contention kindleth a fire: and a hasty quarrel sheddeth blood: and a tongue that beareth witness bringeth death. **14** If thou blow the spark, it shall burn as a fire: and if thou spit upon it, it shall be quenched: both come out of the mouth. **15** The whisperer and the double tongued is accursed: for he hath troubled many that were at peace.

16 The tongue of a third person hath disquieted many, and scattered them from nation to nation. **17** It hath destroyed the strong cities of the rich, and hath overthrown the houses of great men. **18** It hath cut in pieces the forces of people, and undone strong nations. **19** The tongue of a third person hath cast out valiant women, and deprived them of their labours. **20** He that hearkeneth to it, shall never have rest, neither shall he have a friend in whom he may repose.

21 The stroke of a whip maketh a blue mark: but the stroke of the tongue will break the bones. **22** Many have fallen by the edge of the sword, but not so many as have perished by their own tongue. **23** Blessed is he that is defended from a wicked tongue, that hath not passed into the wrath thereof, and that hath not drawn the yoke thereof, and hath not been bound in its bands. **24** For its yoke is a yoke of iron: and its bands are bands of brass. **25** The death thereof is a most evil death: and hell is preferable to it.

26 Its continuance shall not be for a long time, but it shall possess the ways of the unjust: and the just shall not be burnt with its flame. **27** They that forsake God shall fall into it, and it shall burn in them, and shall not be quenched, and it shall be sent upon them as a lion, and as a leopard it shall tear them. **28** Hedge in thy ears with thorns, hear not a wicked tongue, and make doors and bars to thy mouth. **29** Melt down thy gold and silver, and make a balance for thy words, and a just bridle for thy mouth: **30** And take heed lest thou slip with thy tongue, and fall in the sight of thy enemies who lie in wait for thee, and thy fall be incurable unto death.

Chapter 29

1 He that sheweth mercy, lendeth to his neighbour: and he that is stronger in hand, keepeth the commandments. **2** Lend to thy neighbour in the time of his need, and pay thou thy neighbour again in due time. **3** Reap thy word, and deal faithfully with him: and thou shalt always find that which is necessary for thee. **4** Many have looked upon a thing lent as a thing found, and have given trouble to them that helped them. **5** Till they receive, they kiss the hands of the lender, and in promises they humble their voice:

6 But when they should repay, they will ask time, and will return tedious and murmuring words, and will complain of the time: **7** And if he be able to pay, he will stand off, he will scarce pay one half, and will count it as if he had found it: **8** But if not, he will defraud him of his money, and he shall get him for an enemy without cause: **9** And he will pay him with reproaches and curses, and instead of honour and good turn will repay him injuries. **10** Many have refused to lend, not out of wickedness, but they were afraid to be defrauded without cause.

11 But yet towards the poor be thou more hearty, and delay not to shew him mercy. **12** Help the poor because of the commandment: and send him not away empty handed because of his poverty. **13** Lose thy money for thy brother and thy friend: and hide it not under a stone to be lost. **14** Place thy treasure in the commandments of the most High, and it shall bring thee more profit than gold. **15** Shut up alms in the heart of the poor, and it shall obtain help for thee against all evil.

16 Better than the shield of the mighty, and better than the spear: **17** It shall fight for thee against thy enemy. **18** A good man is surety for his neighbour: and he that hath lost shame, will leave him to himself. **19** Forget not the kindness of thy surety: for he hath given his life for thee. **20** The sinner and the unclean fleeth from his surety.

21 A sinner attributeth to himself the goods of his surety: and he that is of an unthankful mind will leave him that delivered him. **22** A man is surety for his neighbour: and when he hath lost all shame, he shall forsake him. **23** Evil suretyship hath undone many of good estate, and hath tossed them as a wave of the sea. **24** It hath made powerful men to go from place to place round about, and they have wandered in strange countries. **25** A sinner that transgresseth the commandment of the Lord, shall fall into an evil suretyship: and he that undertaketh many things, shall fall into judgment.

26 Recover thy neighbour according to thy power, and take heed to thyself that thou fall not. **27** The chief thing for man's life is water and bread, and clothing, and a house to cover shame. **28** Better is the poor man's fare under a roof of boards, than sumptuous cheer abroad in another man's house. **29** Be contented with little instead of much, and thou shalt not hear the reproach of going abroad. **30** It is a miserable life to go as a guest from house to house: for where a man is a stranger, he shall not deal confidently, nor open his mouth.

31 He shall entertain and feed, and give drink to the unthankful, and moreover he shall hear bitter words. **32** Go, stranger, and furnish the table, and give others to eat what thou hast in thy hand. **33** Give place to the honourable presence of my friends: for I want my house, my brother being to be lodged with me. **34** These things are grievous to a man of understanding: the upbraiding of houseroom, and the reproaching of the lender.

Chapter 30

1 He that loveth his son, frequently chastiseth him, that he may rejoice in his latter end, and not grope after the doors of his neighbours. **2** He that instructeth his son shall be praised in him, and shall glory in him in the midst of them of his household. **3** He that teacheth his son, maketh his enemy jealous, and in the midst of his friends he shall glory in him. **4** His father is dead, and he is as if he were not dead: for he hath left one behind him that is like himself. **5** While he lived he saw and rejoiced in him: and when he died he was not sorrowful, neither was he confounded before his enemies.

6 For he left behind him a defender of his house against his enemies, and one that will requite kindness to his friends. **7** For the souls of his sons he shall bind up his wounds, and at every cry his bowels shall be troubled. **8** A horse not broken becometh stubborn, and a child left to himself will become headstrong. **9** Give thy son his way, and he shall make thee afraid: play with him, and he shall make thee sorrowful. **10** Laugh not with him, lest thou have sorrow, and at the last thy teeth be set on edge.

11 Give him not liberty in his youth, and wink not at his devices. **12** Bow down his neck while he is young, and beat his sides while he is a child, lest he grow stubborn, and regard thee not, and so be a sorrow of heart to thee. **13** Instruct thy son, and labour about him, lest his lewd behaviour be an offence to thee. **14** Better is a poor man who is sound, and strong of constitution, than a rich man who is weak and afflicted with evils. **15** Health of the soul in holiness of justice, is better then all gold and silver: and a sound body, than immense revenues.

16 There is no riches above the riches of the health of the body: and there is no pleasure above the joy of the heart. **17** Better is death than a bitter life: and everlasting rest, than continual sickness. **18** Good things that are hidden in a mouth that is shut, are as masses of meat set about a grave. **19** What good shall an offering do to an idol? for it can neither eat, nor smell: **20** So is he that is persecuted by the Lord, bearing the reward of his iniquity:

21 He seeth with his eyes, and groaneth, as an eunuch embracing a virgin, and sighing. **22** Give not up thy soul to sadness, and afflict not thyself in thy own counsel. **23** The joyfulness of the heart, is the life of a man, and a never failing treasure of holiness: and the joy of a man is length of life. **24** Have pity on thy own soul, pleasing God, and contain thyself: gather up thy heart in his holiness: and drive away sadness far from thee. **25** For sadness hath killed many, and there is no profit in it.

26 Envy and anger shorten a man's days, and pensiveness will bring old age before the time. **27** A cheerful and good heart is always feasting: for his banquets are prepared with diligence.

Chapter 31

1 Watching for riches consumeth the flesh, and the thought thereof driveth away sleep. **2** The thinking beforehand turneth away the understanding, and a grievous sickness maketh the soul sober. **3** The rich man hath laboured in gathering riches together, and when he resteth he shall be filled with his goods. **4** The poor man hath laboured in his low way of life, and in the end he is still poor. **5** He that loveth gold, shall not be justified: and he that followeth after corruption, shall be filled with it.

6 Many have been brought to fall for gold, and the beauty thereof hath been their ruin. **7** Gold is a stumblingblock to them that sacrifice to it: woe to them that eagerly follow after it, and every fool shall perish by it. **8** Blessed is the rich man that is found without blemish: and that hath not gone after gold, nor put his trust in money nor in treasures. **9** Who is he, and we will praise him? for he hath done wonderful things in his life. **10** Who hath been tried thereby, and made perfect, he shall have glory everlasting. He that could have transgressed, and hath not transgressed: and could do evil things, and hath not done them:

11 Therefore are his goods established in the Lord, and all the church of the saints shall declare his alms. **12** Art thou set at a great table? be not the first to open thy mouth upon it. **13** Say not: There are many things which are upon it. **14** Remember that a wicked eye is evil. **15** What is created more wicked than an eye? therefore shall it weep over all the face when it shall see.

16 Stretch not out thy hand first, lest being disgraced with envy thou be put to confusion. **17** Be not hasty in a feast. **18** Judge of the disposition of thy neighbour by thyself. **19** Use as a frugal man the things that are set before thee: lest if thou eatest much, thou be hated. **20** Leave off first, for manners' sake: and exceed not, lest thou offend.

21 And if thou sittest among many, reach not thy hand out first of all: and be not the first to ask for drink. **22** How sufficient is a little wine for a man well taught, and in sleeping thou shalt not be uneasy with it, and thou shalt feel no pain. **23** Watching, and choler, and gripes, are with an intemperate man: **24** Sound and wholesome sleep with a moderate man: he shall sleep till morning, and his soul shall be delighted with him. **25** And if thou hast been forced to eat much, arise, go out, and vomit: and it shall refresh thee, and thou shalt not bring sickness upon thy body.

26 Hear me, my son, and despise me not: and in the end thou shalt find my words. **27** In all thy works be quick, and no infirmity shall come to thee. **28** The lips of many shall bless him that is liberal of his bread, and the testimony of his truth is faithful. **29** Against him that is niggardly of his bread, the city will murmur, and the testimony of his niggardliness is true. **30** Challenge not them that love wine: for wine hath destroyed very many.

31 Fire trieth hard iron: so wine drunk to excess shall rebuke the hearts of the proud. **32** Wine taken with sobriety is equal life to men: if thou drink it moderately, thou shalt be sober. **33** What is his life, who is diminished with wine? **34** What taketh away life? death. **35** Wine was created from the beginning to make men joyful, and not to make them drunk.

36 Wine drunken with moderation is the joy of the soul and the heart. **37** Sober drinking is health to soul and body. **38** Wine drunken with excess raiseth quarrels; and wrath, and many ruins. **39** Wine drunken with excess is bitterness of the soul. **40** The heat of drunkenness is the stumblingblock of the fool, lessening strength and causing wounds.

41 Rebuke not thy neighbour in a banquet of wine: and despise him not in his mirth. **42** Speak not to him words of reproach: and press him not in demanding again.

Chapter 32

1 Have they made thee ruler? be not lifted up: be among them as one of them. **2** Have care of them, and so sit down, and when thou hast acquitted thyself of all thy charge, take thy place: **3** That thou mayst rejoice for them, and receive a crown as an ornament of grace, and get the honour of the contribution. **4** Speak, thou that art elder: for it becometh thee, **5** To speak the first word with care knowledge, and hinder not music.

6 Where there is no hearing, pour not out words, and be not lifted up out season with thy wisdom. **7** A concert of music in a banquet wine is as a carbuncle set in gold. **8** As a signet of an emerald in a work of gold: so is the melody of music with pleasant and moderate wine. **9** Hear in silence, and for thy reverence good grace shall come to thee. **10** Young man, scarcely speak in thy own cause.

11 If thou be asked twice, let thy answer be short. **12** In many things be as if thou wert ignorant, and hear in silence and withal seeking. **13** In the company of great men take not upon thee: and when the ancients are present, speak not much. **14** Before a storm goeth lightning: and before shamefacedness goeth favour: and for thy reverence good grace shall come to thee. **15** And at the time of rising be not slack: but be first to run home to thy house, and there withdraw thyself, and there take thy pastime.

16 And do what thou hast a mind, but not in sin or proud speech. **17** And for all these things bless the Lord, that made thee, and that replenisheth thee with all his good things. **18** He that feareth the Lord, will receive his discipline: and they that will seek him early, shall find a blessing. **19** He that seeketh the law, shall be filled with it: and he that dealeth deceitfully, shall meet with a stumblingblock therein. **20** They that fear the Lord, shall find just judgment, and shall kindle justice as a light.

21 A sinful man will flee reproof, and will find an excuse according to his will. **22** A man of counsel will not neglect understanding, a strange and proud man will not dread fear: **23** Even after he hath done with fear without counsel, he shall be controlled by the things of his own seeking. **24** My son, do thou nothing without counsel, and thou shalt not repent when thou hast done. **25** Go not in the way of ruin, and thou shalt not stumble against the stones; trust not thyself to a rugged way, lest thou set a stumblingblock to thy soul.

26 And beware of thy own children, and take heed of them of thy household. **27** In every work of thine regard thy soul in faith: for this is the keeping of the commandments. **28** He that believeth God, taketh heed to the commandments: and he that trusteth in him, shall fare never the worse.

Chapter 33

1 No evils shall happen to him that feareth the Lord, but in temptation God will keep him, and deliver him from evils. **2** A wise man hateth not the commandments and justices, and he shall not be dashed in pieces as a ship in a storm. **3** A man of understanding is faithful to the law of God, and the law is faithful to him. **4** He that cleareth up a question, shall prepare what to say, and so having prayed he shall be heard, and shall keep discipline, and then he shall answer. **5** The heart of a fool is as a wheel of a cart: and his thoughts are like a rolling axletree.

6 A friend that is a mocker, is like a stallion horse: he neigheth under every one that sitteth upon him. **7** Why doth one day excel another, and one light another, and one year another year, when all come of the sun? **8** By the knowledge of the Lord they were distinguished, the sun being made, and keeping his commandment. **9** And he ordered the seasons, and holidays of them, and in them they celebrated festivals at an hour. **10** Some of them God made high and great days, and some of them he put in the number of ordinary days. And all men are from the ground, and out of the earth, from whence Adam was created.

11 With much knowledge the Lord hath divided them and diversified their ways. **12** Some of them hath he blessed, and exalted: and some of them hath he sanctified, and set near himself: and some of them hath he cursed and brought low, and turned them from their station. **13** As the potter's clay is in his hand, to fashion and order it: **14** All his ways are according to his ordering: so man is in the hand of him that made him, and he will render to him according to his judgment. **15** Good is set against evil, and life against death: so also is the sinner against a just man. And so look upon all the works of the most High. Two and two, and one against another.

16 And I awaked last of all, and as one that gathereth after the grapegatherers. **17** In the blessing of God I also have hoped: and as one that gathereth grapes, have I filled the winepress. **18** See that I have not laboured for myself only, but for all that seek discipline. **19** Hear me, ye great men, and all ye people, and hearken with your ears, ye rulers of the church. **20** Give not to son or wife, brother or friend, power over thee while thou livest; and give not thy estate to another, lest then repent, and thou entreat for the same.

21 As long as thou livest, and hast breath in thee, let no man change thee. **22** For it is better that thy children should ask of thee, than that thou look toward the hands of thy children. **23** In all thy works keep the pre-eminence. **24** Let no stain sully thy glory. In the time when thou shalt end the days of thy life, and in the time of thy decease, distribute thy inheritance. **25** Fodder, and a wand, and a burden are for an ass: bread, and correction, and work for a slave.

26 He worketh under correction, and seeketh to rest: let his hands be idle, and he seeketh liberty. **27** The yoke and the thong bend a stiff neck, and continual labours bow a slave. **28** Torture and fetters are for a malicious slave: send him to work, that he be not idle: **29** For idleness hath taught much evil. **30** Set him to work: for so it is fit for him. And if he be not obedient, bring him down with fetters, but be not excessive towards any one: and do no grievous thing without judgment.

31 If thou have a faithful servant, let him be to thee as thy own soul: treat him as a brother: because in the blood of thy soul thou hast gotten him. **32** If thou hurt him unjustly, he will run away: **33** And if he rise up and depart, thou knowest not whom to ask, and in what way to seek him.

Chapter 34

1 The hopes of a man that is void of understanding are vain and deceitful: and dreams lift up fools. **2** The man that giveth heed to lying visions, is like to him that catcheth at a shadow, and followeth after the wind. **3** The vision of dreams is the resemblance of one thing to another: as when a man's likeness is before the face of a man. **4** What can be made clean by the unclean? and what truth can come from that which is false? **5** Deceitful divinations and lying omens and the dreams of evildoers, are vanity:

6 And the heart fancieth as that of a woman in travail: except it be a vision sent forth from the most High, set not thy heart upon them. **7** For dreams have deceived many, and they have failed that put their trust in them. **8** The word of the law shall be fulfilled without a lie, and wisdom shall be made plain in the mouth of the faithful. **9** What doth he know, that hath not been tried? A man that hath much experience, shall think of many things: and he that hath learned many things, shall shew forth understanding. **10** He that hath no experience, knoweth little: and he that hath been experienced in many things, multiplieth prudence.

11 He that hath not been tried, what manner of things doth he know? he that hath been surprised, shall abound with subtlety. **12** I have seen many things by travelling, and many customs of things. **13** Sometimes I have been in danger of death for these things, and I have been delivered by the grace of God. **14** The spirit of those that fear God; is sought after, and by his regard shall be blessed. **15** For their hope is on him that saveth them, and the eyes of God are upon them that love him.

16 He that feareth the Lord shall tremble at nothing, and shall not be afraid for he is his hope. **17** The soul of him that feareth the Lord is blessed. **18** To whom doth he look, and who in his strength? **19** The eyes of the Lord are upon them that fear him, he is their powerful protector, and strong stay, a defence from the heat, and a cover from the sun at noon, **20** A preservation from stumbling, and a help from falling; he raiseth up the soul, and enlighteneth the eyes, and giveth health, and life, and blessing.

21 The offering of him that sacrificeth of a thing wrongfully gotten, is stained, and the mockeries of the unjust are not acceptable. **22** The Lord is only for them that wait upon him in the way of truth and justice. **23** The most High approveth not the gifts of the wicked: neither hath he respect to the oblations of the unjust, nor will he be pacified for sins by the multitude of their sacrifices. **24** He that offereth sacrifice of the goods of the poor, is as one that sacrificeth the son in the presence of his father. **25** The bread of the needy, is the life of the poor: he that defraudeth them thereof, is a man of blood.

26 He that taketh away the bread gotten by sweat, is like him that killeth his neighbour. **27** He that sheddeth blood, and he that defraudeth the labourer of his hire, are brothers. **28** When one buildeth up, and another pulleth down: what profit have they but the labour? **29** When one prayeth, and another curseth: whose voice will God hear? **30** He that washeth himself after touching the dead, if he toucheth him again, what doth his washing avail?

31 So a man that fasteth for his sins, and doth the same again, what doth his humbling himself profit him? who will hear his prayer?

Chapter 35

1 He that keepeth the law, multiplieth offerings. **2** It is a wholesome sacrifice to take heed to the commandments, and to depart from all iniquity. **3** And to depart from injustice, is to offer a propitiatory sacrifice for injustices, and a begging of pardon for sins. **4** He shall return thanks, that offereth fine flour: and he that doth mercy, offereth sacrifice. **5** To depart from iniquity is that which pleaseth the Lord, and to depart from injustice, is an entreaty for sins.

6 Thou shalt not appear empty in the sight of the Lord. **7** For all these things are to be done because of the commandment of God. **8** The oblation of the just maketh the altar fat, and is an odour of sweetness in the sight of the most High. **9** The sacrifice of the just is acceptable, and the Lord will not forget the memorial thereof. **10** Give glory to God with a good heart: and diminish not the firstfruits of thy hands.

11 In every gift shew a cheerful countenance, and sanctify thy tithes with joy. **12** Give to the most High according to what he hath given to thee, and with a good eye do according to the ability of thy hands: **13** For the Lord maketh recompense, and will give thee seven times as much. **14** Do not offer wicked gifts, for such he will not receive. **15** And look not upon an unjust sacrifice, for the Lord is judge, and there is not with him respect of person.

16 The Lord will not accept any person against a poor man, and he will hear the prayer of him that is wronged. **17** He will not despise the prayers of the fatherless; nor the widow, when she poureth out her complaint. **18** Do not the widow's tears run down the cheek, and her cry against him that causeth them to fall? **19** For from the cheek they go up even to heaven, and the Lord that heareth will not be delighted with them. **20** He that adoreth God with joy, shall be accepted, and his prayer shall approach even to the clouds.

21 The prayer of him that humbleth himself, shall pierce the clouds: and till it come nigh he will not be comforted: and he will not depart till the most High behold. **22** And the Lord will not be slack, but will judge for the just, and will do judgment: and the Almighty will not have patience with them, that he may crush their back: **23** And he will repay vengeance to the Gentiles, till he have taken away the multitude of the proud, and broken the sceptres of the unjust, **24** Till he have rendered to men according to their deeds: and according to the works of Adam, and according to his presumption, **25** Till he have judged the cause of his people, and he shall delight the just with his mercy.

26 The mercy of God is beautiful in the time of affliction, as a cloud of rain in the time of drought.

Chapter 36

1 Have mercy upon us, O God of all, and behold us, and shew us the light of thy mercies: **2** And send thy fear upon the nations, that have not sought after thee: that they may know that there is no God beside thee, and that they may shew forth thy wonders. **3** Lift up thy hand over the strange nations, that they may see thy power. **4** For as thou hast been sanctified in us in their sight, so thou shalt be magnified among them in our presence, **5** That they may know thee, as we also have known thee, that there is no God beside thee, O Lord.

6 Renew thy signs, and work new miracles. **7** Glorify thy hand, and thy right arm. **8** Raise up indignation, and pour out wrath. **9** Take away the adversary, and crush the enemy. **10** Hasten the time, and remember the end, that they may declare thy wonderful works.

11 Let him that escapeth be consumed by the rage of the fire: and let them perish that oppress thy people. **12** Crush the head of the princes of the enemies that say: There is no other beside us. **13** Gather together all the tribes of Jacob: that they may know that there is no God besides thee, and may declare thy great works: and thou shalt inherit them as from the beginning. **14** Have mercy on thy people, upon whom thy name is invoked: and upon Israel, whom thou hast raised up to be thy firstborn. **15** Have mercy on Jerusalem, the city which thou hast sanctified, the city of thy rest.

16 Fill Sion with thy unspeakable words, and thy people with thy glory. **17** Give testimony to them that are thy creatures from the beginning, and raise up the prophecies which the former prophets spoke in thy name. **18** Reward them that patiently wait for thee, that thy prophets may be found faithful: and hear the prayers of thy servants, **19** According to the blessing of Aaron over thy people, and direct us into the way of justice, and let all know that dwell upon the earth, that thou art God the beholder of all ages. **20** The belly will devour all meat, yet one is better than another.

21 The palate tasteth venison and the wise heart false speeches. **22** A perverse heart will cause grief, and a man of experience will resist it. **23** A woman will receive every man: yet one daughter is better than another. **24** The beauty of a woman cheereth the countenance of her husband, and a man desireth nothing more. **25** If she have a tongue that can cure, and likewise mitigate and shew mercy: her husband is not like other men.

26 He that possesseth a good wife, beginneth a possession: she is a help like to himself, and a pillar of rest. **27** Where there is no hedge, the possession shall be spoiled: and where there is no wife, he mourneth that is in want. **28** Who will trust him that hath no rest, and that lodgeth wheresoever the night taketh him, as a robber well appointed, that skippeth from city to city.

Chapter 37

1 Every friend will say: I also am his friend: but there is a friend, that is only a friend in name. Is not this a grief even to death? **2** But a companion and a friend shall be turned to an enemy. **3** O wicked presumption, whence camest thou to cover the earth with thy malice, and deceitfulness? **4** There is a companion who rejoiceth with his friend in his joys, but in the time of trouble, he will be against him. **5** There is a companion who condoleth with his friend for his belly's sake, and he will take up a shield against enemy.

6 Forget not thy friend in thy mind, and be not unmindful of him in thy riches. **7** Consult not with him that layeth a snare for thee, and hide thy counsel from them that envy thee. **8** Every counsellor giveth out counsel, but there is one that is a counsellor for himself. **9** Beware of a counsellor. And know before what need he hath: for he will devise to his own mind: **10** Lest he thrust a stake into the ground, and say to thee:

11 Thy way is good; and then stand on the other side to see what shall befall thee. **12** Treat not with a man without religion concerning holiness, nor with an unjust man concerning justice, nor with a woman touching her of whom she is jealous, nor with a coward concerning war, nor with a merchant about traffic, nor with a buyer of selling, nor with an envious man of giving thanks, **13** Nor with the ungodly of piety, nor with the dishonest of honesty, nor with the held labourer of every work, **14** Nor with him that worketh by the year of the finishing of the year, nor with an idle servant of much business: give no heed to these in any matter of counsel. **15** But be continually with a holy man, whomsoever thou shalt know to observe the fear of God,

16 Whose soul is according to thy own soul: and who, when thou shalt stumble in the dark, will be sorry for thee. **17** And establish within thyself a heart of good counsel: for there is no other thing of more worth to thee than it. **18** The soul of a holy man discovereth sometimes true things, more than seven watchmen that sit in a high piece to watch. **19** But above all these things pray to the most High, that he may direct thy way in truth. **20** In all thy works let the true word go before thee, and steady counsel before every action.

21 A wicked word shall change the beast: out of which four manner of things arise, good and evil, life and death: and the tongue is continually the ruler of them. There is a man that is subtle and a teacher of many, and yet is unprofitable to his own soul. **22** A skillful man hath taught many, and is sweet to his own soul. **23** He that speaketh sophistically, is hateful: he shall be destitute of every thing. **24** Grace is not given him from the Lord: for he is deprived of all wisdom. **25** There is a wise man that is wise to his own soul: and the fruit of his understanding is commendable.

26 A wise man instructeth his own people, and the fruits of his understanding are faithful. **27** A wise man shall be filled with blessings, and they that see shall praise him. **28** The life of a man is in the number of his days: but the days of Israel are innumerable. **29** A wise man shall inherit honour among his people, and his name shall live for ever. **30** My son, prove thy soul in thy life: and if it be wicked, give it no power:

31 For all things are not expedient for all, and every kind pleaseth not every soul. **32** Be not greedy in any feasting, and pour not out thyself upon any meat: **33** For in many meats there will be sickness, and greediness will turn to choler. **34** By surfeiting many have perished: but he that is temperate, shall prolong life.

Chapter 38

1 Honour the physician for the need thou hast of him: for the most High hath created him. **2** For all healing is from God, and he shall receive gifts of the king. **3** The skill of the physician shall lift up his head, and in the sight of great men he shall be praised. **4** The most High hath created medicines out of the earth, and a wise man will not abhor them. **5** Was not bitter water made sweet with wood?

6 The virtue of these things is come to the knowledge of men, and the most High hath given knowledge to men, that he may be honoured in his wonders. **7** By these he shall cure and shall allay their pains, and of these the apothecary shall make sweet confections, and shall make up ointments of health, and of his works there shall be no end. **8** For the peace of God is over all the face of the earth. **9** My son, in thy sickness neglect not thyself, but pray to the Lord, and he shall heal thee. **10** Turn away from sin and order thy hands aright, and cleanse thy heart from all offence.

11 Give a sweet savour, and a memorial of fine flour, and make a fat offering, and then give place to the physician. **12** For the Lord created him: and let him not depart from thee, for his works are necessary. **13** For there is a time when thou must fall into their hands: **14** And they shall beseech the Lord, that he would prosper what they give for ease and remedy, for their conversation. **15** He that sinneth in the sight of his Maker, shall fall into the hands of the physician.

16 My son, shed tears over the dead, and begin to lament as if thou hadst suffered some great harm, and according to judgment cover his body, and neglect not his burial. **17** And for fear of being ill spoken of weep bitterly for a, day, and then comfort thyself in thy sadness. **18** And make mourning for him according to his merit for a day, or two, for fear of detraction. **19** For of sadness cometh death, and it overwhelmeth the strength, and the sorrow of the heart boweth down the neck. **20** In withdrawing aside sorrow remaineth: and the substance of the poor is according to his heart.

21 Give not up thy heart to sadness, but drive it from thee: and remember the latter end. **22** Forget it not: for there is no returning, and thou shalt do him no good, and shalt hurt thyself. **23** Remember my judgment: for also shall be so: yesterday for me, and today for thee. **24** When the dead is at rest, let his remembrance rest, and comfort him in the departing of his spirit. **25** The wisdom of a scribe cometh by his time of leisure: and he that is less in action, shall receive wisdom.

26 With what wisdom shall he be furnished that holdeth the plough, and that glorieth in the goad, that driveth the oxen therewith, and is occupied in their labours, and his whole talk is about the offspring of bulls? **27** He shall give his mind to turn up furrows, and his care is to give the kine fodder. **28** So every craftsman and workmaster that laboureth night and day, he who maketh graven seals, and by his continual diligence varieth the figure: he shall give his mind to the resemblance of the picture, and by his watching shall finish the work. **29** So doth the smith sitting by the anvil and considering the iron work. The vapour of the fire wasteth his flesh, and he fighteth with the heat of the furnace. **30** The noise of the hammer is always in his ears, and his eye is upon the pattern of the vessel he maketh.

31 He setteth his mind to finish his work, and his watching to polish them, to perfection. **32** So doth the potter sitting at his work, turning the wheel about with his feet, who is always carefully set to his work, and maketh all his work by number: **33** He fashioneth the clay with his arm, and boweth down his strength before his feet: **34** He shall give his mind to finish the glazing, and his watching to make clean the furnace. **35** All these trust to their hands, and every one is wise in his own art.

36 Without these a city is not built. **37** And they shall not dwell, nor walk about therein, and they shall not go up into the assembly. **38** Upon the judges' seat they shall not sit, and the ordinance of judgment they shall not understand, neither shall they declare discipline and judgment, and they shall not be found where parables are spoken: **39** But they shall strengthen the state of the world, and their prayer shall be in the work of their craft, applying their soul, and searching in the law of the most High.

Chapter 39

1 The wise men will seek out the wisdom of all the ancients, and will be occupied in the prophets. **2** He will keep the sayings of renowned men, and will enter withal into the subtilties of parables. **3** He will search out the hidden meanings of proverbs, and will be conversant in the secrets of parables. **4** He shall serve among great men, and: appear before the governor. **5** He shall pass into strange countries: for he shall try good and evil among men.

6 He will give his heart to resort early to the Lord that made him, and he will pray in the sight of the most High. **7** He will open his mouth in prayer, and will make supplication for his sins. **8** For if it shall please the great Lord, he will fill him with the spirit of understanding: **9** And he will pour forth the words of his wisdom as showers, and in his prayer he will confess to the Lord. **10** And he shall direct his counsel, and his knowledge, and in his secrets shall he meditate.

11 He shall shew forth the discipline he hath learned, and shall glory in the law of the covenant of the Lord. **12** Many shall praise his wisdom, and it shall never be forgotten. **13** The memory of him shall not depart away, and his name shall be in request from generation to generation. **14** Nations shall declare his wisdom, and the church shall shew forth his praise. **15** If he continue, he shall leave a name above a thousand: and if he rest, it shall be to his advantage.

16 I will yet meditate that I may declare: for I am filled as with a holy transport. **17** By a voice he saith: Hear me, ye divine offspring, and bud forth as the rose planted by the brooks of waters. **18** Give ye a sweet odour as frankincense. **19** Send forth flowers, as the lily, and yield a smell, and bring forth leaves in grace, and praise with canticles, and bless the Lord in his works. **20** Magnify his name, and give glory to him with the voice of your lips, and with the canticles of your mouths, and with harps, and in praising him, you shall say in this manner:

21 All the works of the Lord are exceeding good. **22** At his word the waters stood as a heap: and at the words of his mouth the receptacles of waters: **23** For at his commandment favour is shewn, and there is no diminishing of his salvation. **24** The works of all flesh are before him, and there is nothing hid from his eyes. **25** He seeth from eternity to eternity, and there is nothing wonderful before him.

26 There is no saying: What is this, or what is that? for all things shall be sought in their time. **27** His blessing hath overflowed like a river. **28** And as a flood hath watered the earth; so shall his wrath inherit the nations, that have not sought after him: **29** Even as he turned the waters into a dry land, and the earth was made dry: and his ways were made plain for their journey: so to sinners they are stumblingblocks in his wrath. **30** Good things were created for the good from the beginning, so for the wicked, good and evil things.

31 The principal things necessary for the life of men, are water, fire, and iron, salt, milk, and bread of flour, and honey, and the cluster of the grape, and oil, and clothing. **32** All these things shall be for good to the holy, so to the sinners and the ungodly they shall be turned into evil. **33** There are spirits that are created for vengeance, and in their fury they lay on grievous torments. **34** In the time of destruction they shall pour out their force: and they shall appease the wrath of him that made them. **35** Fire, hail, famine, and death, all these were created for vengeance.

36 The teeth of beasts, and scorpions, and serpents, and the sword taking vengeance upon the ungodly unto destruction. **37** In his commandments they shall feast, and they shall be ready upon earth when need is, and when their time is come they shall not transgress his word. **38** Therefore from the beginning I was resolved, and I have meditated, and thought on these things and left them in writing. **39** All the works of the Lord are good, and he will furnish every work in due time. **40** It is not to be said: This is worse than that: for all shall be well approved in their time.

41 Now therefore with the whole heart and mouth praise ye him, and bless the name of the Lord.

Chapter 40

1 Great labour is created for all men, and a heavy yoke is upon the children of Adam, from the day of their coming out of their mother's womb, until the day of their burial into the mother of all. **2** Their thoughts, and fears of the heart, their imagination of things to come, and the day of their end: **3** From him that sitteth on a glorious throne, unto him that is humbled in earth and ashes: **4** From him that weareth purple, and beareth the crown, even to him that is covered with rough linen: wrath, envy, trouble, unquietness, and the fear of death, continual anger, and strife, **5** And in the time of rest upon his bed, the sleep of the night changeth his knowledge.

6 A little and as nothing is his rest, and afterward in sleep, as in the day of keeping watch. **7** He is troubled in the vision of his heart, as if he had escaped in the day of battle. In the time of his safety he rose up, and wondereth that there is no fear: **8** Such things happen to all flesh, from man even to beast, and upon sinners are sevenfold more. **9** Moreover, death, and bloodshed, strife, and sword, oppressions, famine, and affliction, and scourges: **10** All these things are created for the wicked, and for their sakes came the flood.

11 All things that are of the earth, shall return to the earth again, and all waters shall return to the sea. **12** All bribery, and injustice shall blotted out, and fidelity shall stand for ever. **13** The riches of the unjust shall be dried up like a river, and shall pass away with a noise like a great thunder in rain. **14** While he openeth his hands he shall rejoice: but transgressors shall pine away in the end. **15** The offspring of the ungodly shall not bring forth many branches, and make a noise as unclean roots upon the top of a rock.

16 The weed growing over every water, and at the bank of the river, shall be pulled up before all grass. **17** Grace is like a paradise in blessings, and mercy remaineth for ever. **18** The life of a labourer that is content with what he hath, shall be sweet, and in it thou shalt find a treasure. **19** Children, and the building of a city shall establish a name, but a blameless wife shall be counted above them both. **20** Wine and music rejoice the heart, but the love of wisdom is above them both.

21 The flute and the psaltery make a sweet melody, but a pleasant tongue is above them both. **22** Thy eye desireth favour and beauty, but more than these green sown fields. **23** A friend and companion meeting together in season, but above them both is a wife with her husband. **24** Brethren are a help in the time of trouble, but mercy shall deliver more than they. **25** Gold and silver make the feet stand sure: but wise counsel is above them both.

26 Riches and strength lift up the heart: but above these is the fear of the Lord. **27** There is no want in the fear of the Lord, and it needeth not to seek for help. **28** The fear of the Lord is like a paradise of blessing, and they have covered it above all glory. **29** My son, in thy lifetime be not indigent: for it is better to die than to want. **30** The life of him that looketh toward another man's table is not to be counted a life: for he feedeth his soul with another man's meat.

31 But a man, well instructed and taught, will look to himself. **32** Begging will be sweet in the mouth of the unwise, but in his belly there shall burn a fire.

Chapter 41

1 O death, how bitter is the remembrance of thee to a man that hath peace in his possessions! **2** To a man that is at rest, and whose ways are prosperous in all things, and that is yet able to take meat! **3** O death, thy sentence is welcome to the man that is in need, and to him whose strength faileth: **4** Who is in a decrepit age, and that is in care about all things, and to the distrustful that loseth patience! **5** Fear not the sentence of death. Remember what things have been before thee, and what shall come after thee: this sentence is from the Lord upon all flesh.

6 And what shall come upon thee by the good pleasure of the most High? Whether ten, or a hundred, or a thousand years. **7** For among the dead there is no accusing of life. **8** The children of sinners become children of abominations, and they that converse near the houses of the ungodly. **9** The inheritance of the children of sinners shall perish, and with their posterity shall be a perpetual reproach. **10** The children will complain of an ungodly father, because for his sake they are in reproach.

11 Woe to you, ungodly men, who have forsaken the law of the most high Lord. **12** And if you be born, you shall be born in malediction: and if you die, in malediction shall be your portion. **13** All things that are of the earth, shall return into the earth: so the ungodly shall from malediction to destruction. **14** The mourning of men is about their body, but the name of the ungodly shall be blotted out. **15** Take care of a good name: for this shall continue with thee, more than a thousand treasures precious and great.

16 A good life hath its number of days: but a good name shall continue for ever. **17** My children, keep discipline in peace: for wisdom that is hid, and a treasure that is not seen, what profit is there in them both? **18** Better is the man that hideth his folly, than the man that hideth his wisdom. **19** Wherefore have a shame of these things I am now going to speak of. **20** For it is not good to keep all shamefacedness: and all things do not please all men in opinion.

21 Be ashamed of fornication before father and mother: and of a lie before a governor and a man in power: **22** Of an offence before a prince, and a judge: of iniquity before a congregation and a people: **23** Of injustice before a companion and friend: and in regard to the place where thou dwellest, **24** Of theft, and of the truth of God, and the covenant: of leaning with thy elbow over meat, and of deceit in giving and taking: **25** Of silence before them that salute thee: of looking upon a harlot: and of turning away thy face from thy kinsman.

26 Turn not away thy face from thy neighbour, and of taking away a portion and not restoring. **27** Gaze not upon another man's wife, and be not inquisitive after his handmaid, and approach not her bed. **28** Be ashamed of upbraiding speeches before friends: and after thou hast given, upbraid not.

Chapter 42

1 Repeat not the word which thou hast heard, and disclose not the thing that is secret; so shalt thou be truly without confusion, and shall find favour before all men: be not ashamed of any of these things, and accept no person to sin thereby: **2** Of the law of the most High, and of his covenant, and of judgment to justify the ungodly: **3** Of the affair of companions and travellers, and of the gift of the inheritance of friends: **4** Of exactness of balance and weights, of getting much or little: **5** Of the corruption of buying, and of merchants, and of much correction of children, and to make the side of a wicked slave to bleed.

6 Sure keeping is good over a wicked wife. **7** Where there are many hands, shut up, and deliver all things in number, and weight: and put all in writing that thou givest out or receivest in. **8** Be not ashamed to inform the unwise and foolish, and the aged, that are judged by young men: and thou shalt be well instructed in all things, and well approved in the sight of all men living. **9** The father waketh for the daughter when no man knoweth, and the care for her taketh away his sleep, when she is young, lest she pass away the flower of her age, and when she is married, lest she should be hateful: **10** In her virginity, lest she should be corrupted, and be found with child in her father's house: and having a husband, lest she should misbehave herself, or at the least become barren.

11 Keep a sure watch over a shameless daughter: lest at any time she make thee become a laughingstock to thy enemies, and a byword in the city, and a reproach among the people, and she make thee ashamed before all the multitude. **12** Behold not everybody's beauty: and tarry not among women. **13** For from garments cometh a moth, and from a woman the iniquity of a man. **14** For better is the iniquity of a man, than a woman doing a good turn, and a woman bringing shame and reproach. **15** I will now remember the works of the Lord, and I will declare the things I have seen. By the words of the Lord are his works.

16 The sun giving light hath looked upon all things, and full of the glory of the Lord is his work. **17** Hath not the Lord made the saints to declare all his wonderful works, which the Lord Almighty hath firmly settled to be established for his glory? **18** He hath searched out the deep, and the heart of men: and considered their crafty devices. **19** For the Lord knoweth all knowledge, and hath beheld the signs of the world, he declareth the things that are past, and the things that are to come, and revealeth the traces of hidden things. **20** No thought escapeth him, and no word can hide itself from him.

21 He hath beautified the glorious works of his wisdom: and he Is from eternity to eternity, and to him nothing may be added, **22** Nor can he be diminished, and he hath no need of any counsellor. **23** O how desirable are all his works, and what we can know is but as a spark! **24** All these things live, and remain for ever, and for every use all things obey him. **25** All things are double, one against another, and he hath made nothing defective.

26 He hath established the good things of every one. And who shall be filled with beholding his glory?

Chapter 43

1 The firmament on high is his beauty, the beauty of heaven with its glorious shew. **2** The sun when he appeareth shewing forth at his rising, an admirable instrument, the work of the most High. **3** At noon he burneth the earth, and who can abide his burning heat? As one keeping a furnace in the works of heat: **4** The sun three times as much, burneth the mountains, breathing out fiery vapours, and shining with his beams, he blindeth the eyes. **5** Great is the Lord that made him, and at his words he hath hastened his course.

6 And the moon in all in her season, is for a declaration of times and a sign of the world. **7** From the moon is the sign of the festival day, a light that decreaseth in her perfection. **8** The month is called after her name, increasing wonderfully in her perfection. **9** Being an instrument of the armies on high, shining gloriously in the Armament of heaven. **10** The glory of the stars is the beauty of heaven; the Lord enlighteneth the world on high.

11 By the words of the holy one they shall stand in judgment, and shall never fail in their watches. **12** Look upon the rainbow, and bless him that made it: it is very beautiful in its brightness. **13** It encompasseth the heaven about with the circle of its glory, the hands of the most High have displayed it. **14** By his commandment he maketh the snow to fall apace, and sendeth forth swiftly the lightnings of his judgment. **15** Through this are the treasures opened, and the clouds fly out like birds.

16 By his greatness he hath fixed the clouds, and the hailstones are broken. **17** At his sight shall the mountains be shaken, and at his will the south wind shall blow. **18** The noise of his thunder shall strike the earth, so doth the northern storm, and the whirlwind: **19** And as the birds lighting upon the earth, he scattereth snow, and the falling thereof, is as the coming down of locusts. **20** The eye admireth at the beauty of the whiteness thereof, and the heart is astonished at the shower thereof.

21 He shall pour frost as salt upon the earth: and when it freezeth, it shall become like the tops of thistles. **22** The cold north wind bloweth, and the water is congealed into crystal; upon every gathering together of waters it shall rest, and shall clothe the waters as a breastplate. **23** And it shall devour the mountains, and burn the wilderness, and consume all that is green as with fire. **24** A present remedy of all is the speedy coming of a cloud, and a dew that meeteth it, by the heat that cometh, shall overpower it. **25** At his word the wind is still, and with his thought he appeaseth the deep, and the Lord hath planted islands therein.

26 Let them that sail on the sea, tell the dangers thereof: and when we hear with our ears, we shall admire. **27** There are great and wonderful works: a variety of beasts, and of all living things, and the monstrous creatures of whales. **28** Through him is established the end of their journey, and by his word all things are regulated. **29** We shall say much, and yet shall want words: but the sum of our words is, He is all. **30** What shall we be able to do to glorify him? for the Almighty himself is above all his works.

31 The Lord is terrible, and exceeding great, and his power is admirable. **32** Glorify the Lord as much as ever you can, for he will yet far exceed, and his magnificence is wonderful. **33** Blessing the

Lord, exalt him as much as you can: for he is above all praise. **34** When you exalt him put forth all your strength, and be not weary: for you can never go far enough. **35** Who shall see him, and declare him? and who shall magnify him as he is from the beginning?

36 There are many things hidden from us that are greater than these: for we have seen but a few of his works. **37** But the Lord hath made all things, and to the godly he hath given wisdom.

Chapter 44

1 Let us now praise men of renown, and our fathers in their generation. **2** The Lord hath wrought great glory through his magnificence from the beginning. **3** Such as have borne rule in their dominions, men of great power, and endued with their wisdom, shewing forth in the prophets the dignity of prophets, **4** And ruling over the present people, and by the strength of wisdom instructing the people in most holy words. **5** Such as by their skill sought out musical tunes, and published canticles of the scriptures.

6 Rich men in virtue, studying beautifulness: living at peace in their houses. **7** All these have gained glory in their generations, and were praised in their days. **8** They that were born of them have left a name behind them, that their praises might be related: **9** And there are some, of whom there is no memorial: who are perished, as if they had never been: and are become as if they had never been born, and their children with them. **10** But these were men of mercy, whose godly deeds have not failed:

11 Good things continue with their seed, **12** Their posterity are a holy inheritance, and their seed hath stood in the covenants. **13** And their children for their sakes remain for ever: their seed and their glory shall not be forsaken. **14** Their bodies are buried in peace, and their name liveth unto generation and generation. **15** Let the people shew forth their wisdom, and the church declare their praise.

16 Henoch pleased God, and was translated into paradise, that he may give repentance to the nations. **17** Noe was found perfect, just, and in the time of wrath he was made a reconciliation. **18** Therefore was there a remnant left to the earth, when the flood came. **19** The covenants of the world were made with him, that all flesh should no more be destroyed with the flood. **20** Abraham was the great father of a multitude of nations, and there was not found the like to him in glory, who kept the law of the most High, and was in covenant with him.

21 In his flesh he established the covenant, and in temptation he was found faithful. **22** Therefore by an oath he gave him glory in his posterity, that he should increase as the dust of the earth, **23** And that he would exalt his seed as the stars, and they should inherit from sea to sea, and from the river to the ends of the earth. **24** And he did in like manner with Isaac for the sake of Abraham his father. **25** The Lord gave him the blessing of all nations, and confirmed his covenant upon the head of Jacob.

26 He acknowledged him in his blessings, and gave him an inheritance, and divided him his portion in twelve tribes. **27** And he preserved for him men of mercy, that found grace in the eyes of all flesh.

Chapter 45

1 Moses was beloved of God, and men: whose memory is in benediction. **2** He made him like the saints in glory, and magnified him in the fear of his enemies, and with his words he made prodigies to cease. **3** He glorified him in the sight of kings, and gave him commandments in the sight of his people, and shewed him his glory. **4** He sanctified him in his faith, and meekness, and chose him out of all flesh. **5** For he heard him, and his voice, and brought him into a cloud.

6 And he gave him commandments before his face, and a law of life and instruction, that he might teach Jacob his covenant, and Israel his judgments. **7** He exalted Aaron his brother, and like to himself of the tribe of Levi: **8** He made an everlasting covenant with him, and gave him the priesthood of the nation, and made him blessed in glory, **9** And he girded him about with a glorious girdle, and clothed him with a robe of glory, and crowned him with majestic attire. **10** He put upon him a garment to the feet, and breeches, and as ephod, and he compassed him with many little bells of gold all round about,

11 That as he went there might be a sound, and a noise made that might be heard in the temple, for a memorial to the children of his people. **12** He gave him a holy robe of gold, and blue, and purple, a woven work of a wise man, endued with judgment and truth: **13** Of twisted scarlet the work of an artist, with precious stones cut and set in gold, and graven by the work of a lapidary for a memorial, according to the number of the tribes of Israel. **14** And a crown of gold upon his mitre wherein was engraved Holiness, an ornament of honour: a work of power, and delightful to the eyes for its beauty. **15** Before him there were none so beautiful, even from the beginning.

16 No stranger was ever clothed with them, but only his children alone, and his grandchildren for ever. **17** His sacrifices were consumed with fire every day. **18** Moses filled his hands and anointed him with holy oil. **19** This was made to him for an everlasting testament, and to his seed as the days of heaven, to execute the office of the priesthood, and to have praise, and to glorify his people in his name. **20** He chose him out of all men living, to offer sacrifice to God, incense, and a good savour, for a memorial to make reconciliation for his people:

21 And he gave him power in his commandments, in the covenants of his judgments, that he should teach Jacob his testimonies, and give light to Israel in his law. **22** And strangers stood up against him, and through envy the men that were with Dathan and Abiron, compassed him about in the wilderness, and the congregation of Core in their wrath. **23** The Lord God saw and it pleased him not, and they were consumed in his wrathful indignation. **24** He wrought wonders upon them, and consumed them with a flame of fire. **25** And he added glory to Aaron, and gave him an inheritance, and divided unto him the firstfruits of the increase of the earth.

26 He prepared them bread in the first place unto fulness: for the sacrifices also of the Lord they shall eat, which he gave to him, and to his seed. **27** But he shall not inherit among the people in the land, and he hath no portion among the people: for he himself is his portion and inheritance. **28** Phinees the son of Eleazar is the third in glory, by imitating him in the fear of the Lord: **29** And he stood up in the shameful fall of the people: in the goodness and readiness of his soul he appeased God for Israel. **30** Therefore he made to him a covenant of peace, to be the prince of the sanctuary, and of his people, that the dignity of priesthood should be to him and to his seed for ever.

31 And a covenant to David the king, the son of Jesse of the tribe of Juda, an inheritance to him and to his seed, that he might give wisdom into our heart to judge his people in justice, that their good things might not be abolished, and he made their glory in their nation everlasting.

Chapter 46

1 Valiant in war was Jesus the son of Nave, who was successor of Moses among the prophets, who was great according to his name, **2** Very great for the saving the elect of God, to overthrow the enemies that rose up against them, that he might get the inheritance for Israel. **3** How great glory did he gain when he lifted up his hands, and stretched out swords against the cities? **4** Who before him hath so resisted? for the Lord himself brought the enemies. **5** Was not the sun stopped in his anger, and one day made as two?

6 He called upon the most high Sovereign when the enemies assaulted him on every side, and the great and holy God heard him by hailstones of exceeding great force. **7** He made a violent assault against the nation of his enemies, and in the descent he destroyed the adversaries. **8** That the nations might know his power, that it is not easy to fight against God. And he followed the mighty one: **9** And in the days of Moses he did a work of mercy, he and Caleb the son of Jephone, in standing against the enemy, and withholding the people from sins, and appeasing the wicked murmuring. **10** And they two being appointed, were delivered out of the danger from among the number of six hundred thousand men on foot, to bring them into their inheritance, into the land that floweth with milk and honey.

11 And the Lord gave strength also to Caleb, and his strength continued even to his old age, so that he went up to the high places of the land, and his seed obtained it for an inheritance: **12** That all the children of Israel might see, that it is good to obey the holy God. **13** Then all the judges, every one by name, whose heart was not corrupted: who turned not away from the Lord, **14** That their memory might be blessed, and their bones spring up out of their place, **15** And their name continue for ever, the glory of the holy men remaining unto their children.

16 Samuel the prophet of the Lord, the beloved of the Lord his God, established a new government, and anointed princes over his people. **17** By the law of the Lord he judged the congregation, and the God of Jacob beheld, and by his fidelity he was proved a prophet. **18** And he was known to be faithful in his words, because he saw the God of light: **19** And called upon the name of the Lord Almighty, in fighting against the enemies who beset him on every side, when he offered a lamb without blemish. **20** And the Lord thundered from heaven, and with a great noise made his voice to be heard.

21 And he crushed the princes of the Tyrians, and all the lords of the Philistines: **22** And before the time of the end of his life in the world, he protested before the Lord, and his anointed: money, or any thing else, even to a shoe, he had not taken of any man, and no man did accuse him. **23** And after this he slept, and he made known to the king, and shewed him the end of his life, and he lifted up his voice from the earth in prophecy to blot out the wickedness of the nation.

Chapter 47

1 Then Nathan the prophet arose in the days of David. **2** And as the fat taken away from the flesh, so was David chosen from among the children of Israel. **3** He played with lions as with lambs: and with bears he did in like manner as with the lambs of the flock, in his youth. **4** Did not he kill the giant, and take away reproach from his people? **5** In lifting up his hand, with the stone in the sling he beat down the boasting of Goliath:

6 For he called upon the Lord the Almighty, and he gave strength in his right hand, to take away the mighty warrior, and to set up the horn of his nation. **7** So in ten thousand did he glorify him, and praised him in the blessings of the Lord, in offering to him a crown of glory: **8** For he destroyed the enemies on every side, and extirpated the Philistines the adversaries unto this day: he broke their horn for ever. **9** In all his works he gave thanks to the holy one, and to the most High, with words of glory. **10** With his whole heart he praised the Lord, and loved God that made him: and he gave him power against his enemies:

11 And he set singers before the altar, and by their voices he made sweet melody. **12** And to the festivals he added beauty, and set in order the solemn times even to the end of his life, that they should praise the holy name of the Lord, and magnify the holiness of God in the morning. **13** The Lord took away his sins, and exalted his horn for ever: and he gave him a covenant of the kingdom, and a throne of glory in Israel. **14** After him arose up a wise son, and for his sake he cast down all the power of the enemies. **15** Solomon reigned in days of peace, and God brought all his enemies under him, that he might build a house in his name, and prepare a sanctuary for ever: O how wise wast thou in thy youth!

16 And thou wast filled as a river with wisdom, and thy soul covered the earth. **17** And thou didst multiply riddles in parables: thy name went abroad to the islands far off, and thou wast beloved in thy peace. **18** The countries wondered at thee for thy canticles, and proverbs, and parables, and interpretations, **19** And at the name of the Lord God, whose surname is, God of Israel. **20** Thou didst gather gold as copper, and didst multiply silver as lead,

21 And thou didst bow thyself to women: and by thy body thou wast brought under subjection. **22** Thou hast stained thy glory, and defiled thy seed so as to bring wrath upon thy children, and to have thy folly kindled, **23** That thou shouldst make the kingdom to be divided, and out of Ephraim a rebellious kingdom to rule. **24** But God will not leave off his mercy, and he will not destroy, nor abolish his own works, neither will he cut up by the roots the offspring of his elect: and he will not utterly take away the seed of him that loveth the Lord. **25** Wherefore he gave a remnant to Jacob, and to David of the same stock.

26 And Solomon had an end with his fathers. **27** And he left behind him of his seed, the folly of the nation, **28** Even Roboam that had little wisdom, who turned away the people through his counsel: **29** And Jeroboam the son of Nabat, who caused Israel to sin, and shewed Ephraim the way of sin, and their sins were multiplied exceedingly. **30** They removed them far away from their land.

31 And they sought out all iniquities, till vengeance came upon them, and put an end to all their sins.

Chapter 48

1 And Elias the prophet stood up, as a fire, and his word burnt like a torch. **2** He brought a famine upon them, and they that provoked him in their envy, were reduced to a small number, for they could not endure the commandments of the Lord. **3** By the word of the Lord he shut up the heaven, and he brought down fire from heaven thrice. **4** Thus was Elias magnified in his wondrous works. And who can glory like to thee? **5** Who raisedst up a dead man from below, from the lot of death, by the word of the Lord God.

6 Who broughtest down kings to destruction, and brokest easily their power in pieces, and the glorious from their bed. **7** Who heardest judgment in Sina, and in Horeb the judgments of vengeance. **8** Who anointedst kings to penance, and madest prophets successors after thee. **9** Who wast taken up in a whirlwind of fire, in a chariot of fiery horses. **10** Who art registered in the judgments of times to appease the wrath of the Lord, to reconcile the heart of the father to the son, and to restore the tribes of Jacob.

11 Blessed are they that saw thee, and were honoured with thy friendship. **12** For we live only in our life, but after death our name shall not be such. **13** Elias was indeed covered with the whirlwind, and his spirit was filled up in Eliseus: in his days he feared not the prince, and no man was more powerful than he. **14** No word could overcome him, and after death his body prophesied. **15** In his life he did great wonders, and is death he wrought miracles.

16 For all this the people repented not, neither did they depart from their sins till they were cast out of their land, and were scattered through all the earth. **17** And there was left but a small people, and a prince in the house of David. **18** Some of these did that which pleased God: but others committed many sins. **19** Ezechias fortified his city, and brought in water into the midst thereof, and he digged a rock with iron, and made a well for water. **20** In his days Sennacherib came up, and sent Rabsaces, and lifted up his hand against them, and he stretched out his hand against Sion, and became proud through his power.

21 Then their hearts and hands trembled, and they were in pain as women in travail. **22** And they called upon the Lord who is merciful, and spreading their hands, they lifted them up to heaven: and the holy Lord God quickly heard their voice. **23** He was not mindful of their sins, neither did he deliver them up to their enemies, but he purified them by the hand of Isaias, the holy prophet. **24** He overthrew the army of the Assyrians, and the angel of the Lord destroyed them. **25** For Ezechias did that which pleased God, and walked valiantly in the way of David his father, which Isaias, the great prophet, and faithful in the sight of God, had commanded him.

26 In his days the sun went backward, and he lengthened the king's life. **27** With a great spirit he saw the things that are to come to pass at last, and comforted the mourners in Sion. **28** He shewed what should come to pass for ever, and secret things before they came.

Chapter 49

1 The memory of Josias is like the composition of a sweet smell made by the art of a perfumer: **2** His remembrance shall be sweet as honey in every mouth, and as music at a banquet of wine. **3** He was directed by God unto the repentance of the nation, and he took away the abominations of wickedness. **4** And he directed his heart towards the Lord, and in the days of sinners he strengthened godliness. **5** Except David, and Ezechias, and Josias, all committed sin.

6 For the kings of Juda forsook the law of the most High, and despised the fear of God. **7** So they gave their kingdom to others, and their glory to a strange nation. **8** They burnt the chosen city of holiness, and made the streets thereof desolate according to the prediction of Jeremias. **9** For they treated him evil, who was consecrated a prophet from his mother's womb, to overthrow, and pluck up, and destroy, and to build again, and renew. **10** It was Ezechiel that saw the glorious vision, which was shewn him upon the chariot of cherubims.

11 For he made mention of the enemies under the figure of rain, and of doing good to them that shewed right ways. **12** And may the bones of the twelve prophets spring up out of their place: for they strengthened Jacob, and redeemed themselves by strong faith. **13** How shall we magnify Zorobabel? for he was as a signet on the right hand; **14** In like manner Jesus the son of Josedec? who in their days built the house, and set up a holy temple to the Lord, prepared for everlasting glory. **15** And let Nehemias be a long time remembered, who raised up for us our walls that were cast down, and set up the gates and the bars, who rebuilt our houses.

16 No man was born upon earth like Henoch: for he also was taken up from the earth. **17** Nor as Joseph, who was a man born prince of his brethren, the support of his family, the ruler of his brethren, the stay of the people: **18** And his bones were visited, and after death they prophesied. **19** Seth and Sem obtained glory among men: and above every soul Adam in the beginning.

Chapter 50

1 Simon the high priest, the son of Onias, who in his life propped up the house, and in his days fortified the temple. **2** By him also the height of the temple was founded, the double building and the high walls of the temple. **3** In his days the wells of water flowed out, and they were filled as the sea above measure. **4** He took care of his nation, and delivered it from destruction. **5** He prevailed to enlarge the city, and obtained glory in his conversation with the people: and enlarged the entrance of the house and the court.

6 He shone in his days as the morning star in the midst of a cloud, and as the moon at the full. **7** And as the sun when it shineth, so did he shine in the temple of God. **8** And as the rainbow giving light in the bright clouds, and as the flower of roses in the days of the spring, and as the lilies that are on the brink of the water, and as the sweet smelling frankincense in the time of summer. **9** As a bright fire, and frankincense burning in the fire. **10** As a massy vessel of gold, adorned with every precious stone.

11 As an olive tree budding forth, and a cypress tree rearing itself on high, when he put on the robe of glory, and was clothed with the perfection of power. **12** When he went up to the holy altar, he honoured the vesture of holiness. **13** And when he took the portions out of the hands of the priests, he himself stood by the altar. And about him was the ring of his brethren: and as the cedar planted in mount Libanus, **14** And as branches of palm trees, they stood round about him, and all the sons of Aaron in their glory. **15** And the oblation of the Lord was in their hands, before all the congregation of Israel: and finishing his service, on the altar, to honour the offering of the most high King,

16 He stretched forth his hand to make a libation, and offered of the blood of the grape. **17** He poured out at the foot of the altar a divine odour to the most high Prince. **18** Then the sons of Aaron shouted, they sounded with beaten trumpets, and made a great noise to be heard for a remembrance before God. **19** Then all the people together made haste, and fell down to the earth upon their faces, to adore the Lord their God, and to pray to the Almighty God the most High. **20** And the singers lifted up their voices. and in the great house the sound of sweet melody was increased.

21 And the people in prayer besought the Lord the most High, until the worship of the Lord was perfected, and they had finished their office. **22** Then coming down, he lifted up his hands over all the congregation of the children of Israel, to give glory to God with his lips, and to glory in his name: **23** And he repeated his prayer, willing to shew the power of God. **24** And now pray ye to the God of all, who hath done great things in all the earth, who hath increased our days from our mother's womb, and hath done with us according to his mercy. **25** May he grant us joyfulness of heart, and that there be peace in our days in Israel for ever:

26 That Israel may believe that the mercy of God is with us, to deliver us in his days. **27** There are two nations which my soul abhorreth: and the third is no nation, which I hate: **28** They that sit on mount Seir, and the Philistines, and the foolish people that dwell in Sichem. **29** Jesus the son of Sirach, of Jerusalem, hath written in this book the doctrine of wisdom and instruction, who renewed wisdom from his heart. **30** Blessed is he that is conversant in these good things: and he that layeth them up in his heart, shall be wise always.

31 For if he do them, he shall be strong to do all things: because the light of God guideth his steps.

Chapter 51

1 A prayer of Jesus the son of Sirach. I will give glory to thee, O Lord, O King, and I will praise thee, O God my Saviour. **2** I will give glory to thy name: for thou hast been a helper and protector to me. **3** And hast preserved my body from destruction, from the snare of an unjust tongue, and from the lips of them that forge lies, and in the sight of them that stood by, thou hast been my helper. **4** And thou hast delivered me, according to the multitude of the mercy of thy name, from them that did roar, prepared to devour. **5** Out of the hands of them that sought my life, and from the gates of afflictions, which compassed me about:

6 From the oppression of the flame which surrounded me, and in the midst of the fire I was not burnt. **7** From the depth of the belly of hell, and from an unclean tongue, and from lying words, from an unjust king, and from a slanderous tongue: **8** My soul shall praise the Lord even to death. **9** And my life was drawing near to hell beneath. **10** They compassed me on every side, and there was no one that would help me. I looked for the succour of men, and there was none.

11 I remembered thy mercy, O Lord, and thy works, which are from the beginning of the world. **12** How thou deliverest them that wait for thee, O Lord, and savest them out of the hands of the nations. **13** Thou hast exalted my dwelling place upon the earth and I have prayed for death to pass away. **14** I called upon the Lord, the father of my Lord, that he would not leave me in the day of my trouble, and in the time of the proud without help. **15** I will praise thy name continually, and will praise it with thanksgiving, and my prayer was heard.

16 And thou hast saved me from destruction, and hast delivered me from the evil time. **17** Therefore I will give thanks, and praise thee, and bless the name of the Lord. **18** When I was yet young, before I wandered about, I sought for wisdom openly in my prayer. **19** I prayed for her before the temple, and unto the very end I will seek after her, and she flourished as a grape soon ripe. **20** My heart delighted in her, my foot walked in the right way, from my youth up I sought after her.

21 I bowed down my ear a little, and received her. **22** I found much wisdom in myself, and I profited much therein. **23** To him that giveth me wisdom, will I give glory. **24** For I have determined to follow her: I have had a zeal for good, and shall not be confounded. **25** My soul hath wrestled for her, and in doing it I have been confirmed.

26 I stretched forth my hands on high, and I bewailed my ignorance of her. **27** I directed my soul to her, and in knowledge I found her. **28** I possessed my heart with her from the beginning: therefore I shall not be forsaken. **29** My entrails were troubled in seeking her: therefore shall I possess a good possession. **30** The Lord hath given me a tongue for my reward: and with it I will praise him.

31 Draw near to me, ye unlearned, and gather yourselves together into the house of discipline. **32** Why are ye slow? and what do you say of these things? your souls are exceeding thirsty. **33** I have opened my mouth, and have spoken: buy her for yourselves without silver, **34** And submit your neck to the yoke, and let your soul receive discipline: for she is near at hand to be found. **35** Behold with your eyes how I have laboured a little, and have found much rest to myself.

36 Receive ye discipline as a great sum of money, and possess abundance of gold by her. **37** Let your soul rejoice in his mercy, and you shall not be confounded in his praise. **38** Work your work before the time, and he will give you your reward in his time.

THE PROPHESY OF BARUCH

Chapter 1

1 And these are the words of the book, which Baruch the son of Nerias, the son of Maasias, the son of Sedecias, the son of Sedei, the son of Helcias, wrote in Babylonia. **2** In the fifth year, in the seventh day of the month, at the time that the Chaldeans took Jerusalem, and burnt it with fire. **3** And Baruch read the words of this book in the hearing of Jechonias the son of Joakim king of Juda, and in the hearing of all the people that came to hear the book. **4** And in the hearing of the nobles, the sons of the kings, and in the hearing of the ancients, and in the hearing of the people, from the least even to the greatest of them that dwelt in Babylonia, by the river Sedi. **5** And when they heard it they wept, and fasted, and prayed before the Lord.

6 And they made a collection of money, according to every man's power. **7** And they sent it to Jerusalem to Joakim the priest, the son of Helcias, the son of Salom, and to the priests, and to all the people, that were found with him in Jerusalem: **8** At the time when he received the vessels of the temple of the Lord, which had been taken away out of the temple, to return them into the land of Juda the tenth day of the month Sivan, the silver vessels, which Sedecias the son of Josias king of Juda had made, **9** After that Nabuchodonosor the king of Babylon had carried away Jechonias, and the princes, and all the powerful men, and the people of the land from Jerusalem, and brought them bound to Babylon. **10** And they said: Behold we have sent you money, buy with it holocausts, and frankincense, and make meat offerings, and offerings for sin at the altar of the Lord our God:

11 And pray ye for the life of Nabuchodonosor the king of Babylon, and for the life of Balthasar his son, that their days may be upon earth as the days of heaven: **12** And that the Lord may give us strength, and enlighten our eyes, that we may live under the shadow of Nabuchodonosor the king of Babylon, and under the shadow of Balthasar his son, and may serve them many days, and may find favour in their sight. **13** And pray ye for us to the Lord our God: for we have sinned against the Lord our God, and his wrath is not turned away from us even to this day. **14** And read ye this book, which we have sent to you to be read in the temple of the Lord, on feasts, and proper days. **15** And you shall say: To the Lord our God belongeth justice, but to us confusion of our face: as it is come to pass at this day to all Juda, and to the inhabitants of Jerusalem,

16 To our kings, and to our princes, and to our priests, and to our prophets, and to our fathers. **17** We have sinned before the Lord our God, and have not believed him, nor put our trust in him: **18** And we were not obedient to him, and we have not hearkened to the voice of the Lord our God, to walk in his commandments, which he hath given us. **19** From the day that he brought our fathers out of the land of Egypt, even to this day, we were disobedient to the Lord our God: and going astray we turned away from hearing his voice. **20** And many evils have cleaved to us, and the curses which the Lord foretold by Moses his servant: who brought our fathers out of the land of Egypt, to give us a land flowing with milk and honey, as at this day.

21 And we have not hearkened to the voice of the Lord our God according to all the words of the prophets whom he sent to us: **22** And we have gone away every man after the inclinations of his own wicked heart, to serve strange gods, and to do evil in the sight of the Lord our God.

Chapter 2

1 Wherefore the Lord our God hath made good his word, that he spoke to us, and to our judges that have judged Israel, and to our kings, and to our princes, and to all Israel and Juda: **2** That the Lord would bring upon us great evils, such as never happened under heaven, as they have come to pass in Jerusalem, according to the things that are written in the law of Moses: **3** That a man should eat the flesh of his own son, and the flesh of his own daughter. **4** And he hath delivered them up to be under the hand of all the kings that are round about us, to be a reproach, and desolation among all the people, among whom the Lord hath scattered us. **5** And we are brought under, and are not uppermost: because we have sinned against the Lord our God, by not obeying his voice.

6 To the Lord our God belongeth justice: but to us, and to our fathers confusion of face, as at this day. **7** For the Lord hath pronounced against us all these evils that are come upon us: **8** And we have not entreated the face of the Lord our God, that we might return every one of us from our most wicked ways. **9** And the Lord hath watched over us for evil, and hath brought it upon us: for the Lord is just in all his works which he hath commanded us: **10** And we have not hearkened to his voice to walk in the commandments of the Lord which he hath set before us.

11 And now, O Lord God of Israel, who hast brought thy people out of the land of Egypt with a strong hand, and with signs, and with wonders, and with thy great power, and with a mighty arm, and hast made thee a name as at this day, **12** We have sinned, we have done wickedly, we have acted unjustly, O Lord our God, against all thy justices. **13** Let thy wrath be turned away from us: for we are left a few among the nations where thou hast scattered us. **14** Hear, O Lord, our prayers, and our petitions, and deliver us for thy own sake: and grant that we may find favour in the sight of them that have led us away: **15** That all the earth may know that thou art the Lord our God, and that thy name is called upon Israel, and upon his posterity.

16 Look down upon us, O Lord, from thy holy house, and incline thy ear, and hear us. **17** Open thy eyes, and behold: for the dead that are in hell, whose spirit is taken away from their bowels, shall not give glory and justice to the Lord: **18** But the soul that is sorrowful for the greatness of evil she hath done, and goeth bowed down, and feeble, and the eyes that fail, and the hungry soul giveth glory and justice to thee the Lord. **19** For it is not for the justices of our fathers that we pour out our prayers, and beg mercy in thy sight, O Lord our God: **20** But because thou hast sent out thy wrath, and thy indignation upon us, as thou hast spoken by the hand of thy servants the prophets, saying:

21 Thus saith the Lord: Bow down your shoulder, and your neck, and serve the king of Babylon: and you shall remain in the land which I have given to your fathers. **22** But if you will not hearken to the voice of the Lord your God, to serve the king of Babylon: I will cause you to depart out of the cities of Juda, and from without Jerusalem. **23** And I will take away from you the voice of mirth, and the voice of joy, and the voice of the bridegroom, and the voice of the bride, and all the land shall be without any footstep of inhabitants. **24** And they hearkened not to thy voice, to serve the king of Babylon: and thou hast made good thy words, which thou spokest by the hands of thy servants the prophets, that the bones of our kings, and the bones of our fathers should be removed out of their place: **25** And behold they are cast out to the heat of the sun, and to the frost of the night: and they have died in grievous pains, by famine, and by the sword, and in banishment.

26 And thou hast made the temple, in which thy name was called upon, as it is at this day, for the iniquity of the house of Israel, and the house of Juda. **27** And thou hast dealt with us, O Lord our God, according to all thy goodness, and according to all that great mercy of thine: **28** As thou spokest by the hand of thy servant Moses, in the day when thou didst command him to write thy law before the children of Israel, **29** Saying: If you will not hear my voice, this great multitude shall be turned into a very small number among the nations, where I will scatter them: **30** For I know that the people will not hear me, for they are a people of a stiff neck: but they shall turn to their heart in the land of their captivity:

31 And they shall know that I am the Lord their God: and I will give them a heart, and they shall understand: and ears, and they shall hear. **32** And they shall praise me in the land of their captivity, and shall be mindful of my name. **33** And they shall turn away themselves from their stiff neck, and from their wicked deeds: for they shall remember the way of their fathers, that sinned against me. **34** And I will bring them back again into the land which I promised with an oath to their fathers, Abraham, Isaac, and Jacob, and they shall be masters thereof: and I will multiply them, and they shall not be diminished. **35** And I will make with them another covenant that shall be everlasting, to be their God, and they shall be my people: and I will no more remove my people, the children of Israel, out of the land that I have given them.

Chapter 3

1 And now, O Lord Almighty, the God of Israel, the soul in anguish, and the troubled spirit crieth to thee: **2** Hear, O Lord, and have mercy, for thou art a merciful God, and have pity on us: for we have sinned before thee. **3** For thou remainest for ever, and shall we perish everlastingly? **4** O Lord Almighty, the God of Israel, hear now the prayer of the dead of Israel, and of their children, that have sinned before thee, and have not hearkened to the voice of the Lord their God, wherefore evils have cleaved fast to us. **5** Remember not the iniquities of our fathers, but think upon thy hand, and upon thy name at this time:

6 For thou art the Lord our God, and we will praise thee, O Lord: **7** Because for this end thou hast put thy fear in our hearts, to the intent that we should call upon thy name, and praise thee in our captivity, for we are converted from the iniquity of our fathers, who sinned before thee. **8** And behold we are at this day in our captivity, whereby thou hast scattered us to be a reproach, and a curse, and an offence, according to all the iniquities of our fathers, who departed from thee, O Lord our God. **9** Hear, O Israel, the commandments of life: give ear, that thou mayst learn wisdom. **10** How happeneth it, O Israel, that thou art in thy enemies' land?

11 Thou art grown old in a strange country, thou art defiled with the dead: thou art counted with them that go down into hell. **12** Thou hast forsaken the fountain of wisdom: **13** For if thou hadst walked in the way of God, thou hadst surely dwelt in peace for ever. **14** Learn where is wisdom, where is strength, where is understanding: that thou mayst know also where is length of days and life, where is the light of the eyes, and peace. **15** Who hath found out her place? and who hath gone in to her treasures?

16 Where are the princes of the nations, and they that rule over the beasts that are upon the earth? **17** That take their diversion with the birds of the air. **18** That hoard up silver and gold, wherein men trust, and there is no end of their getting? who work in silver and are solicitous, and their works are unsearchable. **19** They are cut off, and are gone down to hell, and others are risen up in their place. **20** Young men have seen the light, and dwelt upon the earth: but the way of knowledge they have not known,
21 Nor have they understood the paths thereof, neither have their children received it, it is far from their face. **22** It hath not been heard of in the land of Chanaan, neither hath it been seen in Theman. **23** The children of Agar also, that search after the wisdom that is of the earth, the merchants of Merrha, and of Theman, and the tellers of fables, and searchers of prudence and understanding: but the way of wisdom they have not known, neither have they remembered her paths. **24** O Israel, how great is the house of God, and how vast is the place of his possession! **25** It is great, and hath no end: it is high and immense.

26 There were the giants, those renowned men that were from the beginning, of great stature, expert in war. **27** The Lord chose not them, neither did they find the way of knowledge: therefore did they perish. **28** And because they had not wisdom, they perished through their folly. **29** Who hath gone up into heaven, and taken her, and brought her down from the clouds? **30** Who hath passed over the sea, and found her, and brought her preferably to chosen gold?

31 There is none that is able to know her ways, nor that can search out her paths: **32** But he that knoweth all things, knoweth her, and hath found her out with his understanding: he that prepared the earth for evermore, and filled it with cattle and fourfooted beasts: **33** He that sendeth forth light, and it goeth: and hath called it, and it obeyeth him with trembling. **34** And the stars have given light in their watches, and rejoiced: **35** They were called, and they said: Here we are: and with cheerfulness they have shined forth to him that made them.

36 This is our God, and there shall no other be accounted of in comparison of him. **37** He found out all the way of knowledge, and gave it to Jacob his servant, and to Israel his beloved. **38** Afterwards he was seen upon earth, and conversed with men.

Chapter 4

1 This is the book of the commandments of God, and the law, that is for ever: all they that keep it, shall come to life: but they that have forsaken it, to death. **2** Return, O Jacob, and take hold of it, walk in the way by its brightness, in the presence of the light thereof. **3** Give not thy honour to another, nor thy dignity to a strange nation. **4** We are happy, O Israel: because the things that are pleasing to God, are made known to us. **5** Be of good comfort, O people of God, the memorial of Israel:

6 You have been sold to the Gentiles, not for your destruction: but because you provoked God to wrath, you are delivered to your adversaries. **7** For you have provoked him who made you, the eternal God, offering sacrifice to devils, and not to God. **8** For you have forgotten God, who brought you up, and you have grieved Jerusalem that nursed you. **9** For she saw the wrath of God coming upon you, and she said: Give ear, all you that dwell near Sion, for God hath brought upon me great mourning: **10** For I have seen the captivity of my people, of my sons, and my daughters, which the Eternal hath brought upon them.

11 For I nourished them with joy: but I sent them away with weeping and mourning. **12** Let no man rejoice over me, a widow, and desolate: I am forsaken of many for the sins of my children, because they departed from the law of God. **13** And they have not known his justices, nor walked by the ways of God's commandments, neither have they entered by the paths of his truth and justice. **14** Let them that dwell about Sion come, and remember the captivity of my sons and daughters, which the Eternal hath brought upon them. **15** For he hath brought a nation upon them from afar, a wicked nation, and of a strange tongue:

16 Who have neither reverenced the ancient, nor pitied children, and have carried away the beloved of the widow, and have left me all alone without children. **17** But as for me, what help can I give you? **18** But he that hath brought the evils upon you, he will deliver you out of the hands of your enemies. **19** Go your way, my children, go your way: for I am left alone. **20** I have put off the robe of peace, and have put upon me the sackcloth of supplication, and I will cry to the most High in my days.

21 Be of good comfort, my children, cry to the Lord, and he will deliver you out of the hand of the princes your enemies. **22** For my hope is in the Eternal that he will save you: and joy is come upon me from the Holy One, because of the mercy which shall come to you from our everlasting Saviour. **23** For I sent you forth with mourning and weeping: but the Lord will bring you back to me with joy and gladness for ever. **24** For as the neighbours of Sion have now seen your captivity from God: so shall they also shortly see your salvation from God, which shall come upon you with great honour, and everlasting glory. **25** My children, suffer patiently the wrath that is come upon you: for thy enemy hath persecuted thee, but thou shalt quickly see his destruction: and thou shalt get up upon his neck.

26 My delicate ones have walked rough ways, for they were taken away as a flock made a prey by the enemies. **27** Be of good comfort, my children, and cry to the Lord: for you shall be remembered by him that hath led you away. **28** For as it was your mind to go astray from God; so when you return again you shall seek him ten times as much. **29** For he that hath brought evils upon you, shall bring you everlasting joy again with your salvation. **30** Be of good heart, O Jerusalem: for he exhorteth thee, that named thee.

31 The wicked that have afflicted thee, shall perish: and they that have rejoiced at thy ruin, shall be punished. **32** The cities which thy children have served, shall be punished: and she that received thy sons. **33** For as she rejoiced at thy ruin, and was glad of thy fall: so shall she be grieved for her own desolation. **34** And the joy of her multitude shall be cut off: and her gladness shall be turned to mourning. **35** For fire shall come upon her from the Eternal, long to endure, and she shall be inhabited by devils for a great time.

36 Look about thee, O Jerusalem, towards the east, and behold the joy that cometh to thee from God. **37** For behold thy children come, whom thou sentest away scattered, they come gathered together from the east even to the west, at the word of the Holy One rejoicing for the honour of God.

Chapter 5

1 Put off, O Jerusalem, the garment of thy mourning, and affliction: and put on the beauty, and honour of that everlasting glory which thou hast from God. **2** God will clothe thee with the double garment of justice, and will set a crown on thy head of everlasting honour. **3** For God will shew his brightness in thee, to every one under heaven. **4** For thy name shall be named to thee by God for ever: the peace of justice, and honour of piety. **5** Arise, O Jerusalem, and stand on high: and look about towards the east, and behold thy children gathered together from the rising to the setting sun, by the word of the Holy One rejoicing in the remembrance of God.

6 For they went out from thee on foot, led by the enemies: but the Lord will bring them to thee exalted with honour as children of the kingdom. **7** For God hath appointed to bring down every high mountain, and the everlasting rocks, and to fill up the valleys to make them even with the ground: that Israel may walk diligently to the honour of God. **8** Moreover the woods, and every sweet-smelling tree have overshadowed Israel by the commandment of God. **9** For God will bring Israel with joy in the light of his majesty, with mercy, and justice, that cometh from him.

Chapter 6

1 For the sins that you have committed before God, you shall be carried away captives into Babylon by Nabuchodonosor the king of Babylon. **2** And when you are come into Babylon, you shall be there many years, and for a long time, even to seven generations: and after that I will bring you away from thence with peace. **3** But now, you shall see in Babylon gods of gold, and of silver, and of stone, and of wood borne upon shoulders, causing fear to the Gentiles. **4** Beware therefore that you imitate not the doings of others, and be afraid, and the fear of them should seize upon you. **5** But when you see the multitude behind, and before, adoring them, say you in your hearts: Thou oughtest to be adored, O Lord.

6 For my angel is with you: And I myself will demand an account of your souls. **7** For their tongue that is polished by the craftsman, and themselves laid over with gold and silver, are false things, and they cannot speak. **8** And as if it were for a maiden that loveth to go gay: so do they take gold and make them up. **9** Their gods have golden crowns upon their heads: whereof the priests secretly convey away from them gold, and silver, and bestow it on themselves. **10** Yea and they give thereof to prostitutes, and they dress out harlots: and again when they receive it of the harlots, they adorn their gods.

11 And these gods cannot defend themselves from the rust, and the moth. **12** But when they have covered them with a purple garment, they wipe their face because of the dust of the house, which is very much among them. **13** This holdeth a sceptre as a man, as a judge of the country, but cannot put to death one that offendeth him. **14** And this hath in his hand a sword, or an axe, but cannot save himself from war, or from robbers, whereby be it known to you, that they are not gods. **15** Therefore fear them not. For as a vessel that a man uses when it is broken becometh useless, even so are their gods:

16 When they are placed in the house, their eyes are full of dust by the feet of them that go in. **17** And as the gates are made sure on every side upon one that hath offended the king, or like a dead man carried to the grave, so do the priests secure the doors with bars and locks, lest they be stripped by thieves. **18** They light candles to them, and in great number, of which they cannot see one: but they are like beams in the house. **19** And they say that the creeping things which are of the earth, gnaw their hearts, while they eat them and their garments, and they feel it not. **20** Their faces are black with the smoke that is made in the house.

21 Owls, and swallows, and other birds fly upon their bodies, and upon their heads, and cats in like manner. **22** Whereby you may know that they are no gods. Therefore fear them not. **23** The gold also which they have, is for shew, but except a man wipe off the rust, they will not shine: for neither when they were molten, did they feel it. **24** Men buy them at a high price, whereas there is no breath in them. **25** And having not the use of feet they are carried upon shoulders, declaring to men how vile they are. Be they confounded also that worship them.

26 Therefore if they fall to the ground, they rise not up again of themselves, nor if a man set them upright, will they stand by themselves, but their gifts shall be set before them, as to the dead. **27** The things that are sacrificed to them, their priests sell and abuse: in like manner also their wives take part of them, but give nothing of it either to the sick, or to the poor. **28** The childbearing and menstruous women touch their sacrifices: knowing therefore by these things that they are not gods, fear them not. **29** For how can they be called gods? because women set offerings before the gods of silver, and of gold, and of wood: **30** And priests sit in their temples, having their garments rent, and their heads and beards shaven, and nothing upon their heads.

31 And they roar and cry before their gods, as men do at the feast when one is dead. **32** The priests take away their garments, and clothe their wives and their children. **33** And whether it be evil that one doth unto them, or good, they are not able to recompense it: neither can they set up a king nor put him down: **34** In like manner they can neither give riches, nor requite evil. If a man make a vow to them, and perform it not, they cannot require it. **35** They cannot deliver a man from death nor save the weak from the mighty.

36 They cannot restore the blind man to his sight: nor deliver a man from distress. **37** They shall not pity the widow, nor do good to the fatherless. **38** Their gods, of wood, and of stone, and of gold, and of silver, are like the stones that are hewn out of the mountains: and they that worship them shall be confounded. **39** How then is it to be supposed, or to be said, that they are gods? **40** Even the Chaldeans themselves dishonour them: who when they hear of one dumb that cannot speak, they present him to Bel, entreating him, that he may speak,

41 As though they could be sensible that have no motion themselves: and they, when they shall perceive this, will leave them: for their gods themselves have no sense. **42** The women also with cords about them, sit in the ways, burning olive stones. **43** And when any one of them, drawn away by some passenger, lieth with him, she upbraideth her neighbour, that she was not thought as worthy as herself, nor her cord broken. **44** But all things that are done about them, are false: how is it then to be thought, or to be said, that they are gods? **45** And they are made by workmen, and by goldsmiths. They shall be nothing else but what the priests will have them to be.

46 For the artificers themselves that make them, are of no long continuance. Can those things then that are made by them be gods? **47** But they have left false things and reproach to them that come after. **48** For when war cometh upon them, or evils, the priests consult with themselves where they may hide themselves with them. **49** How then can they be thought to be gods, that can neither deliver themselves from war, nor save themselves from evils? **50** For seeing they are but of wood, and laid over with gold, and with silver, it shall be known hereafter that they are false things, by all nations and kings: and it shall be manifest that they are no gods, but the work of men's hands, and that there is no work of God in them.

51 Whence, therefore, is it known that they are not gods, but the work of men's hands, and no work of God is in them? **52** They cannot set up a king over the land, nor give rain to men. **53** They determine no causes, nor deliver countries from oppression; because they can do nothing, and are as daws between heaven and earth. **54** For when fire shall fall upon the house of these gods of wood, and of silver, and of gold, their priests indeed will flee away, and be saved: but they themselves shall be burnt in the midst like beams. **55** And they cannot withstand a king and war. How then can it be supposed, or admitted that they are gods?

56 Neither are these gods of wood, and of stone, and laid over with gold, and with silver, able to deliver themselves from thieves or robbers: they that are stronger than them, **57** Shall take from them the gold, and silver, and the raiment wherewith they are clothed, and shall go their way, neither shall they help themselves. **58** Therefore it is better to be a king that sheweth his power: or else a profitable vessel in the house, with which the owner thereof will be well satisfied: or a door in the house, to keep things safe that are therein, than such false gods. **59** The sun, and the moon, and the stars being bright, and sent forth for profitable uses, are obedient. **60** In like manner the lightning, when it breaketh forth, is easy to be seen: and after the same manner the wind bloweth in every country.

61 And the clouds when God commandeth them to go over the whole world, do that which is commanded them. **62** The fire also being sent from above to consume mountains and woods, doth as it is commanded. But these neither in shew, nor in power are like to any one of them. **63** Wherefore it is neither to be thought, nor to be said, that they are gods: since they are neither able to judge causes, nor to do any good to men. **64** Knowing, therefore, that they are not gods, fear them not. **65** For neither can they curse kings, nor bless them.

66 Neither do they shew signs in the heaven to the nations, nor shine as the sun, nor give light as the moon. **67** Beasts are better than they, which can fly under a covert, and help themselves. **68** Therefore there is no manner of appearance that they are gods: so fear them not. **69** For as a scarecrow in a garden of cucumbers keepeth nothing, so are their gods of wood, and of silver, and laid over with gold. **70** They are no better than a white thorn in a garden, upon which every bird sitteth. In like manner also their gods of wood, and laid over with gold, and with silver, are like to a dead body cast forth in the dark.

71 By the purple also and the scarlet which are motheaten upon them, you shall know that they are not gods. And they themselves at last are consumed, and shall be a reproach in the country. **72** Better, therefore, is the just man that hath no idols: for he shall be far from reproach.

THE FIRST BOOK OF MACHABEES

Chapter 1

1 Now it came to pass, after that Alexander the son of Philip the Macedonian, who first reigned in Greece, coming out of the land of Cethim, had overthrown Darius king of the Persians and Medes: **2** He fought many battles, and took the strong holds of all, and slew the kings of the earth: **3** And he went through even to the ends of the earth, and took the spoils of many nations: and the earth was quiet before him. **4** And he gathered a power, and a very strong army: and his heart was exalted and lifted up. **5** And he subdued countries of nations, and princes: and they became tributaries to him.

6 And after these things, he fell down upon his bed, and knew that he should die. **7** And he called his servants the nobles that were brought up with him from his youth: and he divided his kingdom among them, while he was yet alive. **8** And Alexander reigned twelve years, and he died. **9** And his servants made themselves kings every one in his place: **10** And they all put crowns upon themselves after his death, and their sons after them many years, and evils were multiplied in the earth.

11 And there came out of them a wicked root, Antiochus the Illustrious, the son of king Antiochus, who had been a hostage at Rome: and he reigned in the hundred and thirty-seventh year of the kingdom of the Greeks. **12** In those days there went out of Israel wicked men, and they persuaded many, saying: Let us go, and make a covenant with the heathens that are round about us: for since we departed from them, many evils have befallen us. **13** And the word seemed good in their eyes. **14** And some of the people determined to do this, and went to the king: and he gave them license to do after the ordinances of the heathens. **15** And they built a place of exercise in Jerusalem, according to the laws of the nations:

16 And they made themselves prepuces, and departed from the holy covenant, and joined themselves to the heathens, and were sold to do evil. **17** And the kingdom was established before Antiochus, and he had a mind to reign over the land of Egypt, that he might reign over two kingdoms. **18** And he entered into Egypt with a great multitude, with chariots and elephants, and horsemen, and a great number of ships: **19** And he made war against Ptolemee king of Egypt, but Ptolemee was afraid at his presence, and fled, and many were wounded unto death. **20** And he took the strong cities in the land of Egypt: and he took the spoils of the land of Egypt.

21 And after Antiochus had ravaged Egypt in the hundred and forty-third year, he returned and went up against Israel. **22** And he went up to Jerusalem with a great multitude. **23** And he proudly entered into the sanctuary, and took away the golden altar, and the candlestick of light, and all the vessels thereof, and the table of proposition, and the pouring vessels, and the vials, and the little mortars of gold, and the veil, and the crowns, and the golden ornament that was before the temple: and he broke them all in pieces. **24** And he took the silver and gold, and the precious vessels: and he took the hidden treasures which he found: and when he had taken all away he departed into his own country. **25** And he made a great slaughter of men, and spoke very proudly.

26 And there was great mourning in Israel, and in every place where they were. **27** And the princes, and the ancients mourned, and the virgins and the young men were made feeble, and the beauty of the women was changed. **28** Every bridegroom took up lamentation: and the bride that sat in the marriage bed, mourned: **29** And the land was moved for the inhabitants thereof, and all the house of Jacob was covered with confusion. **30** And after two full years the king sent the chief collector of his tributes to the cities of Juda, and he came to Jerusalem with a great multitude.

31 And he spoke to them peaceable words in deceit: and they believed him. **32** And he fell upon the city suddenly, and struck it with a great slaughter, and destroyed much people in Israel. **33** And he took the spoils of the city, and burnt it with fire, and threw down the houses thereof, and the walls thereof round about: **34** And they took the women captive, and the children, and the cattle they possessed. **35** And they built the city of David with a great and strong wall, and with strong towers, and made it a fortress for them:

36 And they placed there a sinful nation, wicked men, and they fortified themselves therein: and they stored up armour, and victuals, and gathered together the spoils of Jerusalem; **37** And laid them up there: and they became a great snare. **38** And this was a place to lie in wait against the sanctuary, and an evil devil in Israel. **39** And they shed innocent blood round about the sanctuary, and defiled the holy place. **40** And the inhabitants of Jerusalem fled away by reason of them, and the city was made the habitation of strangers, and she became a stranger to her own seed, and her children forsook her.

41 Her sanctuary was desolate like a wilderness, her festival days were turned into mourning, her sabbaths into reproach, her honours were brought to nothing. **42** Her dishonour was increased according to her glory, and her excellency was turned into mourning. **43** And king Antiochus wrote to all his kingdom, that all the people should be one: and every one should leave his own law. **44** And all nations consented according to the word of king Antiochus. **45** And many of Israel consented to his service, and they sacrificed to idols, and profaned the sabbath.

46 And the king sent letters by the hands of messengers to Jerusalem, and to all the cities of Juda: that they should follow the law of the nations of the earth, **47** And should forbid holocausts and sacrifices, and atonements to be made in the temple of God. **48** And should prohibit the sabbath, and the festival days, to be celebrated. **49** And he commanded the holy places to be profaned, and the holy people of Israel. **50** And he commanded altars to be built, and temples, and idols, and swine's flesh to be immolated, and unclean beasts.

51 And that they should leave their children uncircumcised, and let their souls be defiled with all uncleannesses, and abominations, to the end that they should forget the law, and should change all the justifications of God. **52** And that whosoever would not do according to the word of king Antiochus should be put to death. **53** According to all these words he wrote to his whole kingdom, and he appointed rulers over the people that should force them to do these things. **54** And they commanded the cities of Juda to sacrifice. **55** Then many of the people were gathered to them that had forsaken the law of the Lord: and they committed evils in the land:

56 And they drove away the people of Israel into lurking holes, and into the secret places of fugitives. **57** On the fifteenth day of the month Casleu, in the hundred and forty-fifth year, king Antiochus set up the abominable idol of desolation upon the altar of God, and they built altars throughout all the cities of Juda round about: **58** And they burnt incense, and sacrificed at the doors of the houses, and in the streets. **59** And they cut in pieces, and burnt with fire the books of the law of God: **60** And every one with whom the books of the testament of the Lord were found, and whosoever observed the law of the Lord, they put to death, according to the edict of the king.

61 Thus by their power did they deal with the people of Israel, that were found in the cities month after month. **62** And on the five and twentieth day of the month they sacrificed upon the altar of the idol that was over against the altar of God. **63** Now the women that circumcised their children, were slain according to the commandment of king Antiochus. **64** And they hanged the children about their necks in all their houses: and those that had circumcised them, they put to death. **65** And many of the people of Israel determined with themselves, that they would not eat unclean things: and they chose rather to die than to be defiled with unclean meats.

66 And they would not break the holy law of God, and they were put to death: **67** And there was very great wrath upon the people.

Chapter 2

1 In those days arose Mathathias the son of John, the son of Simeon, a priest of the sons of Joarib, from Jerusalem, and he abode in the mountain of Modin. **2** And he had five sons: John who was surnamed Gaddis: **3** And Simon, who was surnamed Thasi: **4** And Judas, who was called Machabeus: **5** And Eleazar, who was surnamed Abaron: and Jonathan, who was surnamed Apphus.

6 These saw the evils that were done in the people of Juda, and in Jerusalem. **7** And Mathathias said: Woe is me, wherefore was I born to see the ruin of my people, and the ruin of the holy city, and to dwell there, when it is given into the hands of the enemies? **8** The holy places are come into the hands of strangers: her temple is become as a man without honour. **9** The vessels of her glory are carried away captive: her old men are murdered in the streets, and her young men are fallen by the sword of the enemies. **10** What nation hath not inherited her kingdom, and gotten of her spoils?

11 All her ornaments are taken away. She that was free is made a slave. **12** And behold our sanctuary, and our beauty, and our glory is laid waste, and the Gentiles have defiled them. **13** To what end then should we live any longer? **14** And Mathathias and his sons rent their garments, and they covered themselves with haircloth, and made great lamentation. **15** And they that were sent from king Antiochus came thither, to compel them that were fled into the city of Modin, to sacrifice, and to burn incense, and to depart from the law of God.

16 And many of the people of Israel consented, and came to them: but Mathathias and his sons stood firm. **17** And they that were sent from Antiochus, answering, said to Mathathias: Thou art a ruler, and an honourable, and great man in this city, and adorned with sons, and brethren. **18** Therefore come thou first, and obey the king's commandment, as all nations have done, and the men of Juda, and they that remain in Jerusalem: and thou, and thy sons, shall be in the number of the king's friends, and enriched with gold, and silver, and many presents. **19** Then Mathathias answered, and said with a loud voice: Although all nations obey king Antiochus, so as to depart every man from the service of the law of his fathers, and consent to his commandments: **20** I and my sons, and my brethren will obey the law of our fathers.

21 God be merciful unto us: it is not profitable for us to forsake the law, and the justices of God: **22** We will not hearken to the words of king Antiochus, neither will we sacrifice, and transgress the commandments of our law, to go another way. **23** Now as he left off speaking these words, there came a certain Jew in the sight of all to sacrifice to the idols upon the altar in the city of Modin, according to the king's commandment. **24** And Mathathias saw and was grieved, and his reins trembled, and his wrath was kindled according to the judgment of the law, and running upon him he slew him upon the altar: **25** Moreover the man whom king Antiochus had sent, who compelled them to sacrifice, he slew at the same time, and pulled down the altar.

26 And shewed zeal for the law, as Phinees did by Zamri the son of Salomi. **27** And Mathathias cried out in the city with a loud voice, saying: Every one that hath zeal for the law, and maintaineth the testament, let him follow me. **28** So he, and his sons fled into the mountains, and left all that they had in the city. **29** Then many that sought after judgment, and justice, went down into the desert: **30** And they abode there, they and their children, and their wives, and their cattle: because afflictions increased upon them.

31 And it was told to the king's men, and to the army that was in Jerusalem in the city of David, that certain men who had broken the king's commandment, were gone away into the secret places in the wilderness, and that many were gone after them. **32** And forthwith they went out towards them, and made war against them on the sabbath day, **33** And they said to them: Do you still resist? come forth, and do according to the edict of king Antiochus, and you shall live. **34** And they said: We will not come forth, neither will we obey the king's edict, to profane the sabbath day. **35** And they made haste to give them battle.

36 But they answered them not, neither did they cast a stone at them, nor stopped up the secret places, **37** Saying: Let us all die in our innocency: and heaven and earth shall be witnesses for us, that you put us to death wrongfully. **38** So they gave them battle on the sabbath: and they were slain with their wives, and their children, and their cattle, to the number of a thousand persons. **39** And Mathathias and his friends heard of it, and they mourned for them exceedingly. **40** And every man said to his neighbour: If we shall all do as our brethren have done, and not fight against the heathens for our lives, and our justifications: they will now quickly root us out of the earth.

41 And they determined in that day, saying: Whosoever shall come up against us to fight on the sabbath day, we will fight against him: and we will not all die, as our brethren that were slain in the secret places. **42** Then was assembled to them the congregation of the Assideans, the stoutest of Israel, every one that had a good will for the law. **43** And all they that fled from the evils, joined themselves to them, and were a support to them. **44** And they gathered an army, and slew the sinners in their wrath, and the wicked men in their indignation: and the rest fled to the nations for safety. **45** And Mathathias and his friends went round about, and they threw down the altars:

46 And they circumcised all the children whom they found in the confines of Israel that were uncircumcised: and they did valiantly. **47** And they pursued after the children of pride, and the work prospered in their hands: **48** And they recovered the law out of the hands of the nations, and out of the hands of the kings: and they yielded not the horn to the sinner. **49** Now the days drew near that Mathathias should die, and he said to his sons: Now hath pride and chastisement gotten strength, and the time of destruction, and the wrath of indignation: **50** Now therefore, O my sons, be ye zealous for the law, and give your lives for the covenant of your fathers.

51 And call to remembrance the works of the fathers, which they have done in their generations: and you shall receive great glory, and an everlasting name. **52** Was not Abraham found faithful in temptation, and it was reputed to him unto justice? **53** Joseph in the time of his distress kept the commandment, and he was made lord of Egypt. **54** Phinees our father, by being fervent in the zeal of God, received the covenant of an everlasting priesthood. **55** Jesus [Josue], whilst he fulfilled the word, was made ruler in Israel.

56 Caleb, for bearing witness before the congregation, received an inheritance. **57** David by his mercy obtained the throne of an everlasting kingdom. **58** Elias, while he was full of zeal for the law, was taken up into heaven. **59** Ananias and Azarias and Misael by believing, were delivered out of the flame. **60** Daniel in his innocency was delivered out of the mouth of the lions.

61 And thus consider through all generations: that none that trust in him fail in strength. **62** And fear not the words of a sinful man, for his glory is dung, and worms: **63** Today he is lifted up, and tomorrow he shall not be found, because he is returned into his earth; and his thought is come to nothing. **64** You therefore, my sons, take courage, and behave manfully in the law: for by it you shall be glorious. **65** And behold, I know that your brother Simon is a man of counsel: give ear to him always, and he shall be a father to you.

66 And Judas Machabeus who is valiant and strong from his youth up, let him be the leader of your army, and he shall manage the war of the people. **67** And you shall take to you all that observe the law: and revenge ye the wrong of your people. **68** Render to the Gentiles their reward, and take heed to the precepts of the law. **69** And he blessed them, and was joined to his fathers. **70** And he died in the hundred and forty-sixth year: and he was buried by his sons in the sepulchres of his fathers in Modin, and all Israel mourned for him with great mourning.

Chapter 3

1 Then his son Judas, called Machabeus, rose up in his stead. **2** And all his brethren helped him, and all they that had joined themselves to his father, and they fought with cheerfulness the battle of Israel. **3** And he got his people great honour, and put on a breastplate as a giant, and girt his warlike armour about him in battles, and protected the camp with his sword. **4** In his acts he was like a lion, and like a lion's whelp roaring for his prey. **5** And he pursued the wicked and sought them out, and them that troubled his people he burnt with fire:

6 And his enemies were driven away for fear of him, and all the workers of iniquity were troubled: and salvation prospered in his hand. **7** And he grieved many kings, and made Jacob glad with his works, and his memory is blessed for ever. **8** And he went through the cities of Juda, and destroyed the wicked out of them, and turned away wrath from Israel. **9** And he was renowned even to the utmost part of the earth, and he gathered them that were perishing. **10** And Apollonius gathered together the Gentiles, and a numerous and great army from Samaria, to make war against Israel.

11 And Judas understood it, and went forth to meet him: and he overthrew him, and killed him: and many fell down slain, the rest fled away. **12** And he took their spoils, and Judas took the sword of Apollonius, and fought with it all his lifetime. **13** And Seron captain of the army of Syria heard that Judas had assembled a company of the faithful, and a congregation with him, **14** And he said: I will get me a name, and will be glorified in the kingdom, and will overthrow Judas, and those that are with him, that have despised the edict of the king. **15** And he made himself ready: and the host of the wicked went up with him, strong succours, to be revenged of the children of Israel.

16 And they approached even as far as Bethoron: and Judas went forth to meet him, with a small company. **17** But when they saw the army coming to meet them, they said to Judas: How shall we, being few, be able to fight against so great a multitude and so strong, and we are ready to faint with fasting today? **18** And Judas said: It is an easy matter for many to be shut up in the hands of a few: and there is no difference in the sight of the God of heaven to deliver with a great multitude, or with a small company: **19** For the success of war is not in the multitude of the army, but strength cometh from heaven. **20** They come against us with an insolent multitude, and with pride, to destroy us, and our wives, and our children, and to take our spoils.

139

21 But we will fight for our lives and our laws: **22** And the Lord himself will overthrow them before our face: but as for you, fear them not. **23** And as soon as he had made an end of speaking, he rushed suddenly upon them: and Seron and his host were overthrown before him: **24** And he pursued him by the descent of Bethoron even to the plain, and there fell of them eight hundred men, and the rest fled into the land of the Philistines. **25** And the fear of Judas and of his brethren, and the dread of them fell upon all the nations round about them.

26 And his fame came to the king, and all nations told of the battles of Judas. **27** Now when king Antiochus heard these words, he was angry in his mind: and he sent and gathered the forces of all his kingdom, an exceeding strong army. **28** And he opened his treasury, and gave out pay to the army for a year: and he commanded them, that they should be ready for all things. **29** And he perceived that the money of his treasures failed, and that the tributes of the country were small because of the dissension, and the evil that he had brought upon the land, that he might take away the laws of old times: **30** And he feared that he should not have as formerly enough, for charges and gifts, which he had given before with a liberal hand: for he had abounded more than the kings that had been before him.

31 And he was greatly perplexed in mind, and purposed to go into Persia, and to take tributes of the countries, and to gather much money. **32** And he left Lysias, a nobleman of the blood royal, to oversee the affairs of the kingdom, from the river Euphrates even to the river of Egypt: **33** And to bring up his son Antiochus, till he came again. **34** And he delivered to him half the army, and the elephants: and he gave him charge concerning all that he would have done, and concerning the inhabitants of Judea, and Jerusalem: **35** And that he should send an army against them, to destroy and root out the strength of Israel, and the remnant of Jerusalem, and to take away the memory of them from that place:

36 And that he should settle strangers to dwell in all their coasts, and divide their land by lot. **37** So the king took the half of the army that remained, and went forth from Antioch the chief city of his kingdom, in the hundred and forty-seventh year: and he passed over the river Euphrates, and went through the higher countries. **38** Then Lysias chose Ptolemee the son of Dorymenus, and Nicanor, and Gorgias, mighty men of the king's friends. **39** And he sent with them forty thousand men, and seven thousand horsemen: to go into the land of Juda, and to destroy it according to the king's orders. **40** So they went forth with all their power, and came, and pitched near Emmaus in the plain country.

41 And the merchants of the countries heard the fame of them:

and they took silver and gold in abundance, and servants: and they came into the camp, to buy the children of Israel for slaves: and there were joined to them the forces of Syria, and of the land of the strangers. **42** And Judas and his brethren saw that evils were multiplied, and that the armies approached to their borders: and they knew the orders the king had given to destroy the people and utterly abolish them. **43** And they said every man to his neighbour: Let us raise up the low condition of our people, and let us fight for our people, and our sanctuary. **44** And the assembly was gathered that they might be ready for battle: and that they might pray, and ask mercy and compassion. **45** Now Jerusalem was not inhabited, but was like a desert: there was none of her children that went in or out: and the sanctuary was trodden down: and the children of strangers were in the castle, there was the habitation of the Gentiles: and joy was taken away from Jacob, and the pipe and harp ceased there.

46 And they assembled together, and came to Maspha over against Jerusalem: for in Maspha was a place of prayer heretofore in Israel. **47** And they fasted that day, and put on haircloth, and put ashes upon their heads: and they rent their garments: **48** And they laid open the books of the law, in which the Gentiles searched for the likeness of their idols: **49** And they brought the priestly ornaments, and the firstfruits and tithes, and stirred up the Nazarites that had fulfilled their days: **50** And they cried with a loud voice toward heaven, saying: What shall we do with these, and whither shall we carry them?

51 For thy holies are trodden down, and are profaned, and thy priests are in mourning, and are brought low. **52** And behold the nations are come together against us to destroy us: thou knowest what they intend against us. **53** How shall we be able to stand before their face, unless thou, O God, help us? **54** Then they sounded with trumpets, and cried out with a loud voice. **55** And after this Judas appointed captains over the people, over thousands, and over hundreds, and over fifties, and over tens.

56 And he said to them that were building houses, or had betrothed wives, or were planting vineyards, or were fearful, that they should return every man to his house, according to the law. **57** So they removed the camp, and pitched on the south side of Emmaus. **58** And Judas said: Gird yourselves, and be valiant men, and be ready against the morning, that you may fight with these nations that are assembled against us to destroy us and our sanctuary. **59** For it is better for us to die in battle, than to see the evils of our nation, and of the holies: **60** Nevertheless as it shall be the will of God in heaven so be it done.

Chapter 4

1 Then Gorgias took five thousand men, and a thousand of the best horsemen: and they removed out of the camp by night. **2** That they might come upon the camp of the Jews, and strike them suddenly: and the men that were of the castle were their guides. **3** And Judas heard of it, and rose up, he and the valiant men, to attack the king's forces that were in Emmaus. **4** For as yet the army was dispersed from the camp. **5** And Gorgias came by night into the camp of Judas, and found no man, and he sought them in the mountains: for he said: These men flee from us.

6 And when it was day, Judas shewed himself in the plain with three thousand men only, who neither had armour nor swords. **7** And they saw the camp of the Gentiles that it was strong, and the men in breastplates, and the horsemen round about them, and these were trained up to war. **8** And Judas said to the men that were with him: Fear ye not their multitude, neither be ye afraid of their assault. **9** Remember in what manner our fathers were saved in the Red Sea, when Pharao pursued them with a great army. **10** And now let us cry to heaven: and the Lord will have mercy on us, and will remember the covenant of our fathers, and will destroy this army before our face this day:

11 And all nations shall know that there is one that redeemeth and delivereth Israel. **12** And the strangers lifted up their eyes, and saw them coming against them. **13** And they went out of the camp to battle, and they that were with Judas sounded the trumpet. **14** And they joined battle: and the Gentiles were routed, and fled into the plain. **15** But all the hindmost of them fell by the sword, and they pursued them as far as Gezeron, and even to the plains of Idumea, and of Azotus, and of Jamnia: and there fell of them to the number of three thousand men.

16 And Judas returned again with his army that followed him, **17** And he said to the people: Be not greedy of the spoils: for there is war before us: **18** And Gorgias and his army are near us in the mountain: but stand ye now against our enemies, and overthrow them, and you shall take the spoils afterwards with safety. **19** And as Judas was speaking these words, behold part of them appeared looking forth from the mountain. **20** And Gorgias saw that his men were put to flight, and that they had set fire to the camp: for the smoke that was seen declared what was done.

21 And when they had seen this, they were seized with great fear, seeing at the same time Judas and his army in the plain ready to fight. **22** So they all fled away into the land of the strangers. **23** And Judas returned to take the spoils of the camp, and they got much gold, and silver, and blue silk, and purple of the sea, and great riches. **24** And returning home they sung a hymn, and blessed God in heaven, because he is good, because his mercy endureth for ever. **25** So Israel had a great deliverance that day.

26 And such of the strangers as escaped, went and told Lysias all that had happened. **27** And when he heard these things, he was amazed and discouraged: because things had not succeeded in Israel according to his mind, and as the king had commanded. **28** So the year following Lysias gathered together threescore thousand chosen men, and five thousand horsemen, that he might subdue them. **29** And they came into Judea, and pitched their tents in Bethoron, and Judas met them with ten thousand men. **30** And they saw that the army was strong, and he prayed, and said: Blessed art thou, O Saviour of Israel, who didst break the violence of the mighty by the hand of thy servant David, and didst deliver up the camp of the strangers into the hands of Jonathan the son of Saul and of his armourbearer.

31 Shut up this army in the hands of thy people Israel, and let them be confounded in their host and their horsemen. **32** Strike them with fear, and cause the boldness of their strength to languish, and let them quake at their own destruction. **33** Cast them down with the sword of them that love thee: and let all that know thy name, praise thee with hymns. **34** And they joined battle: and there fell of the army of Lysias five thousand men. **35** And when Lysias saw that his men were put to flight, and how bold the Jews were, and that they were ready either to live, or to die manfully, he went to Antioch, and chose soldiers, that they might come again into Judea with greater numbers.

36 Then Judas, and his brethren said: Behold our enemies are discomfited: let us go up now to cleanse the holy places and to repair them. **37** And all the army assembled together, and they went up into mount Sion. **38** And they saw the sanctuary desolate, and the altar profaned, and the gates burnt, and shrubs growing up in the courts as in a forest, or on the mountains, and the chambers joining to the temple thrown down. **39** And they rent their garments, and made great lamentation, and put ashes on their heads: **40** And they fell face down to the ground on their faces, and they sounded with the trumpets of alarm, and they cried towards heaven.

41 Then Judas appointed men to fight against them that were in the castle, till they had cleansed the holy places. **42** And he chose priests without blemish, whose will was set upon the law of God: **43** And they cleansed the holy places, and took away the stones that had been defiled into an unclean place. **44** And he considered about the altar of holocausts that had been profaned, what he should do with it. **45** And a good counsel came into their minds, to pull it down: lest it should be a reproach to them, because the Gentiles had defiled it; so they threw it down.

46 And they laid up the stones in the mountain of the temple in a convenient place, till there should come a prophet, and give answer concerning them. **47** Then they took whole stones according to the law, and built a new altar according to the former: **48** And they built up the holy places, and the things that were within the temple: and they sanctified the temple, and the courts. **49** And they made new holy vessels, and brought in the candlestick, and the altar of incense, and the table into the temple. **50** And they put incense upon the altar, and lighted up the lamps that were upon the candlestick, and they gave light in the temple.

51 And they set the loaves upon the table, and hung up the veils, and finished all the works that they had begun to make. **52** And they arose before the morning on the five and twentieth day of the ninth month (which is the month of Casleu) in the hundred and forty-eighth year. **53** And they offered sacrifice according to the law upon the new altar of holocausts which they had made. **54** According to the time, and according to the day wherein the heathens had defiled it, in the same was it dedicated anew with canticles, and harps, and lutes, and cymbals. **55** And all the people fell upon their faces, and adored, and blessed up to heaven, him that had prospered them.

56 And they kept the dedication of the altar eight days, and they offered holocausts with joy, and sacrifices of salvation, and of praise. **57** And they adorned the front of the temple with crowns of gold, and escutcheons, and they renewed the gates, and the chambers, and hanged doors upon them. **58** And there was exceeding great joy among the people, and the reproach of the Gentiles was turned away. **59** And Judas, and his brethren, and all the church of Israel decreed, that the day of the dedication of the altar should be kept in its season from year to year for eight days, from the five and twentieth day of the month of Casleu, with joy and gladness. **60** They built up also at that time mount Sion, with high walls, and strong towers round about, lest the Gentiles should at any time come, and tread it down as they did before.

61 And he placed a garrison there to keep it, and he fortified it to secure Bethsura, that the people might have a defence against Idumea.

Chapter 5

1 Now it came to pass, when the nations round about heard that the altar and the sanctuary were built up as before, that they were exceeding angry. **2** And they thought to destroy the generation of Jacob that were among them, and they began to kill some of the people, and to persecute them. **3** Then Judas fought against the children of Esau in Idumea, and them that were in Acrabathane: because they beset the Israelites around about, and he made a great slaughter of them. **4** And he remembered the malice of the children of Bean: who were a snare and a stumblingblock to the people, by lying in wait for them in the way. **5** And they were shut up by him in towers, and he set upon them, and devoted them to utter destruction, and burnt their towers with fire, and all that were in them.

6 Then he passed over to the children of Ammon, where he found a mighty power, and much people, and Timotheus was their captain: **7** And he fought many battles with them, and they were discomfited in their sight, and he smote them: **8** And he took the city of Gazer and her towns, and returned into Judea. **9** And the Gentiles that were in Galaad, assembled themselves together against the Israelites that were in their quarters to destroy them: and they fled into the fortress of Datheman. **10** And they sent letters to Judas and his brethren, saying, The heathens that are round about are gathered together against us, to destroy us:

11 And they are preparing to come, and to take the fortress into which we are fled: and Timotheus is the captain of their host. **12** Now therefore come, and deliver us out of their hands, for many of us are slain. **13** And all our brethren that were in the places of Tubin, are killed: and they have carried away their wives, and their children, captives, and taken their spoils, and they have slain there almost a thousand men. **14** And while they were yet reading these letters, behold there came other messengers out of Galilee with their garments rent, who related according to these words: **15** Saying, that they of Ptolemais, and of Tyre, and of Sidon, were assembled against them, and all Galilee is filled with strangers, in order to consume us.

16 Now when Judas and all the people heard these words, a great assembly met together to consider what they should do for their brethren that were in trouble, and were assaulted by them. **17** And Judas said to Simon his brother: Choose thee men, and go, and deliver thy brethren in Galilee: and I, and my brother Jonathan will go into the country of Galaad. **18** And he left Joseph the son of Zacharias, and Azarias captains of the people with the remnant of the army in Judea to keep it: **19** And he commanded them, saying: Take ye the charge of this people: but make no war against the heathens, till we return. **20** Now three thousand men were allotted to Simon, to go into Galilee: and eight thousand to Judas to go into the land of Galaad.

21 And Simon went into Galilee, and fought many battles with the heathens: and the heathens were discomfited before his face, and he pursued them even to the gate of Ptolemais. **22** And there fell of the heathens almost three thousand men, and he took the spoils of them, **23** And he took with him those that were in Galilee and in Arbatis with their wives, and children, and all that they had, and he brought them into Judea with great joy. **24** And Judas Machabeus, and Jonathan his brother passed over the Jordan, and went three days' journey through the desert. **25** And the Nabutheans met them, and received them in a peaceable manner, and told them all that happened to their brethren in the land of Galaad,

26 And that many of them were shut up in Barasa, and in Bosor, and in Alima, and in Casphor, and in Mageth, and in Carnaim: all these strong and great cities. **27** Yea, and that they were kept shut up in the rest of the cities of Galaad, and that they had appointed to bring their army on the morrow near to these cities, and to take them and to destroy them all in one day. **28** Then Judas and his army suddenly turned their march into the desert, to Bosor, and took the city: and he slew every male by the edge of the sword, and took all their spoils, and burnt it with fire. **29** And they removed from thence by night, and went till they came to the fortress. **30** And it came to pass that early in the morning, when they lifted up their eyes, behold there were people without number, carrying ladders and engines to take the fortress, and assault them.

31 And Judas saw that the fight was begun, and the cry of the battle went up to heaven like a trumpet, and a great cry out of the city: **32** And he said to his host: Fight ye today for your brethren. **33** And he came with three companies behind them, and they sounded their trumpets, and cried out in prayer. **34** And the host of Timotheus understood that it was Machabeus, and they fled away before his face: and they made a great slaughter of them: and there fell of them in that day almost eight thousand men. **35** And Judas turned aside to Maspha, and assaulted, and took it, and he slew every male thereof, and took the spoils thereof, and burnt it with fire.

36 From thence he marched, and took Casbon, and Mageth, and Bosor, and the rest of the cities of Galaad. **37** But after this Timotheus gathered another army, and camped over against Raphon beyond the torrent. **38** And Judas sent men to view the army: and they brought him word, saying: All the nations, that are round about us, are assembled unto him an army exceeding great: **39** And they have hired the Arabians to help them, and they have pitched their tents beyond the torrent, ready to come to fight against thee. And Judas went to meet them. **40** And Timotheus said to the captains of his army: When Judas and his army come near the torrent of water, if he pass over unto us first, we shall not be able to withstand him: for he will certainly prevail over us.

41 But if he be afraid to pass over, and camp on the other side of the river, we will pass over to them and shall prevail against him. **42** Now when Judas came near the torrent of water, he set the scribes of the people by the torrent, and commanded them, saying: Suffer no man to stay behind: but let all come to the battle. **43** And he passed over to them first, and all the people after him, and all the heathens were discomfited before them, and they threw away their weapons, and fled to the temple that was in Carnaim. **44** And he took that city, and the temple he burnt with fire, with all things that were therein: and Carnaim was subdued, and could not stand against the face of Judas. **45** And Judas gathered together all the Israelites that were in the land of Galaad, from the least even to the greatest, and their wives, and children, and an army exceeding great, to come into the land of Juda.

46 And they came as far as Ephron: now this was a great city situate in the way, strongly fortified, and there was no means to turn from it on the right hand or on the left, but the way was through the midst of it. **47** And they that were in the city, shut themselves in, and stopped up the gates with stones: and Judas sent to them with peaceable words, **48** Saying: Let us pass through your land, to go into our country: and no man shall hurt you: we will only pass through on foot. But they would not open to them. **49** Then Judas commanded proclamation to be made in the camp, that they should make an assault every man in the place where he was. **50** And the men of the army drew near, and he assaulted that city all the day, and all the night, and the city was delivered into his hands:

51 And they slew every male with the edge of the sword, and he razed the city, and took the spoils thereof, and passed through all the city over them that were slain. **52** Then they passed over the Jordan to the great plain that is over against Bethsan. **53** And Judas gathered together the hindmost, and he exhorted the people all the way through, till they came into the land of Juda. **54** And they went up to mount Sion with joy and gladness, and offered holocausts, because not one of them was slain, till they had returned in peace. **55** Now in the days that Judas and Jonathan were in the land of Galaad, and Simon his brother in Galilee before Ptolemais,

56 Joseph the son of Zacharias, and Azarias captain of the soldiers, heard of the good success, and the battles that were fought. **57** And he said: Let us also get us a name, and let us go fight against the Gentiles that are round about us. **58** And he gave charge to them that were in his army, and they went towards Jamnia. **59** And Gorgias and his men went out of the city, to give them battle. **60** And Joseph and Azarias were put to flight, and were pursued unto the borders of Judea: and there fell, on that day, of the people of Israel about two thousand men, and there was a great overthrow of the people:

61 Because they did not hearken to Judas, and his brethren, thinking that they should do manfully. **62** But they were not of the seed of those men by whom salvation was brought to Israel. **63** And the men of Juda were magnified exceedingly in the sight of all Israel, and of all the nations where their name was heard. **64** And people assembled to them with joyful acclamations. **65** Then Judas and his brethren went forth and attacked the children of Esau, in the land toward the south, and he took Chebron, and her towns: and he burnt the walls thereof and the towers all round it.

66 And he removed his camp to go into the land of the aliens, and he went through Samaria. **67** In that day some priests fell in battle, while desiring to do manfully they went out unadvisedly to fight. **68** And Judas turned to Azotus into the land of the strangers, and he threw down their altars, and he burnt the statues of their gods with fire: and he took the spoils of the cities, and returned into the land of Juda.

Chapter 6

1 Now king Antiochus was going through the higher countries, and he heard that the city of Elymais in Persia was greatly renowned, and abounding in silver and gold. **2** And that there was in it a temple, exceeding rich: and coverings of gold, and breastplates, and shields which king Alexander, son of Philip the Macedonian that reigned first in Greece, had left there. **3** Lo, he came, and sought to take the city and to pillage it: But he was not able, because the design was known to them that were in the city. **4** And they rose up against him in battle, and he fled away from thence, and departed with great sadness, and returned towards Babylonia. **5** And whilst he was in Persia, there came one that told him, how the armies that were in the land of Juda were put to flight:

6 And that Lysias went with a very great power, and was put to flight before the face of the Jews, and that they were grown strong by the armour, and power, and store of spoils, which they had gotten out of the camps which they had destroyed: **7** And that they had thrown down the abomination which he had set up upon the altar in Jerusalem, and that they had compassed about the sanctuary with high walls as before, and Bethsura also his city. **8** And it came to pass when the king heard these words, that he was struck with fear, and exceedingly moved: and he laid himself down upon his bed, and fell sick for grief, because it had not fallen out to him as he imagined. **9** And he remained there many days: for great grief came more and more and more upon him, and he made account that he should die. **10** And he called for all his friends, and said to them: Sleep is gone from my eyes, and I am fallen away, and my heart is cast down for anxiety.

11 And I said in my heart: Into how much tribulation am I come, and into what floods of sorrow, wherein now I am: I that was pleasant and beloved in my power! **12** But now I remember the evils that I have done in Jerusalem, from whence also I took away all the spoils of gold, and of silver that were in it, and I sent to destroy the inhabitants of Juda without cause. **13** I know therefore that for this cause these evils have found me: and behold I perish with great grief in a strange land. **14** Then he called Philip, one of his friends, and he made him regent over all his kingdom. **15** And he gave him the crown, and his robe, and his ring, that he should go to Antiochus his son, and should bring him up for the kingdom.

16 So king Antiochus died there in the year one hundred and forty-nine. **17** And Lysias understood that the king was dead, and he set up Antiochus his son to reign, whom he brought up young: and he called his name Eupator. **18** Now they that were in the castle, had shut up the Israelites round about the holy places: and they were continually seeking their hurt, and to strengthen the Gentiles. **19** And Judas purposed to destroy them: and he called together all the people, to besiege them. **20** And they came together, and besieged them in the year one hundred and fifty, and they made battering slings and engines.

21 And some of the besieged got out: and some wicked men of Israel joined themselves unto them. **22** And they went to the king, and said: How long dost thou delay to execute the judgment, and to revenge our brethren? **23** We determined to serve thy father and to do according to his orders, and obey his edicts: **24** And for this they of our nation are alienated from us, and have slain as many of us as they could find, and have spoiled our inheritances. **25** Neither have they put forth their hand against us only, but also against all our borders.

26 And behold they have approached this day to the castle of Jerusalem to take it, and they have fortified the stronghold of Bethsura: **27** And unless thou speedily prevent them, they will do greater things than these, and thou shalt not be able to subdue them. **28** Now when the king heard this, he was angry: and he called together all his friends, and the captains of his army, and them that were over the horsemen. **29** There came also to him from other realms, and from the islands of the sea hired troops. **30** And the number of his army was an hundred thousand footmen, and twenty thousand horsemen, and thirty-two elephants, trained to battle.

31 And they went through Idumea, and approached to Bethsura, and fought many days, and they made engines: but they sallied forth and burnt them with fire, and fought manfully. **32** And Judas departed from the castle, and removed the camp to Bethzacharam, over against the king's camp. **33** And the king rose before it was light, and made his troops march on fiercely towards the way of Bethzacharam: and the armies made themselves ready for the battle, and they sounded the trumpets: **34** And they shewed the elephants the blood of grapes, and mulberries to provoke them to fight. **35** And they distributed the beasts by the legions: and there stood by every elephant a thousand men in coats of mail, and with helmets of brass on their heads: and five hundred horsemen set in order were chosen for every beast.

36 These before the time wheresoever the beast was, they were there: and withersoever it went, they went, and they departed not from it. **37** And upon the beast, there were strong wooden towers, which covered every one of them: and engines upon them: and upon every one thirty-two valiant men, who fought from above; and an Indian to rule the beast. **38** And the rest of the horsemen he placed on this side and on that side at the two wings, with trumpets to stir up the army, and to hasten them forward that stood thick together in the legions thereof. **39** Now when the sun shone upon the shields of gold, and of brass, the mountains glittered therewith, and they shone like lamps of fire. **40** And part of the king's army was distinguished by the high mountains, and the other part by the low places: and they marched on warily and orderly.

41 And all the inhabitants of the land were moved at the noise of their multitude, and the marching of the company, and the rattling of the armour, for the army was exceeding great and strong. **42** And Judas and his army drew near for battle: and there fell of the king's army six hundred men. **43** And Eleazar the son of Saura saw one of the beasts harnessed with the king's harness: and it was higher than the other beasts: and it seemed to him that the king was on it: **44** And he exposed himself to deliver his people and to get himself an everlasting name. **45** And he ran up to it boldly in the midst of the legion, killing on the right hand, and on the left, and they fell by him on this side and that side.

46 And he went between the feet of the elephant, and put himself under it: and slew it, and it fell to the ground upon him, and he died there. **47** Then they seeing the strength of the king and the fierceness of his army, turned away from them. **48** But the king's army went up against them to Jerusalem: and the king's army pitched their tents against Judea and mount Sion. **49** And he made peace with them that were in Bethsura: and they came forth out of the city, because they had no victuals, being shut up there, for it was the year of rest to the land. **50** And the king took Bethsura: and he placed there a garrison to keep it.

51 And he turned his army against the sanctuary for many days: and he set up there battering slings, and engines and instruments to cast fire, and engines to cast stones and javelins, and pieces to shoot arrows, and slings. **52** And they also made engines against their engines, and they fought for many days. **53** But there were no victuals in the city, because it was the seventh year: and such as had stayed in Judea of them that came from among the nations, had eaten the residue of all that which had been stored up. **54** And there remained in the holy places but a few, for the famine had prevailed over them: and they were dispersed every man to his own place. **55** Now Lysias heard that Philip, whom king Antiochus while he lived had appointed to bring up his son Antiochus, and to reign, to be king,

56 Was returned from Persia, and Media, with the army that went with him, and that he sought to take upon him the affairs of the kingdom: **57** Wherefore he made haste to go, and say to the king and to the captains of the army: We decay daily, and our provision of victuals is small, and the place that we lay siege to is strong, and it lieth upon us to take order for the affairs of the kingdom. **58** Now therefore let us come to an agreement with these men, and make peace with them and with all their nation. **59** And let us covenant with them, that they may live according to their own laws as before. For because of our despising their laws, they have been provoked, and have done all these things. **60** And the proposal was acceptable in the sight of the king, and of the princes: and he sent to them to make peace: and they accepted of it.

61 And the king and the princes swore to them: and they came out of the stronghold. **62** Then the king entered into mount Sion, and saw the strength of the place: and he quickly broke the oath that he had taken, and gave commandment to throw down the wall round about. **63** And he departed in haste, and returned to Antioch, where he found Philip master of the city: and he fought against him, and took the city.

Chapter 7

1 In the hundred and fifty-first year Demetrius the son of Seleucus departed from the city of Rome, and came up with a few men into a city of the sea coast, and reigned there. **2** And it came to pass, as he entered into the house of the kingdom of his fathers, that the army seized upon Antiochus, and Lysias, to bring them unto him. **3** And when he knew it, he said: Let me not see their face. **4** So the army slew them. And Demetrius sat upon the throne of his kingdom: **5** And there came to him the wicked and ungodly men of Israel: And Alcimus was at the head of them, who desired to be made high priest.

6 And they accused the people to the king, saying: Judas and his brethren have destroyed all thy friends, and he hath driven us out of our land. **7** Now therefore send some man whom thou trustest, and let him go, and see all the havock he hath made amongst us, and in the king's lands: and let him punish all his friends and their helpers. **8** Then the king chose Bacchides, one of his friends that ruled beyond the great river in the kingdom, and was faithful to the king: and he sent him, **9** To see the havock that Judas had made: and the wicked Alcimus he made high priest, and commanded him to take revenge upon the children of Israel. **10** And they arose, and came with a great army into the land of Juda: and they sent messengers, and spoke to Judas and his brethren with peaceable words deceitfully.

11 But they gave no heed to their words: for they saw that they were come with a great army. **12** Then there assembled to Alcimus and Bacchides a company of the scribes to require things that are just: **13** And first the Assideans that were among the children of Israel, and they sought peace of them. **14** For they said: One that is a priest of the seed of Aaron is come, he will not deceive us. **15** And he spoke to them peaceably: and he swore to them, saying: We will do you no harm nor your friends.

16 And they believed him. And he took threescore of them, and slew them in one day, according to the word that is written: **17** The flesh of thy saints, and the blood of them they have shed round about Jerusalem, and there was none to bury them. **18** Then fear and trembling fell upon all the people: for they said: There is no truth, nor justice among them: for they have broken the covenant, and the oath which they made. **19** And Bacchides removed the camp from Jerusalem, and pitched in Bethzecha: and he sent, and took many of them that were fled away from him, and some of the people he killed, and threw them into a great pit. **20** Then he committed the country to Alcimus, and left with him troops to help him. So Bacchides went away to the king:

21 But Alcimus did what he could to maintain his chief priesthood. **22** And they that disturbed the people resorted to him, and they got the land of Juda into their power, and did much hurt in Israel. **23** And Judas saw all the evils that Alcimus, and they that were with him, did to the children of Israel, much more than the Gentiles. **24** And he went out into all the coasts of Juda round about, and took vengeance upon the men that had revolted, and they ceased to go forth any more into the country. **25** And Alcimus saw that Judas, and they that were with him prevailed: and he knew that he could not stand against them, and he went back to the king, and accused them of many crimes.

26 And the king sent Nicanor one of his principal lords, who was a great enemy to Israel: and he commanded him to destroy the people. **27** And Nicanor came to Jerusalem with a great army, and he sent to Judas and to his brethren deceitfully with friendly words, **28** Saying: Let there be no fighting between me and you: I will come with a few men to see your faces with peace. **29** And he came to Judas, and they saluted one another peaceably: and the enemies were prepared to take away Judas by force. **30** And the thing was known to Judas that he was come to him with deceit: and he was much afraid of him, and would not see his face any more.

31 And Nicanor knew that his counsel was discovered: and he went out to fight against Judas near Capharsalama. **32** And there fell of Nicanor's army almost five thousand men, and they fled into the city of David. **33** And after this Nicanor went up into mount Sion: and some of the priests and the people came out to salute him peaceably, and to shew him the holocausts that were offered for the king. **34** But he mocked them and despised them, and abused them: and he spoke proudly, **35** And swore in anger, saying: Unless Judas and his army be delivered into my hands, as soon as ever I return in peace, I will burn this house. And he went out in a great rage.

36 And the priests went in, and stood before the face of the altar and the temple: and weeping, they said: **37** Thou, O Lord, hast chosen this house for thy name to be called upon therein, that it might be a house of prayer and supplication for thy people. **38** Be avenged of this man, and his army, and let them fall by the sword: remember their blasphemies, and suffer them not to continue any longer. **39** Then Nicanor went out from Jerusalem, and encamped near to Bethoron: and an army of Syria joined him. **40** But Judas pitched in Adarsa with three thousand men: and Judas prayed, and said:

41 O Lord, when they that were sent by king Sennacherib blasphemed thee, an angel went out, and slew of them a hundred and eighty-five thousand: **42** Even so destroy this army in our sight today, and let the rest know that he hath spoken ill against thy sanctuary: and judge thou him according to his wickedness. **43** And the armies joined battle on the thirteenth day of the month Adar: and the army of Nicanor was defeated, and he himself was first slain in the battle. **44** And when his army saw that Nicanor was slain, they threw away their weapons, and fled: **45** And they pursued after them one day's journey from Adazer, even till ye come to Gazara, and they sounded the trumpets after them with signals.

46 And they went forth out of all the towns of Judea round about, and they pushed them with the horns, and they turned again to them, and they were all slain with the sword, and there was not left of them so much as one. **47** And they took the spoils of them for a booty, and they cut off Nicanor's head, and his right hand, which he had proudly stretched out, and they brought it, and hung it up over against Jerusalem. **48** And the people rejoiced exceedingly, and they spent that day with great joy. **49** And he ordained that this day should be kept every year, being the thirteenth of the month of Adar. **50** And the land of Juda was quiet for a short time.

Chapter 8

1 Now Judas heard of the fame of the Romans, that they are powerful and strong, and willingly agree to all things that are requested of them: and that whosoever have come to them, they have made amity with them, and that they are mighty in power. **2** And they heard of their battles, and their noble acts, which they had done in Galatia, how they conquered them, and brought them under tribute: **3** And how great things they had done in the land of Spain, and that they had brought under their power the mines of silver and of gold that are there, and had gotten possession of all the place by their counsel and patience: **4** And had conquered places that were very far off from them, and kings that came against them from the ends of the earth, and had overthrown them with great slaughter: and the rest pay them tribute every year. **5** And that they had defeated in battle Philip, and Perses the king of the Ceteans, and the rest that had borne arms against them, and had conquered them:

6 And how Antiochus the great king of Asia, who went to fight against them, having a hundred and twenty elephants, with horsemen, and chariots, and a very great army, was routed by them: **7** And how they took him alive, and appointed to him, that both he and they that should reign after him, should pay a great tribute, and that he should give hostages, and that which was agreed upon, **8** And the country of the Indians, and of the Medes, and of the Lydians, some of their best provinces: and those which they had taken from them they gave to king Eumenes [King of Pergamus]. **9** And that they who were in Greece had a mind to go and to destroy them: and they had knowledge thereof, **10** And they sent a general against them, and fought with them, and many of them were slain, and they carried away their wives and their children captives, and spoiled them, and took possession of their land, and threw down their walls, and brought them to be their servants unto this day.

11 And the other kingdoms, and islands, that at any time had resisted them, they had destroyed and brought under their power. **12** But with their friends, and such as relied upon them, they kept amity, and had conquered kingdoms that were near, and that were far off: for all that heard their name, were afraid of them. **13** That whom they had a mind to help to a kingdom, those reigned: and whom they would, they deposed from a kingdom: and they were greatly exalted. **14** And none of all these wore a crown, or was clothed in purple, to be magnified thereby. **15** And that they made themselves a senate house, and consulted daily three hundred and twenty men, that sat in council always for the people, that they might do the things that were right.

16 And that they committed their government to one man every year, to rule over all their country, and they all obey one, and there is no envy, nor jealousy amongst them. **17** So Judas chose Eupolemus the son of John, the son of Jacob, and Jason the son of Eleazar, and he sent them to Rome to make a league of amity and confederacy with them. **18** And that they might take off from them the yoke of the Grecians, for they saw that they oppressed the kingdom of Israel with servitude. **19** And they went to Rome, a very long journey, and they entered into the senate house, and said: **20** Judas Machabeus, and his brethren, and the people of the Jews have sent us to you, to make alliance and peace with you, and that we may be registered your confederates and friends.

21 And the proposal was pleasing in their sight. **22** And this is the copy of the writing that they wrote back again, graven in tables of brass, and sent to Jerusalem, that it might be with them there for a memorial of the peace and alliance. **23** GOOD SUCCESS BE TO THE ROMANS, and to the people of the Jews, by sea and by land for ever: and far be the sword and enemy from them. **24** But if there come first any war upon the Romans, or any of their confederates, in all their dominions: **25** The nation of the Jews shall help them according as the time shall direct, with all their heart:

26 Neither shall they give them, whilst they are fighting, or furnish them with wheat, or arms, or money, or ships, as it hath seemed good to the Romans: and they shall obey their orders, without taking any thing of them. **27** In like manner also if war shall come first upon the nation of the Jews, the Romans shall help them with all their heart, according as the time shall permit them. **28** And there shall not be given to them that come to their aid, either wheat, or arms, or money, or ships, as it hath seemed good to the Romans: and they shall observe their orders without deceit. **29** According to these articles did the Romans covenant with the people of the Jews. **30** And if after this one party or the other shall have a mind to add to these articles, or take away anything, they may do it at their pleasure: and whatsoever they shall add, or take away, shall be ratified.

31 Moreover concerning the evils that Demetrius the king hath done against them, we have written to him, saying: Why hast thou made thy yoke heavy upon our friends, and allies, the Jews? **32** If therefore they come again to us complaining of thee, we will do them justice, and will make war against thee by sea and land.

Chapter 9

1 In the meantime when Demetrius heard that Nicanor and his army were fallen in battle, he sent again Bacchides and Alcimus into Judea; and the right wing of his army with them. **2** And they took the road that leadeth to Galgal, and they camped in Masaloth, which is in Arabella: and they made themselves masters of it, and slew many people. **3** In the first month of the hundred and fifty-second year they brought the army to Jerusalem: **4** And they arose, and went to Berea with twenty thousand men, and two thousand horsemen. **5** Now Judas had pitched his tents in Laisa, and three thousand chosen men with him:

6 And they saw the multitude of the army that they were many, and they were seized with great fear: and many withdrew themselves out of the camp, and there remained of them no more than eight hundred men. **7** And Judas saw that his army slipped away, and the battle pressed upon him, and his heart was cast down: because he had not time to gather them together, and he was discouraged. **8** Then he said to them that remained: Let us arise, and go against our enemies, if we may be able to fight against them. **9** But they dissuaded him, saying: We shall not be able, but let us save our lives now, and return to our brethren, and then we will fight against them: for we are but few. **10** Then Judas said: God forbid we should do this thing, and flee away from them: but if our time be come, let us die manfully for our brethren, and let us not stain our glory.

11 And the army removed out of the camp, and they stood over against them: and the horsemen were divided into two troops, and the slingers, and the archers went before the army, and they that were in the front were all men of valour. **12** And Bacchides was in the right wing, and the legion drew near on two sides, and they sounded the trumpets: **13** And they also were on Judas' side, even they also cried out, and the earth shook at the noise of the armies: and the battle was fought from morning even unto the evening. **14** And Judas perceived that the stronger part of the army of Bacchides was on the right side, and all the stout of heart came together with him: **15** And the right wing was discomfited by them, and he pursued them even to the mount Azotus.

16 And they that were in the left wing saw that the right wing was discomfited, and they followed after Judas, and them that were with him, at their back: **17** And the battle was hard fought, and there fell many wounded of the one side and of the other. **18** And Judas was slain, and the rest fled away. **19** And Jonathan and Simon took Judas their brother, and buried him in the sepulchre of their fathers in the city of Modin. **20** And all the people of Israel bewailed him with great lamentation, and they mourned for him many days.

21 And said: How is the mighty man fallen, that saved the people of Israel! **22** But the rest of the words of the wars of Judas, and of the noble acts that he did, and of his greatness, are not written: for they were very many. **23** And it came to pass after the death of Judas, that the wicked began to put forth their heads in all the confines of Israel, and all the workers of iniquity rose up. **24** In those days there was a very great famine, and they and all their country yielded to Bacchides. **25** And Bacchides chose the wicked men, and made them lords of the country:

26 And they sought out, and made diligent search after the friends of Judas, and brought them to Bacchides, and he took vengeance of them, and abused them. **27** And there was a great tribulation in Israel, such as was not since the day, that there was no prophet seen in Israel. **28** And all the friends of Judas came together, and said to Jonathan: **29** Since thy brother Judas died, there is not a man like him to go forth against our enemies, Bacchides, and them that are the enemies of our nation. **30** Now therefore we have chosen thee this day to be our prince, and captain in his stead to fight our battles.

31 So Jonathan took upon him the government at that time, and rose up in the place of Judas his brother. **32** And Bacchides had knowledge of it, and sought to kill him. **33** And Jonathan and Simon his brother, knew it, and all that were with them: and they fled into the desert of Thecua, and they pitched by the water of the lake of Asphar, **34** And Bacchides understood it, and he came himself with all his army over the Jordan on the sabbath day. **35** And Jonathan sent his brother a captain of the people, to desire the Nabutheans his friends, that they would lend them their equipage, which was copious.

36 And the children of Jambri came forth out of Madaba, and took John, and all that he had, and went away with them. **37** After this it was told Jonathan, and Simon his brother, that the children of Jambri made a great marriage, and were bringing the bride out of Madaba, the daughter of one of the great princes of Chanaan, with great pomp. **38** And the remembered the blood of John their brother: and they went up, and hid themselves under the covert of the mountain. **39** And they lifted up their eyes, and saw: and behold a tumult, and great preparation: and the bridegroom came forth, and his friends, and his brethren to meet them with timbrels, and musical instruments, and many weapons. **40** And they rose up against them from the place where they lay in ambush, and slew them, and there fell many wounded, and the rest fled into the mountains, and they took all their spoils:

41 And the marriage was turned into mourning, and the noise of their musical instruments into lamentation. **42** And they took revenge for the blood of their brother: and they returned to the bank of the Jordan. **43** And Bacchides heard it, and he came on the sabbath day even to the bank of the Jordan with a great power. **44** And Jonathan said to his company: Let us arise, and fight against our enemies: for it is not now as yesterday, and the day before. **45** And behold the battle is before us, and the water of the Jordan on this side and on that side, and banks, and marshes, and woods: and there is no place for us to turn aside.

46 Now therefore cry ye to heaven, that ye may be delivered from the hand of your enemies. And they joined battle. **47** And Jonathan stretched forth his hand to strike Bacchides, but he turned away from him backwards. **48** And Jonathan, and they that were with him leaped into the Jordan, and swam over the Jordan to them: **49** And there fell of Bacchides' side that day a thousand men: and they returned to Jerusalem, **50** And they built strong cities in Judea, the fortress that was in Jericho, and in Ammaus, and in Bethoron, and in Bethel, and Thamnata, and Phara, and Thopo, with high walls, and gates, and bars.

51 And he placed garrisons in them, that they might wage war against Israel: **52** And he fortified the city of Bethsura, and Gazara, and the castle, and set garrisons in them, and provisions of victuals: **53** And he took the sons of the chief men of the country for hostages, and put them in the castle in Jerusalem in custody. **54** Now in the year one hundred and fifty-three, the second month, Alcimus commanded the walls of the inner court of the sanctuary to be thrown down, and the works of the prophets to be destroyed: and he began to be destroyed: and he began to destroy. **55** At that time Alcimus was struck: and his works were hindered, and his mouth was stopped, and he was taken with a palsy, so that he could no more speak a word, nor give order concerning his house.

56 And Alcimus died at that time in great torment. **57** And Bacchides saw that Alcimus was dead: and he returned to the king, and the land was quiet for two years. **58** And all the wicked held a council, saying: Behold Jonathan, and they that are with him, dwell at ease, and without fear: now therefore let us bring Bacchides hither, and he shall take them all in one night. **59** So they went, and gave him counsel. **60** And he arose to come with a great army: and he sent secretly letters to his adherents that were in Judea, to seize upon Jonathan, and them that were with him: but they could not, for their design was known to them.

61 And he apprehended of the men of the country, that were the principal authors of the mischief, fifty men, and slew them. **62** And

Jonathan, and Simon, and they that were with him retired into Bethbessen, which is in the desert: and he repaired the breaches thereof, and they fortified it. **63** And when Bacchides knew it, he gathered together all his multitude: and sent word to them that were of Judea. **64** And he came, and camped above Bethbessen, and fought against it many days, and made engines. **65** But Jonathan left his brother Simon in the city, and went forth into the country: and came with a number of men.

66 And struck Odares, and his brethren, and the children of Phaseron in their tents, and he began to slay, and to increase in forces. **67** But Simon and they that were with him, sallied out of the city, and burnt the engines. **68** And they fought against Bacchides, and he was discomfited by them: and they afflicted him exceedingly, for his counsel, and his enterprise was in vain. **69** And he was angry with the wicked men that had given him counsel to come into their country, and he slew many of them: and he purposed to return with the rest into their country. **70** And Jonathan had knowledge of it, and he sent ambassadors to him to make peace with him, and to restore to him the prisoners.

71 And he accepted it willingly, and did according to his words, and swore that he would do him no harm all the days of his life. **72** And he restored to him the prisoners which he before had taken out of the land of Juda: and he returned and went away into his own country, and he came no more into their borders. **73** So the sword ceased from Israel: and Jonathan dwelt in Machmas, and Jonathan began there to judge the people, and he destroyed the wicked out of Israel.

Chapter 10

1 Now in the hundred and sixtieth year Alexander the son of Antiochus, surnamed the Illustrious, came up and took Ptolemais, and they received him, and he reigned there. **2** And king Demetrius heard of it, and gathered together an exceeding great army, and went forth against him to fight. **3** And Demetrius sent a letter to Jonathan with peaceable words, to magnify him. **4** For he said: Let us first make a peace with him, before he make one with Alexander against us. **5** For he will remember all the evils that we have done against him, and against his brother, and against his nation.

6 And he gave him authority to gather together an army, and to make arms, and that he should be his confederate: and the hostages that were in the castle, he commanded to be delivered to him. **7** And Jonathan came to Jerusalem, and read the letters in the hearing of all the people, and of them that were in the castle. **8** And they were struck with great fear, because they heard that the king had given him authority to gather together an army. **9** And the hostages were delivered to Jonathan, and he restored them to their parents. **10** And Jonathan dwelt in Jerusalem, and began to build, and to repair the city.

11 And he ordered workmen to build the walls, and mount Sion round about with square stones for fortification: and so they did. **12** And the strangers that were in the strong holds, which Bacchides had built, fled away. **13** And every man left his place, and departed into his own country: **14** Only in Bethsura there remained some of them, that had forsaken the law, and the commandments of God: for this was a place of refuge for them. **15** And king Alexander heard of the promises that Demetrius had made Jonathan: and they told him of the battles, and the worthy acts that he, and his brethren had done, and the labours that they had endured.

16 And he said: Shall we find such another man? now therefore we will make him our friend and our confederate. **17** So he wrote a letter, and sent it to him according to these words, saying: **18** King Alexander to his brother Jonathan, greeting. **19** We have heard of thee, that thou art a man of great power, and fit to be our friend: **20** Now therefore we make thee this day high priest of thy nation, and that thou be called the king's friend, (and he sent him a purple robe, and a crown of gold,) and that thou be of one mind with us in our affairs, and keep friendship with us.

21 Then Jonathan put on the holy vestment in the seventh month, in the year one hundred and threescore, at the feast day of the tabernacles: and he gathered together an army, and made a great number of arms. **22** And Demetrius heard these words, and was exceeding sorry, and said: **23** What is this that we have done, that Alexander hath prevented us to gain the friendship of the Jews to strengthen himself? **24** I also will write to them words of request, and offer dignities, and gifts: that they may be with me to aid me. **25** And he wrote to them in these words: King Demetrius to the nation of the Jews, greeting.

26 Whereas you have kept covenant with us, and have continued in our friendship, and have not joined with our enemies, we have heard of it, and are glad. **27** Wherefore now continue still to keep fidelity towards us, and we will reward you with good things, for what you have done in our behalf. **28** And we will remit to you many charges, and will give you gifts. **29** And now I free you, and all the Jews from tributes, and I release you from the customs of salt, and remit the crowns, and the thirds of the seed: **30** And the half of the fruit of trees, which is my share, I leave to you from this day forward, so that it shall not be taken of the land of Juda, and of the three cities that are added thereto out of Samaria and Galilee, from this day forth and for ever:

31 And let Jerusalem be holy and free, with the borders thereof: and let the tenths, and tributes be for itself. **32** I yield up also the power of the castle that is in Jerusalem, and I give it to the high priest, to place therein such men as he shall choose to keep it. **33** And every soul of the Jews that hath been carried captive from the land of Juda in all my kingdom, I set at liberty freely, that all be discharged from tributes even of their cattle. **34** And I will that all the feasts, and the sabbaths, and the new moons, and the days appointed, and three days before the solemn day, and three days after the solemn day, be all days of immunity and freedom, for all the Jews that are in my kingdom: **35** And no man shall have power to do any thing against them, or to molest any of them, in any cause.

36 And let there be enrolled in the king's army to the number of thirty thousand of the Jews: and allowance shall be made them as is due to all the king's forces, and certain of them shall be appointed to be in the fortresses of the great king: **37** And some of them shall be set over the affairs of the kingdom, that are of trust, and let the governors be taken from among themselves, and let them walk in their own laws, as the king hath commanded in the land of Juda. **38** And the three cities that are added to Judea, out of the country of Samaria, let them be accounted with Judea: that they may be under one, and obey no other authority but that of the high priest: **39** Ptolemais, and the confines thereof, I give as a free gift to the holy places, that are in Jerusalem, for the necessary charges of the holy things. **40** And I give every year fifteen thousand sicles of silver out of the king's accounts, of what belongs to me:

41 And all that is above, which they that were over the affairs the years before, had not paid, from this time they shall give it to the works of the house. **42** Moreover the five thousand sicles of silver which they received from the account of the holy places, every year, shall also belong to the priests that execute the ministry. **43** And whosoever shall flee into the temple that is in Jerusalem, and in all the borders thereof, being indebted to the king for any matter, let them be set at liberty, and all that they have in my kingdom, let them have it free. **44** For the building also, or repairing the works of the holy places, the charges shall be given out of the king's revenues: **45** For the building also of the walls of Jerusalem, and the fortifying thereof round about, the charges shall be given out of the king's account, as also for the building of the walls in Judea.

46 Now when Jonathan, and the people heard these words, they gave no credit to them nor received them: because they remembered the great evil that he had done in Israel, for he had afflicted them exceedingly. **47** And their inclinations were towards Alexander, because he had been the chief promoter of peace in their regard, and him they always helped. **48** And king Alexander gathered together a great army, and moved his camp near to Demetrius. **49** And the two kings joined battle, and the army of Demetrius fled away, and Alexander pursued after him, and pressed them close. **50** And the battle was hard fought till the sun went down: and Demetrius was slain that day.

51 And Alexander sent ambassadors to Ptolemee king of Egypt, with words to this effect, saying: **52** Forasmuch as I am returned into my kingdom, and am set in the throne of my ancestors and have gotten the dominion, and have overthrown Demetrius, and possessed our country, **53** And have joined battle with him, and both he and his army have been destroyed by us, and we are placed in the throne of his kingdom: **54** Now therefore let us make friendship one with another: and give me now thy daughter to wife, and I will be thy son in law, and I will give both thee and her gifts worthy of thee. **55** And king Ptolemee answered, saying: Happy is the day wherein thou didst return to the land of thy fathers, and sattest in the throne of their kingdom.

56 And now I will do to thee as thou hast written: but meet me at Ptolemais, that we may see one another, and I may give her to thee as thou hast said. **57** So Ptolemee went out of Egypt, with Cleopatra his daughter, and he came to Ptolemais in the hundred and sixty-second year. **58** And king Alexander met him, and he gave him his daughter Cleopatra: and he celebrated her marriage at Ptolemais, with great glory, after the manner of kings. **59** And king Alexander wrote to Jonathan, that he should come and meet him. **60** And he went honourably to Ptolemais, and he met there the two kings, and he gave them much silver, and gold, and presents: and he found favour in their sight.

61 And some pestilent men of Israel, men of a wicked life, assembled themselves against him to accuse him: and the king gave no heed to them. **62** And he commanded that Jonathan's garments should be taken off, and that he should be clothed with purple: and they did so. And the king made him sit by himself. **63** And he said to his princes: Go out with him into the midst of the city, and make proclamation, that no man complain against him of any matter, and that no man trouble him for any manner of cause. **64** So when his accusers saw his glory proclaimed, and him clothed with purple, they all fled away. **65** And the king magnified him, and enrolled him amongst his chief friends, and made him governor and partaker of his dominion.

66 And Jonathan returned into Jerusalem with peace and joy. **67** In the year one hundred and sixty-five Demetrius the son of Demetrius came from Crete into the land of his fathers. **68** And king Alexander heard of it, and was much troubled, and returned to

Antioch. **69** And king Demetrius made Apollonius his general, who was governor of Celesyria: and he gathered together a great army, and came to Jamnia: and he sent to Jonathan the high priest, **70** Saying: Thou alone standest against us, and I am laughed at, and reproached, because thou shewest thy power against us in the mountains.

71 Now therefore if thou trustest in thy forces, come down to us into the plain, and there let us try one another: for with me is the strength of war. **72** Ask, and learn who I am, and the rest that help me, who also say that your foot cannot stand before our face, for thy fathers have twice been put to flight in their own land: **73** And now how wilt thou be able to abide the horsemen, and so great an army in the plain, where there is no stone, nor rock, nor place to flee to? **74** Now when Jonathan heard the words of Apollonius, he was moved in his mind: and he chose ten thousand men, and went out of Jerusalem, and Simon his brother met him to help him. **75** And they pitched their tents near Joppe, but they shut him out of the city: because a garrison of Apollonius was in Joppe, and he laid siege to it.

76 And they that were in the city being affrighted, opened the gates to him: so Jonathan took Joppe. **77** And Apollonius heard of it, and he took three thousand horsemen, and a great army. **78** And he went to Azotus as one that was making a journey, and immediately he went forth into the plain: because he had a great number of horsemen, and he trusted in them. And Jonathan followed after him to Azotus, and they joined battle. **79** And Apollonius left privately in the camp a thousand horsemen behind them. **80** And Jonathan knew that there was an ambush behind him, and they surrounded his army, and cast darts at the people from morning till evening.

81 But the people stood still, as Jonathan had commanded them: and so their horses were fatigued. **82** Then Simon drew forth his army, and attacked the legion: for the horsemen were wearied: and they were discomfited by him, and fled. **83** And they that were scattered about the plain, fled into Azotus, and went into Bethdagon their idol's temple, there to save themselves. **84** But Jonathan set fire to Azotus, and the cities that were around it, and took the spoils of them, and the temple of Dagon: and all them that were fled into it, he burnt with fire. **85** So they that were slain by the sword, with them that were burnt, were almost eight thousand men.

86 And Jonathan removed his army from thence, and camped against Ascalon: and they went out of the city to meet him with great honour. **87** And Jonathan returned into Jerusalem with his people, having many spoils. **88** And it came to pass: When Alexander the king heard these words, that he honoured Jonathan yet more. **89** And he sent him a buckle of gold, as the custom is, to be given to such as are of the royal blood. And he gave him Accaron and all the borders thereof in possession.

Chapter 11

1 And the king of Egypt gathered together an army, like the sand that lieth upon the sea shore, and many ships: and he sought to get the kingdom of Alexander by deceit, and join it to his own kingdom. **2** And he went out into Syria with peaceable words, and they opened to him the cities, and met him: for king Alexander had ordered them to go forth to meet him, because he was his father in law. **3** Now when Ptolemee entered into the cities, he put garrisons of soldiers in every city. **4** And when he came near to Azotus, they shewed him the temple of Dagon that was burnt with fire, and Azotus, and the suburbs thereof that were destroyed, and the bodies that were cast abroad, and the graves of them that were slain in the battle, which they had made near the way. **5** And they told the king that Jonathan had done these things, to make him odious: but the king held his peace.

6 And Jonathan came to meet the king at Joppe with glory, and they saluted one another, and they lodged there. **7** And Jonathan went with the king as far as the river, called Eleutherus: and he returned into Jerusalem. **8** And king Ptolemee got the dominion of the cities by the sea side, even to Seleucia, and he devised evil designs against Alexander. **9** And he sent ambassadors to Demetrius, saying: Come, let us make a league between us, and I will give thee my daughter whom Alexander hath, and thou shalt reign in the kingdom of thy father. **10** For I repent that I have given him my daughter: for he hath sought to kill me.

11 And he slandered him, because he coveted his kingdom. **12** And he took away his daughter, and gave her to Demetrius, and alienated himself from Alexander, and his enmities were made manifest. **13** And Ptolemee entered into Antioch, and set two crowns upon his head, that of Egypt, and that of Asia. **14** Now king Alexander was in Cilicia at that time: because they that were in those places had rebelled. **15** And when Alexander heard of it, he came to give him battle, and king Ptolemee brought forth his army, and met him with a strong power, and put him to flight.

16 And Alexander fled into Arabia, there to be protected: and king Ptolemee was exalted. **17** And Zabdiel the Arabian took off Alexander's head, and sent it to Ptolemee. **18** And king Ptolemee died the third day after: and they that were in the strong holds were destroyed by them that were within the camp. **19** And Demetrius reigned in the hundred and sixty-seventh year. **20** In those days Jonathan gathered together them that were in Judea, to take the castle that was in Jerusalem: and they made many engines of war against it.

21 Then some wicked men that hated their own nation, went away to king Demetrius, and told him that Jonathan was besieging the castle. **22** And when he heard it, he was angry: and forthwith he came to Ptolemais, and wrote to Jonathan, that he should not besiege the castle, but should come to him in haste, and speak to him. **23** But when Jonathan heard this, he bade them besiege it still: and he chose some of the ancients of Israel, and of the priests, and put himself in danger. **24** And he took gold, and silver, and raiment, and many other presents, and went to the king to Ptolemais, and he found favour in his sight. **25** And certain wicked men of his nation made complaints against him.

26 And the king treated him as his predecessor had done before: and he exalted him in the sight of all his friends. **27** And he confirmed him in the high priesthood, and all the honours he had before, and he made him the chief of his friends. **28** And Jonathan requested of the king that he would make Judea free from tribute, and the three governments, and Samaria, and the confines thereof: and he promised him three hundred talents. **29** And the king consented: and he wrote letters to Jonathan of all these things to this effect. **30** King Demetrius to his brother Jonathan, and to the nation of the Jews, greeting.

31 We send you here a copy of the letter, which we have written to Lasthenes our parent concerning you, that you might know it. **32** King Demetrius to Lasthenes his parent, greeting. **33** We have determined to do good to the nation of the Jews who are our friends, and keep the things that are just with us, for their good will which they bear towards us. **34** We have ratified therefore unto them all the borders of Judea, and the three cities, Apherema, Lydda, and Ramatha, which are added to Judea, out of Samaria, and all their confines, to be set apart to all them that sacrifice in Jerusalem, instead of the payments which the king received of them every year, and for the fruits of the land, and of the trees. **35** And as for other things that belonged to us of the tithes, and of the tributes, from this time we discharge them of them: the saltpans also, and the crowns that were presented to us.

36 We give all to them, and nothing hereof shall be revoked from this time forth and for ever. **37** Now therefore see that thou make a copy of these things, and let it be given to Jonathan, and set upon the holy mountain, in a conspicuous place. **38** And king Demetrius seeing that the land was quiet before him, and nothing resisted him, sent away all his forces, every man to his own place, except the foreign army, which he had drawn together from the islands of the nations: so all the troops of his fathers hated him. **39** Now there was one Tryphon who had been of Alexander's party before: who seeing that all the army murmured against Demetrius, went to Emalchuel the Arabian, who brought up Antiochus the son of Alexander. **40** And he pressed him much to deliver him to him, that he might be king in his father's place: and he told him all that Demetrius had done, and how his soldiers hated him. And he remained there many days.

41 And Jonathan sent to king Demetrius, desiring that he would cast out them that were in the castle in Jerusalem, and those that were in the strong holds: because they fought against Israel. **42** And Demetrius sent to Jonathan, saying: I will not only do this for thee, and for thy people, but I will greatly honour thee, and thy nation, when opportunity shall serve. **43** Now therefore thou shalt do well if thou send me men to help me: for all my army is gone from me. **44** And Jonathan sent him three thousand valiant men to Antioch: and they came to the king, and the king was very glad of their coming. **45** And they that were of the city assembled themselves together, to the number of a hundred and twenty thousand men, and would have killed the king.

46 And the king fled into the palace, and they of the city kept the passages of the city, and began to fight. **47** And the king called the Jews to his assistance: and they came to him all at once, and they all dispersed themselves through the city. **48** And they slew in that day a hundred thousand men, and they set fire to the city, and got many spoils that day, and delivered the king. **49** And they that were of the city saw that the Jews had got the city as they would: and they were discouraged in their minds, and cried to the king, making supplication, and saying: **50** Grant us peace, and let the Jews cease from assaulting us, and the city.

51 And they threw down their arms, and made peace, and the Jews were glorified in the sight of the king, and in the sight of all that were in his realm, and were renowned throughout the kingdom, and returned to Jerusalem with many spoils. **52** So king Demetrius sat in the throne of his kingdom: and the land was quiet before him. **53** And he falsified all whatsoever he had said, and alienated himself from Jonathan, and did not reward him according to the benefits he had received from him, but gave him great trouble. **54** And after this Tryphon returned, and with him Antiochus the young boy, who was made king, and put on the diadem. **55** And there assembled unto him all the hands which Demetrius had sent away, and they fought against Demetrius, who turned his back and fled.

56 And Tryphon took the elephants, and made himself master of

Antioch. **57** And young Antiochus wrote to Jonathan, saying: I confirm thee in the high priesthood, and I appoint thee ruler over the four cities, and to be one of the king's friends. **58** And he sent him vessels of gold for his service, and he gave him leave to drink in gold, and to be clothed in purple, and to wear a golden buckle: **59** And he made his brother Simon governor from the borders of Tyre even to the confines of Egypt. **60** Then Jonathan went forth and passed through the cities beyond the river: and all the forces of Syria gathered themselves to him to help him, and he came to Ascalon, and they met him honourably out of the city.

61 And he went from thence to Gaza: and they that were in Gaza shut him out: and he besieged it, and burnt all the suburbs round about, and took the spoils. **62** And the men of Gaza made supplication to Jonathan, and he gave them the right hand: and he took their sons for hostages, and sent them to Jerusalem: and he went through the country as far as Damascus. **63** And Jonathan heard that the generals of Demetrius were come treacherously to Cades, which is in Galilee, with a great army, purposing to remove him from the affairs of the kingdom: **64** And he went against them: but left his brother Simon in the country. **65** And Simon encamped against Bethsura, and assaulted it many days, and shut them up.

66 And they desired him to make peace, and he granted it them: and he cast them out from thence, and took the city, and placed a garrison in it. **67** And Jonathan, and his army encamped by the water of Genesar, and before it was light they were ready in the plain of Asor. **68** And behold the army of the strangers met him in the plain, and they laid an ambush for him in the mountains: but he went out against them. **69** And they that lay in ambush arose out of their places, and joined battle. **70** And all that were on Jonathan's side fled, and none was left of them, but Mathathias the son of Absalom, and Judas the son of Calphi, chief captain of the army.

71 And Jonathan rent his garments, and cast earth upon his head, and prayed. **72** And Jonathan turned again to them to battle, and he put them to flight, and they fought. **73** And they of his part that fled saw this, and they turned again to him, and they all with him pursued the enemies even to Cades to their own camp, and they came even thither. **74** And there fell of the aliens in that day three thousand men: and Jonathan returned to Jerusalem.

Chapter 12

1 And Jonathan saw that the time served him, and he chose certain men and sent them to Rome, to confirm and to renew the amity with them: **2** And he sent letters to the Spartans, and to other places according to the same form. **3** And they went to Rome, and entered into the senate house, and said: Jonathan the high priest, and the nation of the Jews have sent us to renew the amity, and alliance as it was before. **4** And they gave them letters to their governors in every place, to conduct them into the land of Juda with peace. **5** And this is a copy of the letters which Jonathan wrote to the Spartans:

6 Jonathan the high priest, and the ancients of the nation, and the priests, and the rest of the people of the Jews, to the Spartans, their brethren, greeting. **7** There were letters sent long ago to Onias the high priest from Arius who reigned then among you, to signify that you are our brethren, as the copy here underwritten doth specify. **8** And Onias received the ambassador with honour: and received the letters wherein there was mention made of the alliance, and amity. **9** We, though we needed none of these things, having for our comfort the holy books that are in our hands, **10** Chose rather to send to you to renew the brotherhood and friendship, lest we should become strangers to you altogether: for there is a long time passed since you sent to us.

11 We therefore at all times without ceasing, both in our festivals, and other days, wherein it is convenient, remember you in the sacrifices that we offer, and in our observances, as it is meet, and becoming to remember brethren. **12** And we rejoice at your glory. **13** But we have had many troubles and wars on every side, and the kings that are round about us, have fought against us. **14** But we would not be troublesome to you, nor the rest of our allies and friends in these wars. **15** For we have had help from heaven, and we have been delivered, and our enemies are humbled.

16 We have chosen therefore Numenius the son of Antiochus, and Antipater the son of Jason, and have sent them to the Romans to renew with them the former amity and alliance. **17** And we have commanded them to go also to you, and to salute you, and to deliver you our letters, concerning the renewing of our brotherhood. **18** And now you shall do well to give us an answer hereto. **19** And this is the copy of the letter which he had sent to Onias: **20** Arius king of the Spartans to Onias the high priest, greeting.

21 It is found in writing concerning the Spartans, and the Jews, that they are brethren, and that they are of the stock of Abraham. **22** And now since this is come to our knowledge, you do well to write to us of your prosperity. **23** And we also have written back to you: That our cattle, and our possessions are yours: and yours, ours. We therefore have commanded that these things should be told you. **24** Now Jonathan heard that the generals of Demetrius were come again with a greater army than before to fight against him. **25** So he went out from Jerusalem, and met them in the land of Amath: for he gave them no time to enter into his country.

26 And he sent spies into their camp, and they came back and brought him word that they designed to come upon them in the night. **27** And when the sun was set, Jonathan commanded his men to watch, and to be in arms all night long ready to fight, and he set sentinels round about the camp. **28** And the enemies heard that Jonathan and his men were ready for battle, and they were struck with fear, and dread in their heart: and they kindled fires in their camp. **29** But Jonathan and they that were with him knew it not till the morning: for they saw the lights burning. **30** And Jonathan pursued after them, but overtook them not: for they had passed the river Eleutherus.

31 And Jonathan turned upon the Arabians that are called Zabadeans: and he defeated them, and took the spoils of them. **32** And he went forward, and came to Damascus, and passed through all that country. **33** Simon also went forth, and came as far as Ascalon, and the neighbouring fortresses, and he turned aside to Joppe, and took possession of it, **34** (For he heard that they designed to deliver the hold to them that took part with Demetrius,) and he put a garrison there to keep it. **35** And Jonathan came back, and called together the ancients of the people, and he took a resolution with them to build fortresses in Judea,

36 And to build up walls in Jerusalem, and raise a mount between the castle and the city, to separate it from the city, that so it might have no communication, and that they might neither buy nor sell. **37** And they came together to build up the city: for the wall that was upon the brook towards the east was broken down, and he repaired that which is called Caphetetha: **38** And Simon built Adiada in Sephela, and fortified it, and set up gates and bars. **39** Now when Tryphon had conceived a design to make himself king of Asia, and to take the crown, and to stretch out his hand against king Antiochus: **40** Fearing lest Jonathan would not suffer him, but would fight against him: he sought to seize upon him, and to kill him. So he rose up and came to Bethsan.

41 And Jonathan went out to meet him with forty thousand men chosen for battle, and came to Bethsan. **42** Now when Tryphon saw that Jonathan came with a great army, he durst not stretch forth his hand against him, **43** But received him with honour, and commended him to all his friends, and gave him presents: and he commanded his troops to obey him, as himself. **44** And he said to Jonathan: Why hast thou troubled all the people, whereas we have no war? **45** Now therefore send them back to their own houses: and choose thee a few men that may be with thee, and come with me to Ptolemais, and I will deliver it to thee, and the rest of the strong holds, and the army, and all that have any charge, and I will return and go away: for this is the cause of my coming.

46 And Jonathan believed him, and did as he said: and sent away his army, and they departed into the land of Juda: **47** But he kept with him three thousand men: of whom he sent two thousand into Galilee, and one thousand went with him. **48** Now as soon as Jonathan entered into Ptolemais, they of Ptolemais shut the gates of the city, and took him: and all them that came in with him they slew with the sword. **49** Then Tryphon sent an army and horsemen into Galilee, and into the great plain to destroy all Jonathan's company. **50** But they, when they understood that Jonathan and all that were with him were taken and slain, encouraged one another, and went out ready for battle.

51 Then they that had come after them, seeing that they stood for their lives, returned back. **52** Whereupon they all came peaceably into the land of Juda. And they bewailed Jonathan, and them that had been with him, exceedingly: and Israel mourned with great lamentation. **53** Then all the heathens that were round about them, sought to destroy them. For they said: **54** They have no prince, nor any to help them: now therefore let us make war upon them, and take away the memory of them from amongst men.

Chapter 13

1 Now Simon heard that Tryphon was gathering together a very great army, to invade the land of Juda, and to destroy it. **2** And seeing that the people was in dread, and in fear, he went up to Jerusalem, and assembled the people: **3** And exhorted them, saying: You know what great battles I and my brethren, and the house of my father, have fought for the laws, and the sanctuary, and the distresses that we have seen: **4** By reason whereof all my brethren have lost their lives for Israel's sake, and I am left alone. **5** And now far be it from me to spare my life in any time of trouble: for I am not better than my brethren.

6 I will avenge then my nation and the sanctuary, and our children, and wives: for all the heathens are gathered together to destroy us out of mere malice. **7** And the spirit of the people was enkindled as soon as they heard these words. **8** And they answered with a loud voice, saying: Thou art our leader in the place of Judas, and Jonathan thy brother. **9** Fight thou our battles, and we will do whatsoever thou shalt say to us. **10** So gathering together all the men of war, he made haste to finish all the walls of Jerusalem, and he fortified it round about.

11 And he sent Jonathan the son of Absalom, and with him a new army into Joppe, and he cast out them that were in it, and himself remained there. **12** And Tryphon removed from Ptolemais with a great army, to invade the land of Juda, and Jonathan was with him in custody. **13** But Simon pitched in Addus, over against the plain. **14** And when Tryphon understood that Simon was risen up in the place of his brother Jonathan, and that he meant to join battle with him, he sent messengers to him, **15** Saying: We have detained thy brother Jonathan for the money that he owed in the king's account, by reason of the affairs which he had the management of.

16 But now send a hundred talents of silver, and his two sons for hostages, that when he is set at liberty he may not revolt from us, and we will release him. **17** Now Simon knew that he spoke deceitfully to him, nevertheless he ordered the money, and the children to be sent: lest he should bring upon himself a great hatred of the people of Israel, who might have said: **18** Because he sent not the money, and the children, therefore is he lost. **19** So he sent the children, and the hundred talents: and he lied, and did not let Jonathan go. **20** And after this Tryphon entered within the country, to destroy it: and they went about by the way that leadeth to Ador: and Simon and his army marched to every place whithersoever they went.

21 And they that were in the castle, sent messengers to Tryphon, that he should make haste to come through the desert, and send them victuals. **22** And Tryphon made ready all his horsemen to come that night: but there fell a very great snow, and he came not into the country of Galaad. **23** And when he approached to Bascama, he slew Jonathan and his sons there. **24** And Tryphon returned, and went into his own country. **25** And Simon sent, and took the bones of Jonathan his brother, and buried them in Modin, in the city of his fathers.

26 And all Israel bewailed him with great lamentation: and they mourned for him many days. **27** And Simon built over the sepulchre of his father and of his brethren, a building lofty to the sight, of polished stone behind and before: **28** And he set up seven pyramids one against another for his father and his mother, and his four brethren: **29** And round about these he set great pillars: and upon the pillars arms for a perpetual memory: and by the arms ships carved, which might be seen by all that sailed on the sea. **30** This is the sepulchre that he made in Modin even unto this day.

31 But Tryphon when he was upon a journey with the young king Antiochus, treacherously slew him. **32** And he reigned in his place, and put on the crown of Asia: and brought great evils upon the land. **33** And Simon built up the strong holds of Judea, fortifying them with high towers, and great walls, and gates, and bars: and he stored up victuals in the fortresses. **34** And Simon chose men and sent to king Demetrius, to the end that he should grant an immunity to the land: for all that Tryphon did was to spoil. **35** And king Demetrius in answer to this request, wrote a letter in this manner:

36 King Demetrius to Simon the high priest, and friend of kings, and to the ancients, and to the nation of the Jews, greeting. **37** The golden crown, and the palm, which you sent, we have received: and we are ready to make a firm peace with you, and to write to the king's chief officers to release you the things that we have released. **38** For all that we have decreed in your favour, shall stand in force. The strong holds that you have built, shall be your own. **39** And as for any oversight or fault committed unto this day, we forgive it, and the crown which you owed: and if any other thing were taxed in Jerusalem, now let it not be taxed. **40** And if any of you be fit to be enrolled among ours, let them be enrolled, and let there be peace between us.

41 In the year one hundred and seventy the yoke of the Gentiles was taken off from Israel. **42** And the people of Israel began to write in the instruments, and public records, The first year under Simon the high priest, the great captain and prince of the Jews. **43** In those days Simon besieged Gaza, and camped round about it, and he made engines, and set them to the city, and he struck one tower, and took it. **44** And they that were within the engine leaped into the city: and there was a great uproar in the city. **45** And they that were in the city went up with their wives and children upon the wall, with their garments rent, and they cried with a loud voice, beseeching Simon to grant them peace.

46 And they said: Deal not with us according to our evil deeds, but according to thy mercy. **47** And Simon being moved, did not destroy them: but yet he cast them out of the city, and cleansed the houses wherein there had been idols, and then he entered into it with hymns, blessing the Lord. **48** And having cast out of it all uncleanness, he placed in it men that should observe the law: and he fortified it, and made it his habitation. **49** But they that were in the castle of Jerusalem were hindered from going out and coming into the country, and from buying and selling: and they were straitened with hunger, and many of them perished through famine. **50** And they cried to Simon for peace, and he granted it to them: and he cast them out from thence, and cleansed the castle from uncleannesses.

51 And they entered into it the three and twentieth day of the second month, in the year one hundred and seventy-one, with thanksgiving, and branches of palm trees, and harps, and cymbals, and psalteries, and hymns, and canticles, because the great enemy was destroyed out of Israel. **52** And he ordained that these days should be kept every year with gladness. **53** And he fortified the mountain of the temple that was near the castle, and he dwelt there himself, and they that were with him. **54** And Simon saw that John his son was a valiant man for war: and he made him captain of all the forces: and he dwelt in Gazara.

Chapter 14

1 In the year one hundred and seventy-two, king Demetrius assembled his army, and went into Media to get him succours to fight against Tryphon. **2** And Arsaces the king of Persia and Media heard that Demetrius was entered within his borders, and he sent one of his princes to take him alive, and bring him to him. **3** And he went and defeated the army of Demetrius: and took him, and brought him to Arsaces, and he put him into custody. **4** And all the land of Juda was at rest all the days of Simon, and he sought the good of his nation: and his power, and his glory pleased them well all his days. **5** And with all his glory he took Joppe for a haven, and made an entrance to the isles of the sea.

6 And he enlarged the bounds of his nation, and made himself master of the country. **7** And he gathered together a great number of captives, and had the dominion of Gazara, and of Bethsura, and of the castle: and took away all uncleanness out of it and there was none that resisted him. **8** And every man tilled his land with peace: and the land of Juda yielded her increase, and the trees of the fields their fruit. **9** The ancient men sat all in the streets, and treated together of the good things of the land, and the young men put on them glory, and the robes of war. **10** And he provided victuals for the cities, and he appointed that they should be furnished with ammunition, so that the fame of his glory was renowned even to the end of the earth.

11 He made peace in the land, and Israel rejoiced with great joy. **12** And every man sat under his vine, and under his fig tree: and there was none to make them afraid. **13** There was none left in the land to fight against them: kings were discomfited in those days. **14** And he strengthened all those of his people that were brought low, and he sought the law, and took away every unjust and wicked man. **15** He glorified the sanctuary, and multiplied the vessels of the holy places.

16 And it was heard at Rome, and as far as Sparta, that Jonathan was dead: and they were very sorry. **17** But when they heard that Simon his brother was made high priest in his place, and was possessed of all the country, and the cities therein: **18** They wrote to him in tables of brass, to renew the friendship and alliance which they had made with Judas, and with Jonathan his brethren. **19** And they were read before the assembly in Jerusalem. And this is the copy of the letters that the Spartans sent. **20** The princes and the cities of the Spartans to Simon the high priest, and to the ancients, and the priests, and the rest of the people of the Jews their brethren, greeting.

21 The ambassadors that were sent to our people, have told us of your glory, and honour, and joy: and we rejoice at their coming. **22** And we registered what was said by them in the councils of the people in this manner: Numenius the son of Antiochus, and Antipater the son of Jason, ambassadors of the Jews, came to us to renew the former friendship with us. **23** And it pleased the people to receive the men honourably, and to put a copy of their words in the public records, to be a memorial to the people of the Spartans. And we have written a copy of them to Simon the high priest. **24** And after this Simon sent Numenius to Rome, with a great shield of gold the weight of a thousand pounds, to confirm the league with them. And when the people of Rome had heard **25** These words, they said: What thanks shall we give to Simon, and his sons?

26 For he hath restored his brethren, and hath driven away in fight the enemies of Israel from them: and they decreed him liberty, and registered it in tables of brass, and set it upon pillars in mount Sion. **27** And this is a copy of the writing: The eighteenth day of the month Elul, in the year one hundred and seventy-two, being the third year under Simon the high priest at Asaramel, **28** In a great assembly of the priests, and of the people, and the princes of the nation, and the ancients of the country, these things were notified: Forasmuch as there have often been wars in our country, **29** And Simon the son of Mathathias of the children of Jarib, and his brethren have put themselves in danger, and have resisted the enemies of their nation, for the maintenance of their holy places, and the law: and have raised their nation to great glory. **30** And Jonathan gathered together his nation, and was made their high priest, and he was laid to his people.

31 And their enemies desired to tread down and destroy their country, and to stretch forth their hands against their holy places. **32** Then Simon resisted and fought for his nation, and laid out much of his money, and armed the valiant men of his nation, and gave them wages: **33** And he fortified the cities of Judea, and Bethsura that lieth in the borders of Judea, where the armour of the enemies was before: and he placed there a garrison of Jews. **34** And he fortified Joppe which lieth by the sea: and Gazara, which bordereth upon Azotus, wherein the enemies dwelt before, and he placed Jews here: and furnished them with all things convenient for their reparation. **35** And the people seeing the acts of Simon, and to what glory he meant to bring his nation, made him their prince, and high priest, because he had done all these things, and for the justice, and faith, which he kept to his nation, and for that he sought by all means to advance his people.

36 And in his days things prospered in his hands, so that the heathens were taken away out of their country, and they also that were in the city of David in Jerusalem in the castle, out of which they issued forth, and profaned all places round about the sanctuary, and did much evil to its purity. **37** And he placed therein Jews for the defence of the country, and of the city, and he raised up the walls of Jerusalem. **38** And king Demetrius confirmed him in the high priesthood. **39** According to these things he made him his friend, and glorified him with great glory. **40** For he had heard that the Romans had called the Jews their friends, and confederates, and brethren, and that they had received Simon's ambassadors with honour:

41 And that the Jews, and their priests, had consented that he should be their prince, and high priest for ever, till there should arise a faithful prophet: **42** And that he should be chief over them, and that he should have the charge of the sanctuary, and that he should appoint rulers over their works, and over the country, and over the armour, and over the strong holds. **43** And that he should have care of the holy places: and that he should be obeyed by all, and that all the writings in the country should be made in his name: and that he should be clothed with purple, and gold: **44** And that it should not be lawful for any of the people, or of the priests, to disannul any of these things, or to gainsay his words, or to call together an assembly in the country without him: or to be clothed with purple, or to wear a buckle of gold: **45** And whosoever shall do otherwise, or shall make void any of these things shall be punished.

46 And it pleased all the people to establish Simon, and to do according to these words. **47** And Simon accepted thereof, and was well pleased to execute the office of the high priesthood, and to be captain, and prince of the nation of the Jews, and of the priests, and to be chief over all. **48** And they commanded that this writing should be put in tables of brass, and that they should be set up within the compass of the sanctuary, in a conspicuous place: **49** And that a copy thereof should be put in the treasury, that Simon and his sons may have it.

Chapter 15

1 And king Antiochus the son of Demetrius sent letters from the isles of the sea to Simon the priest, and prince of the nation of the Jews, and to all the people: **2** And the contents were these: King Antiochus to Simon the high priest, and to the nation of the Jews, greeting. **3** Forasmuch as certain pestilent men have usurped the kingdom of our fathers, and my purpose is to challenge the kingdom, and to restore it to its former estate: and I have chosen a great army, and have built ships of war. **4** And I design to go through the country that I may take revenge of them that have destroyed our country, and that have made many cities desolate in my realm. **5** Now therefore I confirm unto thee all the oblations which all the kings before me remitted to thee, and what other gifts soever they remitted to thee:

6 And I give thee leave to coin thy own money in thy country: **7** And let Jerusalem be holy and free, and all the armour that hath been made, and the fortresses which thou hast built, and which thou keepest in thy hands, let them remain to thee. **8** And all that is due to the king, and what should be the king's hereafter, from this present and for ever, is forgiven thee. **9** And when we shall have recovered our kingdom, we will glorify thee, and thy nation, and the temple with great glory, so that your glory shall be made manifest in all the earth. **10** In the year one hundred and seventy-four Antiochus entered into the land of his fathers, and all the forces assembled to him, so that few were left with Tryphon.

11 And king Antiochus pursued after him, and he fled along by the sea coast and came to Dora. **12** For he perceived that evils were gathered together upon him, and his troops had forsaken him. **13** And Antiochus camped above Dora with a hundred and twenty thousand men of war, and eight thousand horsemen: **14** And he invested the city, and the ships drew near by sea: and they annoyed the city by land, and by sea, and suffered none to come in, or to go out. **15** And Numenius, and they that had been with him, came from the city of Rome, having letters written to the kings, and countries, the contents whereof were these:

16 Lucius the consul of the Romans, to king Ptolemee [brother and successor to the former], greeting. **17** The ambassadors of the Jews our friends came to us, to renew the former friendship and alliance, being sent from Simon the high priest, and the people of the Jews. **18** And they brought also a shield of gold of a thousand pounds. **19** It hath seemed good therefore to us to write to the kings, and countries, that they should do them no harm, nor fight against them, their cities, or countries: and that they should give no aid to them that fight against them. **20** And it hath seemed good to us to receive the shield of them.

21 If therefore any pestilent men are fled out of their country to you, deliver them to Simon the high priest, that he may punish them according to their law. **22** These same things were written to king Demetrius, and to Attalus, and to Ariarathes, and to Arsaces, **23** And to all the countries; and to Lampsacus, and to the Spartans, and to Delus, and Myndus, and Sicyon, and Caria, and Samus, and Pamphylia, and Lycia, and Alicarnassus, and Cos, and

Side, and Aradus, and Rhodes, and Phaselis, and Gortyna, and Gnidus, and Cyprus, and Cyrene. **24** And they wrote a copy thereof to Simon the high priest, and to the people of the Jews. **25** But king Antiochus moved his camp to Dora the second time, assaulting it continually, and making engines: and shut up Tryphon, that he could not go out.

26 And Simon sent to him two thousand chosen men to aid him, silver also, and gold, and abundance of furniture. **27** And he would not receive them, but broke all the covenant that he had made with him before, and alienated himself from him. **28** And he sent to him Athenobius one of his friends, to treat with him, saying: You hold Joppe, and Gazara, and the castle that is in Jerusalem, which are cities of my kingdom: **29** Their borders you have wasted, and you have made great havock in the land, and have got the dominion of many places in my kingdom. **30** Now therefore deliver up the cities that you have taken, and the tributes of the places whereof you have gotten the dominion without the borders of Judea.

31 But if not, give me for them five hundred talents of silver, and for the havock that you have made, and the tributes of the cities other five hundred talents: or else we will come and fight against you. **32** So Athenobius the king's friend came to Jerusalem, and saw the glory of Simon and his magnificence in gold, and silver, and his great equipage, and he was astonished, and told him the king's words. **33** And Simon answered him, and said to him: We have neither taken other men's land, neither do we hold that which is other men's: but the inheritance of our fathers, which was for some time unjustly possessed by our enemies. **34** But we having opportunity claim the inheritance of our fathers. **35** And as to thy complaints concerning Joppe and Gazara, they did great harm to the people, and to our country: yet for these we will give a hundred talents. And Athenobius answered him not a word:

36 But returning in a rage to the king, made report to him of these words, and of the glory of Simon, and of all that he had seen, and the king was exceeding angry. **37** And Tryphon fled away by ship to Orthosias. **38** And the king appointed Cendebeus captain of the sea coast, and gave him an army of footmen and horsemen. **39** And he commanded him to march with his army towards Judea: and he commanded him to build up Gedor, and to fortify the gates of the city, and to war against the people. But the king himself pursued after Tryphon. **40** And Cendebeus came to Jamnia, and began to provoke the people, and to ravage Judea, and to take the people prisoners, and to kill, and to build Gedor.

41 And he placed there horsemen, and an army: that they might issue forth, and make incursions upon the ways of Judea, as the king had commanded him.

Chapter 16

1 Then John [surnamed Hircanus] came up from Gazara, and told Simon his father what Cendebeus had done against their people. **2** And Simon called his two eldest sons, Judas and John, and said to them: I and my brethren, and my father's house, have fought against the enemies of Israel from our youth even to this day: and things have prospered so well in our hands that we have delivered Israel oftentimes. **3** And now I am old, but be you instead of me, and my brethren, and go out, and fight for our nation: and the help from heaven be with you. **4** Then he chose out of the country twenty thousand fighting men, and horsemen, and they went forth against Cendebeus: and they rested in Modin. **5** And they arose in the morning, and went into the plain: and behold a very great army of footmen and horsemen came against them, and there was a running river between them.

6 And he and his people pitched their camp over against them, and he saw that the people were afraid to go over the river, so he went over first: then the men seeing him, passed over after him. **7** And he divided the people, and set the horsemen in the midst of the footmen: but the horsemen of the enemies were very numerous. **8** And they sounded the holy trumpets: and Cendebeus and his army were put to flight: and there fell many of them wounded, and the rest fled into the strong hold. **9** At that time Judas John's brother was wounded: but John pursued after them, till he came to Cedron, which he had built: **10** And they fled even to the towers that were in the fields of Azotus, and he burnt them with fire. And there fell of them two thousand men, and he returned into Judea in peace.

11 Now Ptolemee the son of Abobus was appointed captain in the plain of Jericho, and he had abundance of silver and gold, **12** For he was son in law of the high priest. **13** And his heart was lifted up, and he designed to make himself master of the country, and he purposed treachery against Simon, and his sons, to destroy them. **14** Now Simon, as he was going through the cities that were in the country of Judea, and taking care for the good ordering of them, went down to Jericho, he and Mathathias and Judas his sons, in the year one hundred and seventy-seven, the eleventh month: the same is the month Sabath. **15** And the son of Abobus received them deceitfully into a little fortress, that is called Doch which he had built: and he made them a great feast, and hid men there.

16 And when Simon and his sons had drunk plentifully, Ptolemee and his men rose up and took their weapons, and entered into the banqueting place, and slew him, and his two sons, and some of his servants. **17** And he committed a great treachery in Israel, and rendered evil for good. **18** And Ptolemee wrote these things and sent to the king that he should send him an army to aid him, and he would deliver him the country, and their cities, and tributes. **19** And he sent others to Gazara to kill John: and to the tribunes he sent letters to come to him, and that he would give them silver, and gold, and gifts. **20** And he sent others to take Jerusalem, and the mountain of the temple.

21 Now one running before, told John in Gazara, that his father and his brethren were slain, and that he hath sent men to kill thee also. **22** But when he heard it he was exceedingly afraid: and he apprehended the men that came to kill him, and he put them to death: for he knew that they sought to take him away. **23** And as concerning the rest of the acts of John, and his wars, and the worthy deeds, which he bravely achieved, and the building of the walls, which he made, and the things that he did: **24** Behold these are written in the book of the days of his priesthood, from the time he was made high priest after his father.

THE SECOND BOOK OF MACHABEES

Chapter 1

1 To the brethren the Jews that are throughout Egypt, the brethren, the Jews that are in Jerusalem, and in the land of Judea, send health, and good peace. **2** May God be gracious to you, and remember his covenant that he made with Abraham, and Isaac, and Jacob, his faithful servants: **3** And give you all a heart to worship him, and to do his will with a great heart, and a willing mind. **4** May he open your heart in his law, and in his commandments, and send you peace. **5** May he hear your prayers, and be reconciled unto you, and never forsake you in the evil time.

6 And now here we are praying for you. **7** When Demetrius reigned, in the year one hundred and sixty-nine, we Jews wrote to you, in the trouble, and violence, that came upon us in those years, after Jason withdrew himself from the holy land, and from the kingdom. **8** They burnt the gate, and shed innocent blood: then we prayed to the Lord, and were heard, and we offered sacrifices, and fine flour, and lighted the lamps, and set forth the loaves. **9** And now celebrate ye the days of Scenopegia [feast of tabernacles] in the month of Casleu. **10** In the year one hundred and eighty-eight, the people that is at Jerusalem, and in Judea, and the senate, and Judas, to Aristobolus, the preceptor of king Ptolemee, who is of the stock of the anointed priests, and to the Jews that are in Egypt, health and welfare.

11 Having been delivered by God out of great dangers, we give him great thanks, forasmuch as we have been in war with such a king. **12** For he made numbers of men swarm out of Persia that have fought against us, and the holy city. **13** For when the leader himself was in Persia, and with him a very great army, he fell in the temple of Nanea, being deceived by the counsel of the priests of Nanea. **14** For Antiochus, with his friends, came to the place as though he would marry her, and that he might receive great sums of money under the title of a dowry. **15** And when the priests of Nanea had set it forth, and he with a small company had entered into the compass of the temple, they shut the temple,

16 When Antiochus was come in: and opening a secret entrance of the temple, they cast stones and slew the leader, and them that were with him, and hewed them in pieces, and cutting off their heads they threw them forth. **17** Blessed be God in all things, who hath delivered up the wicked. **18** Therefore whereas we purpose to keep the purification of the temple on the five and twentieth day of the month of Casleu, we thought it necessary to signify it to you: that you also may keep the day of Scenopegia, and the day of the fire, that was given when Nehemias offered sacrifice, after the temple and the altar was built. **19** For when our fathers were led into Persia, the priests that then were worshippers of God took privately the fire from the altar, and hid it in a valley where there was a deep pit without water, and there they kept it safe, so that the place was unknown to all men. **20** But when many years had passed, and it pleased God that Nehemias should be sent by the king of Persia, he sent some of the posterity of those priests that had hid it, to seek for the fire: and as they told us, they found no fire, but thick water.

21 Then he bade them draw it up, and bring it to him: and the priest Nehemias commanded the sacrifices that were laid on, to be sprinkled with the same water, both the wood, and the things that were laid upon it. **22** And when this was done, and the time came that the sun shone out, which before was in a cloud, there was a great fire kindled, so that all wondered. **23** And all the priests made prayer, while the sacrifice was consuming, Jonathan beginning, and the rest answering. **24** And the prayer of Nehemias was after this manner: O Lord God, Creator of all things, dreadful and strong, just and merciful, who alone art the good king, **25** Who alone art gracious, who alone art just, and almighty, and eternal, who deliverest Israel from all evil, who didst choose the fathers and didst sanctify them:

26 Receive the sacrifice for all thy people Israel, and preserve thy own portion, and sanctify it. **27** Gather together our scattered people, deliver them that are slaves to the Gentiles, and look upon them that are despised and abhorred: that the Gentiles may know that thou art our God. **28** Punish them that oppress us, and that treat us injuriously with pride. **29** Establish thy people in thy holy place, as Moses hath spoken. **30** And the priests sung hymns till the sacrifice was consumed.

31 And when the sacrifice was consumed, Nehemias commanded the water that was left to be poured out upon the great stones. **32** Which being done, there was kindled a flame from them: but it was consumed by the light that shined from the altar. **33** And when this matter became public, it was told to the king of Persia, that in the place where the priests that were led away, had hid the fire, there appeared water, with which Nehemias and they that were with him had purified the sacrifices. **34** And the king considering, and diligently examining the matter, made a temple for it, that he might prove what had happened. **35** And when he had proved it, he gave the priests many goods, and divers presents, and he took and distributed them to them with his own hand.

36 And Nehemias called this place Nephthar, which is interpreted purification. But many call it Nephi.

Chapter 2

1 Now it is found in the descriptions of Jeremias the prophet, that he commanded them that went into captivity, to take the fire, as it hath been signified, and how he gave charge to them that were carried away into captivity. **2** And how he gave them the law that they should not forget the commandments of the Lord, and that they should not err in their minds, seeing the idols of gold, and silver, and the ornaments of them. **3** And with other such like speeches, he exhorted them that they would not remove the law from their heart. **4** It was also contained in the same writing, how the prophet, being warned by God, commanded that the tabernacle and the ark should accompany him, till he came forth to the mountain where Moses went up, and saw the inheritance of God. **5** And when Jeremias came thither he found a hollow cave: and he carried in thither the tabernacle, and the ark, and the altar of incense, and so stopped the door.

6 Then some of them that followed him, came up to mark the place: but they could not find it. **7** And when Jeremias perceived it, he blamed them, saying: The place shall be unknown, till God gather together the congregation of the people, and receive them to mercy. **8** And then the Lord will shew these things, and the majesty of the Lord shall appear, and there shall be a cloud as it was also shewed to Moses, and he shewed it when Solomon prayed that the place might be sanctified to the great God. **9** For he treated wisdom in a magnificent manner: and like a wise man, he offered the sacrifice of the dedication, and of the finishing of the temple. **10** And as Moses prayed to the Lord and fire came down from heaven, and consumed the holocaust: so Solomon also prayed, and fire came down from heaven and consumed the holocaust.

11 And Moses said: Because the sin offering was not eaten, it was consumed. **12** So Solomon also celebrated the dedication eight days. **13** And these same things were set down in the memoirs and commentaries of Nehemias: and how he made a library, and gathered together out of the countries, the books both of the prophets, and of David, and the epistles of the kings, and concerning the holy gifts. **14** And in like manner Judas also gathered together all such things as were lost by the war we had, and they are in our possession. **15** Wherefore if you want these things, send some that may fetch them to you.

16 As we are then about to celebrate the purification, we have written unto you: and you shall do well, if you keep the same days. **17** And we hope that God who hath delivered his people, and hath rendered to all the inheritance, and the kingdom, and the priesthood, and the sanctuary, **18** As he promised in the law, will shortly have mercy upon us, and will gather us together from every land under heaven into the holy place. **19** For he hath delivered us out of great perils, and hath cleansed the place. **20** Now as concerning Judas Machabeus. and his brethren, and the purification of the great temple, and the dedication of the altar:

21 As also the wars against Antiochus the Illustrious, and his son Eupator: **22** And the manifestations that came from heaven to them, that behaved themselves manfully on the behalf of the Jews, so that, being but a few, they made themselves masters of the whole country, and put to flight; the barbarous multitude: **23** And recovered again the most renowned temple in all the world, and delivered the city, and restored the laws that were abolished, the Lord with all clemency shewing mercy to them. **24** And all such things as have been comprised in five books by Jason of Cyrene, we have attempted to abridge in one book. **25** For considering the multitude of books, and the difficulty that they find that desire to undertake the narrations of histories, because of the multitude of the matter,

26 We have taken care for those indeed that are willing to read, that it might be a pleasure of mind: and for the studious, that they may more easily commit to memory: and that all that read might receive profit. **27** And as to ourselves indeed, in undertaking this work of abridging, we have taken in hand no easy task, yea rather a business full of watching and sweat. **28** But as they that prepare a feast, and seek to satisfy the will of others: for the sake of many, we willingly undergo the labour. **29** Leaving to the authors the exact handling of every particular, and as for ourselves, according to the plan proposed, studying to be brief. **30** For as the master builder of a new house must have care of the whole building: but he that taketh care to paint it, must seek out fit things for the adorning of it: so must it be judged for us.

31 For to collect all that is to be known, to put the discourse in order, and curiously to discuss every particular point, is the duty of the author of a history: **32** But to pursue brevity of speech, and to avoid nice declarations of things, is to be granted to him that maketh an abridgment. **33** Here then we will begin the narration: let this be enough by way of a preface: for it is a foolish thing to make a long prologue, and to be short in the story itself.

Chapter 3

1 Therefore when the holy city was inhabited with all peace, and the laws as yet were very well kept, because of the godliness of Onias the high priest, and the hatred his soul had of evil, **2** It came to pass that even the kings themselves, and the princes esteemed the place worthy of the highest honour, and glorified the temple with very great gifts: **3** So that Seleucus king of Asia allowed out of his revenues all the charges belonging to the ministry of the sacrifices. **4** But one Simon of the tribe of Benjamin, who was appointed overseer of the temple, strove in opposition to the high priest, to bring about some unjust thing in the city. **5** And when he could not overcome Onias he went to Apollonius the son of Tharseas, who at that time was governor of Celesyria and Phenicia:

6 And told him, that the treasury in Jerusalem was full of immense sums of money, and the common store was infinite, which did not belong to the account of the sacrifices: and that it was possible to bring all into the king's hands. **7** Now when Apollonius had given the king notice concerning the money that he was told of, he called for Heliodorus, who had the charge over his affairs, and sent him with commission to bring him the foresaid money. **8** So Heliodorus forthwith began his journey, under a colour of visiting the cities of Celesyria and Phenicia, but indeed to fulfill the king's purpose. **9** And when he was come to Jerusalem, and had been courteously received in the city by the high priest, he told him what information had been given concerning the money: and declared the cause for which he was come: and asked if these things were so indeed. **10** Then the high priest told him that these were sums deposited, and provisions for the subsistence of the widows and the fatherless.

11 And that some part of that which wicked Simon had given intelligence of, belonged to Hircanus son of Tobias, a man of great dignity: and that the whole was four hundred talents of silver, and two hundred of gold: **12** But that to deceive them who had trusted to the place and temple which is honoured throughout the whole world, for the reverence and holiness of it, was a thing which could not by any means be done. **13** But he, by reason of the orders he had received from the king, said that by all means the money must be carried to the king. **14** So on the day he had appointed, Heliodorus entered in to order this matter. But there was no small terror throughout the whole city. **15** And the priests prostrated themselves before the altar in their priests' vestments, and called upon him from heaven, who made the law concerning things given to be kept, that he would preserve them safe, for them that had deposited them.

16 Now whosoever saw the countenance of the high priest, was wounded in heart: for his face, and the changing of his colour declared the inward sorrow of his mind. **17** For the man was so compassed with sadness and horror of the body, that it was manifest to them that beheld him, what sorrow he had in his heart. **18** Others also came flocking together out of their houses, praying and making public supplication, because the place was like to come into contempt. **19** And the women, girded with haircloth about their breasts, came together in the streets. And the virgins also that were shut up, came forth, some to Onias, and some to the walls, and others looked out of the windows. **20** And all holding up their hands towards heaven, made supplication.

21 For the expectation of the mixed multitude, and of the high priest who was in an agony, would have moved any one to pity. **22** And these indeed called upon almighty God, to preserve the things that had been committed to them, safe and sure for those that had committed them. **23** But Heliodorus executed that which he had resolved on, himself being present in the same place with his guard about the treasury. **24** But the spirit of the almighty God gave a great evidence of his presence, so that all that had presumed to obey him, falling down by the power of God, were struck with fainting and dread. **25** For there appeared to them a horse with a terrible rider upon him, adorned with a very rich covering: and he ran fiercely and struck Heliodorus with his fore feet, and he that sat upon him seemed to have armour of gold.

26 Moreover there appeared two other young men beautiful and strong, bright and glorious, and in comely apparel: who stood by him, on either side, and scourged him without ceasing with many stripes. **27** And Heliodorus suddenly fell to the ground, and they took him up covered with great darkness, and having put him into a litter they carried him out. **28** So he that came with many servants, and all his guard into the aforesaid treasury, was carried out, no one being able to help him, the manifest power of God being known. **29** And he indeed by the power of God lay speechless, and without all hope of recovery. **30** But they praised the Lord because he had glorified his place: and the temple, that a little before was full of fear and trouble, when the almighty Lord appeared, was filled with joy and gladness.

31 Then some of the friends of Heliodorus forthwith begged of Onias, that he would call upon the most High to grant him his life, who was ready to give up the ghost. **32** So the high priest considering that the king might perhaps suspect that some mischief had been done to Heliodorus by the Jews, offered a sacrifice of health for the recovery of the man. **33** And when the high priest was praying, the same young men in the same clothing stood by

Heliodorus, and said to him: Give thanks to Onias the priest: because for his sake the Lord hath granted thee life. **34** And thou having been scourged by God, declare unto all men the great works and the power of God. And having spoken thus, they appeared no more. **35** So Heliodorus after he had offered a sacrifice to God, and made great vows to him, that had granted him life, and given thanks to Onias, taking his troops with him, returned to the king.

36 And he testified to all men the works of the great God, which he had seen with his own eyes. **37** And when the king asked Heliodorus, who might be a fit man to be sent yet once more to Jerusalem, he said: **38** If thou hast any enemy or traitor to thy kingdom, send him thither, and thou shalt receive him again scourged, if so be he escape: for there is undoubtedly in that place a certain power of God. **39** For he that hath his dwelling in the heavens, is the visitor, and protector of that place, and he striketh and destroyeth them that come to do evil to it. **40** And the things concerning Heliodorus, and the keeping of the treasury fell out in this manner.

Chapter 4

1 But Simon, of whom we spoke before, and of his country, spoke ill of Onias, as though he had incited Heliodorus to do these things, and had been the promoter of evils: **2** And he presumed to call him a traitor to the kingdom, who provided for the city, and defended his nation, and was zealous for the law of God. **3** But when the enmities proceeded so far, that murders also were committed by some of Simon's friends: **4** Onias considering the danger of this contention, and that Apollonius, who was the governor of Celesyria and Phenicia, was outrageous, which increased the malice of Simon, went to the king, **5** Not to be an accuser of his countrymen, but with a view to the common good of all the people.

6 For he saw that, except the king took care, it was impossible that matters should be settled in peace, or that Simon would cease from his folly. **7** But after the death of Seleucus, when Antiochus, who was called the Illustrious, had taken possession of the kingdom, Jason the brother of Onias ambitiously sought the high priesthood: **8** And went to the king, promising him three hundred and sixty talents of silver, and out of other revenues fourscore talents. **9** Besides this he promised also a hundred and fifty more, if he might have license to set him up a place for exercise, and a place for youth, and to entitle them, that were at Jerusalem, Antiochians. **10** Which when the king had granted, and he had gotten the rule into his hands, forthwith he began to bring over his countrymen to the fashion of the heathens.

11 And abolishing those things, which had been decreed of special favour by the kings in behalf of the Jews, by the means of John the father of that Eupolemus, who went ambassador to Rome to make amity and alliance, he disannulled the lawful ordinances of the citizens, and brought in fashions that were perverse. **12** For he had the boldness to set up, under the very castle, a place of exercise, and to put all the choicest youths in brothel houses. **13** Now this was not the beginning, but an increase, and progress of heathenish and foreign manners, through the abominable and unheard of wickedness of Jason, that impious wretch and no priest. **14** Insomuch that the priests were not now occupied about the offices of the altar, but despising the temple and neglecting the sacrifices, hastened to be partakers of the games, and of the unlawful allowance thereof, and of the exercise of the discus. **15** And setting nought by the honours of their fathers, they esteemed the Grecian glories for the best:

16 For the sake of which they incurred a dangerous contention, and followed earnestly their ordinances, and in all things they coveted to be like them, who were their enemies and murderers. **17** For acting wickedly against the laws of God doth not pass unpunished: but this the time following will declare. **18** Now when the game that was used every fifth year was kept at Tyre, the king being present, **19** The wicked Jason sent from Jerusalem sinful men to carry three hundred didrachmas of silver for the sacrifice of Hercules; but the bearers thereof desired it might not be bestowed on the sacrifices, because it was not necessary, but might be deputed for other charges. **20** So the money was appointed by him that sent it to the sacrifice of Hercules: but because of them that carried it was employed for the making of galleys.

21 Now when Apollonius the son of Mnestheus was sent into Egypt to treat with the nobles of king Philometor, and Antiochus understood that he was wholly excluded from the affairs of the kingdom, consulting his own interest, he departed thence and came to Joppe, and from thence to Jerusalem: **22** Where he was received in a, magnificent manner by Jason, and the city, and came in with torch lights, and with praises, and from thence he returned with his army into Phenicia. **23** Three years afterwards Jason sent Menelaus, brother of the aforesaid Simon, to carry money to the king, and to bring answers from him concerning certain necessary affairs. **24** But he being recommended to the king, when he had magnified the appearance of his power, got the high priesthood for himself, by offering more than Jason by three hundred talents of silver. **25** So having received the king's mandate, he returned bringing nothing worthy of the high priesthood: but having the mind of a cruel tyrant, and the rage of a savage beast.

26 Then Jason, who had undermined his own brother, being himself undermined, was driven out a fugitive into the country of the Ammonites. **27** So Menelaus got the principality: but as for the money he had promised to the king he took no care, when Sostratus the governor of the castle called for it. **28** For to him appertained the gathering of the taxes: wherefore they were both called before the king. **29** And Menelaus was removed from the priesthood, Lysimachus his brother succeeding: and Sostratus was made governor of the Cyprians. **30** When these things were in doing, it fell out that they of Tharsus and Mallos raised a sedition, because they were given for a gift to Antiochis, the king's concubine.

31 The king therefore went in all haste to appease them, leaving Andronicus, one of his nobles, for his deputy. **32** Then Menelaus supposing that he had found a convenient time, having stolen certain vessels of gold out of the temple, gave them to Andronicus, and others he had sold at Tyre, and in the neighbouring cities. **33** Which when Onias understood most certainly, he reproved him, keeping himself in a safe place at Antioch beside Daphne. **34** Whereupon Menelaus coming to Andronicus, desired him to kill Onias. And he went to Onias, and gave him his right hand with an oath, and (though he were suspected by him) persuaded him to come forth out of the sanctuary, and immediately slew him, without any regard to justice. **35** For which cause not only the Jews, but also the other nations, conceived indignation, and were much grieved for the unjust murder of so great a man.

36 And when the king was come back from the places of Cilicia, the Jews that were at Antioch, and also the Greeks went to him: complaining of the unjust murder of Onias. **37** Antiochus therefore was grieved in his mind for Onias, and being moved to pity, shed tears, remembering the sobriety and modesty of the deceased. **38** And being inflamed to anger, he commanded Andronicus to be stripped of his purple, and to be led about through all the city: and that in the same place wherein he had committed the impiety against Onias, the sacrilegious wretch should be put to death, the Lord repaying him his deserved punishment. **39** Now when many sacrileges had been committed by Lysimachus in the temple by the counsel of Menelaus, and the rumour of it was spread abroad, the multitude gathered themselves together against Lysimachus, a great quantity of gold being already carried away. **40** Wherefore the multitude making an insurrection, and their minds being filled with anger, Lysimachus armed about three thousand men, and began to use violence, one Tyrannus being captain, a man far gone both in age, and in madness.

41 But when they perceived the attempt of Lysimachus, some caught up stones, some strong clubs: and some threw ashes upon Lysimachus, **42** And many of them were wounded, and some struck down to the ground, but all were put to flight: and as for the sacrilegious fellow himself, they slew him beside the treasury. **43** Now concerning these matters, an accusation was laid against Menelaus. **44** And when the king was come to Tyre, three men were sent from the ancients to plead the cause before him. **45** But Menelaus being convicted, promised Ptolemee [son of Dorymenus] to give him much money to persuade the king to favour him.

46 So Ptolemee went to the king in a certain court where he was, as it were to cool himself, and brought him to be of another mind: **47** So Menelaus who was guilty of all the evil, was acquitted by him of the accusations: and those poor men, who, if they had pleaded their cause even before Scythians, should have been judged innocent, were condemned to death. **48** Thus they that prosecuted the cause for the city, and for the people, and the sacred vessels, did soon suffer unjust punishment. **49** Wherefore even the Tyrians being moved with indignation, were liberal towards their burial. **50** And so through the covetousness of them that were in power, Menelaus continued in authority, increasing in malice to the betraying of the citizens.

Chapter 5

1 At the same time Antiochus prepared for a second journey into Egypt. **2** And it came to pass that through the whole city of Jerusalem for the space of forty days there were seen horsemen running in the air, in gilded raiment, and armed with spears, like bands of soldiers. **3** And horses set in order by ranks, running one against another, with the shakings of shields, and a multitude of men in helmets, with drawn swords, and casting of darts, and glittering of golden armour, and of harnesses of all sorts. **4** Wherefore all men prayed that these prodigies might turn to good. **5** Now when there was gone forth a false rumour, as though Antiochus had been dead, Jason taking with him no fewer than a thousand men, suddenly assaulted the city: and though the citizens ran together to the wall, the city at length was taken, and Menelaus fled into the castle.

6 But Jason slew his countrymen without mercy, not considering that prosperity against one's own kindred is a very great evil, thinking they had been enemies, and not citizens, whom he conquered. **7** Yet he did not get the principality, but received confusion at the end, for the reward of his treachery, and fled again into the country of the Ammonites. **8** At the last having been shut up by Aretas the king of the Arabians, in order for his destruction, flying from city to city, hated by all men, as a forsaker of the laws, and execrable, as an enemy of his country and countrymen, he was thrust out into Egypt: **9** And he that had driven many out of their country, perished in a strange land, going to Lacedemon, as if for kindred sake he should have refuge there: **10** But he that had cast out many unburied, was himself cast forth both unlamented and unburied, neither having foreign burial, nor being partaker of the sepulchre of his fathers.

11 Now when these things were done, the king suspected that the Jews would forsake the alliance: whereupon departing out of Egypt with a furious mind, he took the city by force of arms. **12** And commanded the soldiers to kill, and not to spare any that came in their way, and to go up into the houses to slay. **13** Thus there was a slaughter of young and old, a destruction of women and children, and killing of virgins and infants. **14** And there were slain in the space of three whole days fourscore thousand, forty thousand were made prisoners, and as many sold. **15** But this was not enough; he presumed also to enter into the temple, the most holy in all the world, Menelaus, that traitor to the laws, and to his country, being his guide.

16 And taking in his wicked hands the holy vessels, which were given by other kings and cities, for the ornament and the glory of the place, he unworthily handled and profaned them. **17** Thus Antiochus going astray in mind, did not consider that God was angry for a while, because of the sins of the inhabitants of the city: and therefore this contempt had happened to the place: **18** Otherwise had they not been involved in many sins, as Heliodorus, who was sent by king Seleucus to rob the treasury, so this man also, as soon as he had come, had been forthwith scourged, and put back from his presumption. **19** But God did not choose the people for the place's sake, but the place for the people's sake. **20** And therefore the place also itself was made partaker of the evils of the people: but afterward shall communicate in the good things thereof, and as it was forsaken in the wrath of almighty God, shall be exalted again with great glory, when the great Lord shall be reconciled.

21 So when Antiochus had taken away out of the temple a thousand and eight hundred talents, he went back in all haste to Antioch, thinking through pride, that he might now make the land navigable, and the sea passable on foot: such was the haughtiness of his mind. **22** He left also governors to afflict the people: at Jerusalem, Philip, a Phrygian by birth, but in manners more barbarous than he that set him there: **23** And in Gazarim, Andronicus and Menelaus, who bore a more heavy hand upon the citizens than the rest. **24** And whereas he was set against the Jews, he sent that hateful prince Apollonius with an army of two and twenty thousand men, commanding him to kill all that were of perfect age, and to sell the women and the younger sort. **25** Who when he was come to Jerusalem, pretending peace, rested till the holy day of the sabbath: and then the Jews keeping holiday, he commanded his men to take arms.

26 And he slew all that were come forth to see: and running through the city with armed men, he destroyed a very great multitude. **27** But Judas Machabeus, who was the tenth, had withdrawn himself into a desert place, and there lived amongst wild beasts in the mountains with his company: and they continued feeding on herbs, that they might not be partakers of the pollution.

Chapter 6

1 But not long after the king sent a certain old man of Antioch, to compel the Jews to depart from the laws of their fathers and of God: **2** And to defile the temple that was in Jerusalem, and to call it the temple of Jupiter Olympius: and that in Gazarim of Jupiter Hospitalis, according as they were that inhabited the place. **3** And very bad was this invasion of evils and grievous to all. **4** For the temple was full of the riot and revellings of the Gentiles: and of men lying with lewd women. And women thrust themselves of their accord into the holy places, and brought in things that were not lawful. **5** The altar also was filled with unlawful things, which were forbidden by the laws.

6 And neither were the sabbaths kept, nor the solemn days of the fathers observed, neither did any man plainly profess himself to be a Jew. **7** But they were led by bitter constraint on the king's birthday to the sacrifices: and when the feast of Bacchus was kept, they were compelled to go about crowned with ivy in honour of Bacchus. **8** And there went out a decree into the neighbouring cities of the Gentiles, by the suggestion of the Ptolemeans, that they also should act in like manner against the Jews, to oblige them to sacrifice: **9** And whosoever would not conform themselves to the ways of the Gentiles, should be put to death: then was misery to be seen. **10** For two women were accused to have circumcised their children: whom, when they had openly led about through the city with the infants hanging at their breasts, they threw down headlong from the walls.

11 And others that had met together in caves that were near, and were keeping the sabbath day privately, being discovered by Philip [governor of Jerusalem], were burnt with fire, because they made a conscience to help themselves with their hands, by reason of the religious observance of the day. **12** Now I beseech those that shall read this book, that they be not shocked at these calamities, but that they consider the things that happened, not as being for the destruction, but for the correction of our nation. **13** For it is a token of great goodness when sinners are not suffered to go on in their ways for a long time, but are presently punished. **14** For, not as with other nations (whom the Lord patiently expecteth, that when the day of judgment shall come, he may punish them in the fulness of their sins:) **15** Doth he also deal with us, so as to suffer our sins to come to their height, and then take vengeance on us.

16 And therefore he never withdraweth his mercy from us: but though he chastise his people with adversity, he forsaketh them not. **17** But let this suffice in a few words for a warning to the readers. And now we must come to the narration. **18** Eleazar one of the chief of the scribes, a man advanced in years, and of a comely countenance, was pressed to open his mouth to eat swine's flesh. **19** But he, choosing rather a most glorious death than a hateful life, went forward voluntarily to the torment. **20** And considering in what manner he was come to it, patiently bearing, he determined not to do any unlawful things for the love of life.

21 But they that stood by, being moved with wicked pity, for the old friendship they had with the man, taking him aside, desired that flesh might be brought, which it was lawful for him to eat, that he might make as if he had eaten, as the king had commanded of the flesh of the sacrifice: **22** That by so doing he might be delivered from death: and for the sake of their old friendship with the man they did him this courtesy. **23** But he began to consider the dignity of his age, and his ancient years, and the inbred honour of his grey head, and his good life and conversation from a child: and he answered without delay, according to the ordinances of the holy law made by God, saying, that he would rather be sent into the other world. **24** For it doth not become our age, said he, to dissemble: whereby many young persons might think that Eleazar, at the age of fourscore and ten years, was gone over to the life of the heathens: **25** And so they, through my dissimulation, and for a little time of a corruptible life, should be deceived, and hereby I should bring a stain and a curse upon my old age.

26 For though, for the present time, I should be delivered from the punishments of men, yet should I not escape the hand of the Almighty neither alive nor dead. **27** Wherefore by departing manfully out of this life, I shall shew myself worthy of my old age: **28** And I shall leave an example of fortitude to young men, if with a ready mind and constancy I suffer an honourable death, for the most venerable and most holy laws. And having spoken thus, he was forthwith carried to execution. **29** And they that led him, and had been a little before more mild, were changed to wrath for the words he had spoken, which they thought were uttered out of arrogancy. **30** But when he was now ready to die with the stripes, he groaned, and said: O Lord, who hast the holy knowledge, thou knowest manifestly that whereas I might be delivered from death, I suffer grevious pains in body: but in soul am well content to suffer these things because I fear thee.

31 Thus did this man die, leaving not only to young men, but also to the whole nation, the memory of his death for an example of virtue and fortitude.

Chapter 7

1 It came to pass also, that seven brethren, together with their mother, were apprehended, and compelled by the king to eat swine's flesh against the law, for which end they were tormented with whips and scourges. **2** But one of them, who was the eldest, said thus: What wouldst thou ask, or learn of us? we are ready to die rather than to transgress the laws of God, received from our fathers. **3** Then the king being angry commanded frying pans, and brazen caldrons to be made hot: which forthwith being heated, **4** He commanded to cut out the tongue of him that had spoken first: and the skin of his head being drawn off, to chop off also the extremities of his hands and feet, the rest of his brethren, and his mother, looking on. **5** And when he was now maimed in all parts, he commanded him, being yet alive, to be brought to the fire, and to be fried in the frying pan: and while he was suffering therein long torments, the rest, together with the mother, exhorted one another to die manfully,

6 Saying: The Lord God will look upon the truth, and will take pleasure in us, as Moses declared in the profession of the canticle: And In his servants he will take pleasure. **7** So when the first was dead after this manner, they brought the next to make him a, mocking stock: and when they had pulled off the skin of his head with the hair, they asked him if he would eat, before he were punished throughout the whole body in every limb. **8** But he answered in his own language, and said: I will not do it. Wherefore he also in the next place, received the torments of the first: **9** And when he was at the last gasp, he said thus: Thou indeed, O most wicked man, destroyest us out of this present life: but the King of the world will raise us up, who die for his laws, in the resurrection of eternal life. **10** After him the third was made a mocking stock, and when he was required, he quickly put forth his tongue, and courageously stretched out his hands:

11 And said with confidence: These I have from heaven, but for the laws of God I now despise them: because I hope to receive them again from him. **12** So that the king, and they that were with him, wondered at the young man's courage, because he esteemed the torments as nothing. **13** And after he was thus dead, they tormented the fourth in the like manner. **14** And when he was now ready to die, he spoke thus: It is better, being put to death by men, to look for hope from God, to be raised up again by him: for, as to thee thou shalt have no resurrection unto life. **15** And when they had brought the fifth, they tormented him. But he looking upon the king,

16 Said: Whereas thou hast power among men, though thou art corruptible, thou dost what thou wilt: but think not that our nation is forsaken by God. **17** But stay patiently a while, and thou shalt see his great power, in what manner he will torment thee and thy seed. **18** After him they brought the sixth, and he being ready to die, spoke thus: Be not deceived without cause: for we suffer these things for ourselves, having sinned against our God, and things worthy of admiration are done to us: **19** But do not think that thou shalt escape unpunished, for that thou attempted to fight against God. **20** Now the mother was to be admired above measure, and worthy to be remembered by good men, who beheld seven sons slain in the space of one day, and bore it with a good courage, for the hope that she had in God:

21 And she bravely exhorted every one of them in her own language, being filled with wisdom: and joining a man's heart to a woman's thought, **22** She said to them: I know not how you were formed in my womb: for I neither gave you breath, nor soul, nor life, neither did I frame the limbs of every one of you. **23** But the Creator of the world, that formed the nativity of man, and that found out the origin of all, he will restore to you again in his mercy, both breath and life, as now you despise yourselves for the sake of his laws. **24** Now Antiochus, thinking himself despised, and withal despising the voice of the upbraider, when the youngest was yet alive, did not only exhort him by words, but also assured him with an oath, that he would make him a rich and a happy man, and, if he would turn from the laws of his fathers, would take him for a friend, and furnish him with things necessary. **25** But when the young man was not moved with these things, the king called the mother, and counselled her to deal with the young man to save his life.

26 And when he had exhorted her with many words, she promised that she would counsel her son. **27** So bending herself towards him, mocking the cruel tyrant, she said in her own language: My son, have pity upon me, that bore thee nine months in my womb, and gave thee suck three years, and nourished thee, and brought thee up unto this age. **28** I beseech thee, my son, look upon heaven and earth, and all that is in them: and consider that God made them out of nothing, and mankind also: **29** So thou shalt not fear this tormentor, but being made a worthy partner with thy brethren, receive death, that in that mercy I may receive thee again with thy brethren. **30** While she was yet speaking these words, the young man said: For whom do you stay? I will not obey the commandment of the king, but the commandment of the law, which was given us by Moses.

31 But thou that hast been the author of all mischief against the Hebrews, shalt not escape the hand of God. **32** For we suffer thus for our sins. **33** And though the Lord our God is angry with us a little while for our chastisement and correction: yet he will be reconciled again to his servants. **34** But thou, O wicked and of all men most flagitious, be not lifted up without cause with vain hopes, whilst thou art raging against his servants. **35** For thou hast not yet escaped the judgment of the almighty God, who beholdeth all things.

36 For my brethren, having now undergone a short pain, are under the covenant of eternal life: but thou by the judgment of God shalt receive just punishment for thy pride. **37** But I, like my brethren, offer up my life and my body for the laws of our fathers: calling upon God to be speedily merciful to our nation, and that thou by torments and stripes mayst confess that he alone is God. **38** But in me and in my brethren the wrath of the Almighty, which hath justly been brought upon all our nation, shall cease. **39** Then the king being incensed with anger, raged against him more cruelly than all the rest, taking it grievously that he was mocked. **40** So this man also died undefiled, wholly trusting in the Lord.

41 And last of all after the sons the mother also was consumed. **42** But now there is enough said of the sacrifices, and of the excessive cruelties.

Chapter 8

1 But Judas Machabeus, and they that were with him, went privately into the towns: and calling together their kinsmen and friends, and taking unto them such as continued in the Jews' religion, they assembled six thousand men. **2** And they called upon the Lord that he would look upon his people that was trodden down by all, and would have pity on the temple, that was defiled by the wicked: **3** That he would have pity also upon the city that was destroyed, that was ready to be made even with the ground, and would hear the voice of the blood that cried to him: **4** That he would remember also the most unjust deaths of innocent children, and the blasphemies offered to his name, and would shew his indignation on this occasion. **5** Now when Machabeus had gathered a multitude, he could not be withstood by the heathens: for the wrath of the Lord was turned into mercy.

6 So coming unawares upon the towns and cities, he set them on fire, and taking possession of the most commodious places, he made no small slaughter of the enemies, **7** And especially in the nights he went upon these expeditions, and the fame of his valour was spread abroad everywhere. **8** Then Philip, seeing that the man gained ground by little and little, and that things for the most part succeeded prosperously with him, wrote to Ptolemee the governor of Celesyria and Phenicia, to send aid to the king's affairs. **9** And he with all speed sent Nicanor the son of Patroclus, one of his special friends, giving him no fewer than twenty thousand armed men of different nations, to root out the whole race of the Jews, joining also with him Gorgias, a good soldier, and of great experience in matters of war. **10** And Nicanor purposed to raise for the king the tribute of two thousand talents, that was to be given to the Romans, by making so much money of the captive Jews:

11 Wherefore he sent immediately to the cities upon the sea coast, to invite men together to buy up the Jewish slaves, promising that they should have ninety slaves for one talent, not reflecting on the vengeance, which was to follow him from the Almighty. **12** Now when Judas found that Nicanor was coming, he imparted to the Jews that were with him, that the enemy was at hand. **13** And some of them being afraid, and distrusting the justice of God, fled away: **14** Others sold all that they had left, and withal besought the Lord, that he would deliver them from the wicked Nicanor, who had sold them before he came near them: **15** And if not for their sakes, yet for the covenant that he had made with their fathers, and for the sake of his holy and glorious name that was invoked upon them.

16 But Machabeus calling together seven thousand that were with him, exhorted them not to be reconciled to the enemies, nor to fear the multitude of the enemies who came wrongfully against them, but to fight manfully: **17** Setting before their eyes the injury they had unjustly done the holy place, and also the injury they had done to the city, which had been shamefully abused, besides their destroying the ordinances of the fathers. **18** For, said he, they trust in their weapons, and in their boldness: but we trust in the Almighty Lord, who at a beck can utterly destroy both them that come against us, and the whole world. **19** Moreover he put them in mind also of the helps their fathers had received from God: and how under Sennacherib a hundred and eighty-five thousand had been destroyed. **20** And of the battle that they had fought against the Galatians in Babylonia, how they, being in all but six thousand, when it came to the point, and the Macedonians their companions were a stand, slew a hundred and twenty thousand, because of the help they had from heaven, and for this they received many favours.

21 With these words they were greatly encouraged, and disposed even to die for the laws and their country. **22** So he appointed his brethren captains over each division of his army, Simon, and Joseph, and Jonathan, giving to each one fifteen hundred men. **23** And after the holy Book had been read to them by Esdras, and he had given them for a watchword, The help of God: himself leading the first band, he joined battle with Nicanor: **24** And the Almighty being their helper, they slew above nine thousand men: and having wounded and disabled the greater part of Nicanor's army, they obliged them to fly. **25** And they took the money of them that came to buy them, and they pursued them on every side.

26 But they came back for want of time: for it was the day before the sabbath: and therefore they did not continue the pursuit. **27** But when they had gathered together their arms and their spoils, they kept the sabbath: blessing the Lord who had delivered them that day, distilling the beginning of mercy upon them. **28** Then after the sabbath they divided the spoils to the feeble and the orphans, and the widows: and the rest they took for themselves and their servants. **29** When this was done, and they had all made a common supplication, they besought the merciful Lord to be reconciled to his servants unto the end. **30** Moreover they slew above twenty thousand of them that were with Timotheus and Bacchides who fought them, and they made themselves masters of the high strong holds: and they divided amongst them many spoils, giving equal portions to the feeble, the fatherless and the widows, yea and the aged also.

31 And when they had carefully gathered together their arms, they laid them all up in convenient places, and the residue of their spoils they carried to Jerusalem: **32** They slew also Philarches who was with Timotheus, a wicked man, who had many ways afflicted the Jews. **33** And when they kept the feast of the victory at Jerusalem, they burnt Callisthenes, that had set fire to the holy gates, who had taken refuge in a certain house, rendering to him a worthy reward for his impieties: **34** But as for that most wicked man Nicanor, who had brought a thousand merchants to the sale of the Jews, **35** Being through the help of the Lord brought down by them, of whom he had made no account, laying; aside his garment of glory, fleeing through the midland country, he came alone to Antioch, being rendered very unhappy by the destruction of his army.

36 And he that had promised to levy the tribute for the Romans by the means of the captives of Jerusalem, now professed that the Jews had God for their protector, and therefore they could not be hurt, because they followed the laws appointed by him.

Chapter 9

1 At that time Antiochus returned with dishonour out of

Persia. **2** For he had entered into the city called Persepolis [Elymais], and attempted to rob the temple, and to oppress the city: but the multitude running together to arms, put them to flight: and so it fell out that Antiochus being put to flight returned with disgrace. **3** Now when he was come about Ecbatana, he received the news of what had happened to Nicanor and Timotheus. **4** And swelling with anger he thought to revenge upon the Jews the injury done by them that had put him to flight. And therefore he commanded his chariot to be driven, without stopping in his journey, the judgment of heaven urging him forward, because he had spoken so proudly, that he would come to Jerusalem, and make it a common burying place of the Jews. **5** But the Lord the God of Israel, that seeth all things, struck him with an incurable and an invisible plague. For as soon as he had ended these words, a dreadful pain in his bowels came upon him, and bitter torments of the inner parts.

6 And indeed very justly, seeing he had tormented the bowels of others with many and new torments, albeit he by no means ceased from his malice. **7** Moreover being filled with pride, breathing out fire in his rage against the Jews, and commanding the matter to be hastened, it happened as he was going with violence that he fell from the chariot, so that his limbs were much pained by a grievous bruising of the body. **8** Thus he that seemed to himself to command even the waves of the sea, being proud above the condition of man, and to weigh the heights of the mountains in a balance, now being cast down to the ground, was carried in a litter, bearing witness to the manifest power of God in himself: **9** So that worms swarmed out of the body of this man, and whilst he lived in sorrow and pain, his flesh fell off, and the filthiness of his smell was noisome to the army. **10** And the man that thought a little before he could reach to the stars of heaven, no man could endure to carry, for the intolerable stench.

11 And by this means, being brought from his great pride, he began to come to the knowledge of himself, being admonished by the scourge of God, his pains increasing every moment. **12** And when he himself could not now abide his own stench, he spoke thus: It is just to be subject to God, and that a mortal man should not equal himself to God. **13** Then this wicked man prayed to the Lord, of whom he was not like to obtain mercy. **14** And the city to which he was going in haste to lay it even with the ground, and to make it a, common buryingplace, he now desireth to make free. **15** And the Jews whom he said he would not account worthy to be so much as buried, but would give them up to be devoured by the birds and wild beasts, and would utterly destroy them with their children, he now promiseth to make equal with the Athenians.

16 The holy temple also which before he had spoiled, he

promiseth to adorn with goodly gifts, and to multiply the holy vessels, and to allow out of his revenues the charges pertaining to the sacrifices. **17** Yea also, that he would become a Jew himself, and would go through every place of the earth, and declare the power of God. **18** But his pains not ceasing (for the just judgment of God was come upon him) despairing of life he wrote to the Jews in the manner of a supplication, a letter in these words: **19** To his very good subjects the Jews, Antiochus king and ruler wisheth much health and welfare, and happiness. **20** If you and your children are well, and if all matters go with you to your mind, we give very great thanks.

21 As for me, being infirm, but yet kindly remembering you, returning out of the places of Persia, and being taken with a grievous disease, I thought it necessary to take care for the common good: **22** Not distrusting my life, but having great hope to escape the sickness. **23** But considering that my father also, at what time he led an army into the higher countries, appointed who should reign after him: **24** To the end that if any thing contrary to expectation should fall out, or any bad tidings should be brought, they that were in the countries, knowing to whom the whole government was left, might not be troubled. **25** Moreover, considering that neighbouring princes and borderers wait for opportunities, and expect what shall be the event, I have appointed my son Antiochus king, whom I often recommended to many of you, when I went into the higher provinces: and I have written to him what I have joined here below.

26 I pray you therefore, and request of you, that remembering favours both public and private, you will every man of you continue to be faithful to me and to my son. **27** For I trust that he will behave with moderation and humanity, and following my intentions, will be gracious unto you. **28** Thus the murderer and blasphemer, being grievously struck, as himself had treated others, died a miserable death in a strange country among the mountains. **29** But Philip that was brought up with him, carried away his body: and out of fear of the son of Antiochus, went into Egypt to Ptolemee Philometor.

Chapter 10

1 But Machabeus, and they that were with him, by the protection of the Lord, recovered the temple and the city again. **2** But he threw down the altars, which the heathens had set up in the streets, as also the temples of the idols. **3** And having purified the temple, they made another altar: and taking fire out of the fiery stones, they offered sacrifices after two years, and set forth incense, and lamps, and the loaves of proposition. **4** And when they had done these things, they besought the Lord, lying prostrate on the ground, that they might no more fall into such evils; but if they should at any time sin, that they might be chastised by him more gently, and not be delivered up to barbarians and blasphemous men. **5** Now upon the same day that the temple had been polluted by the strangers, on the very same day it was cleansed again, to wit, on the five and twentieth day of the month of Casleu.

6 And they kept eight days with joy, after the manner of the feast of the tabernacles, remembering that not long before they had kept the feast of the tabernacles when they were in the mountains, and in dens like wild beasts. **7** Therefore they now, carried boughs, and green branches, and palms for Him that had given them good success in cleansing his place. **8** And they ordained by a common statute, and decree, that all the nation of the Jews should keep those days every year. **9** And this was the end of Antiochus that was called the Illustrious. **10** But now we will relate the acts of Eupator the son of that wicked Antiochus, abridging the account of the evils that happened in the wars.

11 For when he was come to the crown, he appointed over the affairs of his realm one Lysias, general of the army of Phenicia and Syria. **12** For Ptolemee that was called Macer, was determined to be strictly just to the Jews, and especially by reason of the wrong that had been done them, and to deal peaceably with them. **13** But being accused for this to Eupator by his friends, and being oftentimes called traitor, because he had left Cyprus which Philometor had committed to him, and coming over to Antiochus the Illustrious, had revolted also from him, he put an end to his life by poison. **14** But Gorgias, who was governor of the holds, taking with him the strangers, often fought against the Jews. **15** And the [faithless] Jews that occupied the most commodious hold, received those that were driven out of Jerusalem, and attempted to make war.

16 Then they that were with Machabeus, beseeching the Lord by prayers to be their helper, made a strong attack upon the strong holds of the Idumeans: **17** And assaulting them with great force, won the holds, killed them that came in the way, and slew altogether no fewer than twenty thousand. **18** And whereas some were fled into very strong towers, having all manner of provision to sustain a siege, **19** Machabeus left Simon and Joseph, and Zacheus, and them that were with them in sufficient number to besiege them, and departed to those expeditions which urged more. **20** Now they that were with Simon, being led with covetousness, were persuaded for the sake of money by some that were in the towers: and taking seventy thousand didrachmas, let some of them escape.

21 But when it was told Machabeus what was done, he assembled the rulers of the people, and accused those men that they had sold their brethren for money, having let their adversaries escape. **22** So he put these traitors to death, and forthwith took the two towers. **23** And having good success in arms and in all things he took in hand, he slew more than twenty thousand in the two holds. **24** But Timotheus who before had been overcome by the Jews, having called together a multitude of foreign troops, and assembled horsemen out of Asia, came as though he would take Judea by force of arms. **25** But Machabeus and they that were with him, when he drew near, prayed to the Lord, sprinkling earth upon their heads and girding their loins with haircloth,

26 And lying prostrate at the foot of the altar, besought him to be merciful to them, and to be an enemy to their enemies, and an adversary to their adversaries, as the law saith. **27** And so after prayer taking their arms, they went forth further from the city, and when they were come very near the enemies they rested. **28** But as soon as the sun was risen both sides joined battle: the one part having with their valour the Lord for a surety of victory and success: but the other side making their rage their leader in battle. **29** But when they were in the heat of the engagement there appeared to the enemies from heaven five men upon horses, comely with golden bridles, conducting the Jews: **30** Two of whom took Machabeus between them, and covered him on every side with their arms, and kept him safe: but cast darts and fireballs against the enemy, so that they fell down, being both confounded with blindness, and filled with trouble.

31 And there were slain twenty thousand five hundred, and six hundred horsemen. **32** But Timotheus fled into Gazara a strong hold, where Chereas was governor. **33** Then Machabeus, and they that were with him, cheerfully laid siege to the fortress four days. **34** But they that were within, trusting to the strength of the place, blasphemed exceedingly, and cast forth abominable words. **35** But when the fifth day appeared, twenty young men of them that were with Machabeus, inflamed in their minds because of the blasphemy, approached manfully to the wall, and pushing forward with fierce courage got up upon it.

36 Moreover others also getting up after them, went to set fire to the towers and the gates, and to burn the blasphemers alive. **37** And having for two days together pillaged and sacked the fortress, they killed Timotheus [different from Timotheus mentioned in 1ˢᵗ Machabees and in the subsequent chapter], who was found hid in a certain place: they slew also his brother Chereas, and Apollophanes. **38** And when this was done, they blessed the Lord with hymns and thanksgiving, who had done great things in Israel, and given them the victory.

Chapter 11

1 A short time after this Lysias the king's lieutenant, and cousin, and who had chief charge over all the affairs, being greatly displeased with what had happened, **2** Gathered together fourscore thousand men, and all the horsemen, and came against the Jews, thinking to take the city, and make it a habitation of the Gentiles: **3** And to make a gain of the temple, as of the other temples of the Gentiles, and to set the high priesthood to sale every year: **4** Never considering the power of God, but puffed up in mind, and trusting in the multitude of his foot soldiers, and the thousands of his horsemen, and his fourscore elephants. **5** So he came into Judea, and approaching to Bethsura, which was in a narrow place, the space of five furlongs from Jerusalem, he laid siege to that fortress.

6 But when Machabeus and they that were with him, understood that the strong holds were besieged, they and all the people besought the Lord with lamentations and tears, that he would send a good angel to save Israel. **7** Then Machabeus himself, first taking his arms, exhorted the rest to expose themselves together with him, to the danger, and to succour their brethren. **8** And when they were going forth together with a willing mind, there appeared at Jerusalem a horseman going before them in white clothing, with golden armour, shaking a spear. **9** Then they all together blessed the merciful Lord, and took great courage, being ready to break through not only men, but also the fiercest beasts, and walls of iron. **10** So they went on courageously, having a helper from Heaven, and the Lord who shewed mercy to them.

11 And rushing violently upon the enemy, like lions, they slew of them eleven thousand footmen, and one thousand six hundred horsemen: **12** And put all the rest to flight: many of them being wounded, escaped naked: yea and Lysias himself fled away shamefully, and escaped. **13** And as he was a man of understanding considering with himself, the loss he had suffered, and perceiving that the Hebrews could not be overcome, because they relied upon the help of the Almighty God, he sent to them: **14** And promised that he would agree to all things that are just, and that he would persuade the king to be their friend. **15** Then Machabeus consented to the request of Lysias, providing for the common good in all things, and whatsoever Machabeus wrote to Lysias concerning the Jews, the king allowed of.

16 For there were letters written to the Jews from Lysias, to this effect: Lysias to the people of the Jews, greeting. **17** John and Abesalom who were sent from you, delivering your writings, requested that I would accomplish those things which were signified by them. **18** Therefore whatsoever things could be reported to the king I have represented to him: and he hath granted as much as the matter permitted. **19** If therefore you will keep yourselves loyal in affairs, hereafter also I will endeavour to be a means of your good. **20** But as concerning other particulars, I have given orders by word both to these, and to them that are sent by me, to commune with you.

21 Fare ye well. In the year one hundred and forty-eight, the four and twentieth day of the month of Dioscorus. **22** But the king's letter contained these words: King Antiochus to Lysias his brother, greeting. **23** Our father being translated amongst the gods, we are desirous that they that are in our realm should live quietly, and apply themselves diligently to their own concerns, **24** And we have heard that the Jews would not consent to my father to turn to the rites of the Greeks, but that they would keep to their own manner of living, and therefore that they request us to allow them to live after their own laws. **25** Wherefore being desirous that this nation also should be at rest, we have ordained and decreed, that the temple should be restored to them, and that they may live according to the custom of their ancestors.

26 Thou shalt do well therefore to send to them, and grant them peace, that our pleasure being known, they may be of good comfort, and look to their own affairs. **27** But the king's letter to the Jews was in this manner: King Antiochus to the senate of the Jews, and to the rest of the Jews, greeting. **28** If you are well, you are as we desire, we ourselves also are well. **29** Menelaus came to us, saying that you desired to come down to your countrymen, that are with us. **30** We grant therefore a safe conduct to all that come and go, until the thirtieth day of the month of Xanthicus,

31 That the Jews may use their own kind of meats, and their own laws as before, and that none of them any manner of ways be molested for things which have been done by ignorance. **32** And we have sent also Menelaus to speak to you. **33** Fare ye well. In the year one hundred and forty-eight, the fifteenth day of the month of Xanthicus. **34** The Romans also sent them a letter, to this effect. Quintus Memmius, and Titus Manilius, ambassadors of the Romans, to the people of the Jews, greeting. **35** Whatsoever Lysias the king's cousin hath granted you, we also have granted.

36 But touching such things as he thought should be referred to the king, after you have diligently conferred among yourselves, send some one forthwith, that we may decree as it is convenient for you: for we are going to Antioch. **37** And therefore make haste to write back, that we may know of what mind you are. **38** Fare ye well. In the year one hundred and forty-eight, the fifteenth day of the month of Xanthicus.

Chapter 12

1 When these covenants were made, Lysias went to the king, and the Jews gave themselves to husbandry. **2** But they that were behind, namely, Timotheus and Apollonius the son of Genneus, also Hieronymus, and Demophon, and besides them Nicanor the governor of Cyprus, would not suffer them to live in peace, and to be quiet. **3** The men of Joppe also were guilty of this kind of wickedness: they desired the Jews who dwelt among them to go with their wives and children into the boats, which they had prepared, as though they had no enmity to them. **4** Which when they had consented to, according to the common decree of the city, suspecting nothing, because of the peace: when they were gone forth into the deep, they drowned no fewer than two hundred of them. **5** But as soon as Judas heard of this cruelty done to his countrymen, he commanded the men that were with him: and after having called upon God the just judge,

6 He came against those murderers of his brethren, and set the haven on fire in the night, burnt the boats, and slew with the sword them that escaped from the fire. **7** And when he had done these things in this manner, he departed as if he would return again, and root out all the Joppites. **8** But when he understood that the men of Jamnia also designed to do in like manner to the Jews that dwelt among them, **9** He came upon the Jamnites also by night, and set the haven on fire with the ships, so that the light of the fire was seen at Jerusalem two hundred and forty furlongs off. **10** And when they were now gone from thence nine furlongs, and were marching towards Timotheus, five thousand footmen and five hundred horsemen of the Arabians set upon them.

11 And after a hard fight, in which by the help of God they got the victory, the rest of the Arabians being overcome, besought Judas for peace, promising to give him pastures, and to assist him in other things. **12** And Judas thinking that they might be profitable indeed in many things, promised them peace, and after having joined hands, they departed to their tents. **13** He also laid siege to a certain strong city, encompassed with bridges and walls, and inhabited by multitudes of different nations, the name of which is Casphin. **14** But they that were within it, trusting in the strength of the walls, and the provision of victuals, behaved in a more negligent manner, and provoked Judas with railing and blaspheming, and uttering such words as were not to be spoken. **15** But Machabeus calling upon the great Lord of the world, who without any battering rams or engines of war threw down the walls of Jericho in the time of Josue, fiercely assaulted the walls.

16 And having taken the city by the will of the Lord, he made an unspeakable slaughter, so that a pool adjoining of two furlongs broad seemed to run with the blood of the slain. **17** From thence they departed seven hundred and fifty furlongs, and came to Characa to the Jews that are called Tubianites. **18** But as for Timotheus, they found him not in those places, for before he had dispatched any thing he went back, having left a very strong garrison in a certain hold: **19** But Dositheus, and Sosipater, who were captains with Machabeus, slew them that were left by Timotheus in the hold, to the number of ten thousand men. **20** And Machabeus having set in order about him six thousand men, and divided them by bands, went forth against Timotheus, who had with him a hundred and twenty thousand footmen, and two thousand five hundred horsemen.

21 Now when Timotheus had knowledge of the coming of Judas, he sent the women and children, and the other baggage before him into a fortress, called Carnion: for it was impregnable and hard to come at, by reason of the straitness of the places. **22** But when the first band of Judas came in sight, the enemies were struck with fear, by the presence of God, who seeth all things, and they were put to flight one from another, so that they were often thrown down by their own companions, and wounded with the strokes of their own swords. **23** But Judas was vehemently earnest in punishing the profane, of whom he slew thirty thousand men. **24** And Timotheus himself fell into the hands of the band of Dositheus and Sosipater, and with many prayers he besought them to let him go with his life, because he had the parents and brethren of many of the Jews, who, by his death, might happen to be deceived. **25** And when he had given his faith that he would restore them according to the agreement, they let him go without hurt, for the saving of their brethren.

26 Then Judas went away to Carnion, where he slew five and twenty thousand persons. **27** And after he had put to flight and destroyed these, he removed his army to Ephron, a strong city, wherein there dwelt a multitude of divers nations: and stout young men standing upon the walls made a vigorous resistance: and in this place there were many engines of war, and a provision of darts. **28** But when they had invocated the Almighty, who with his power breaketh the strength of the enemies, they took the city; and slew five and twenty thousand of them that were within. **29** From thence they departed to Scythopolis [formerly, Bethsan], which lieth six hundred furlongs from Jerusalem. **30** But the Jews that were among the Scythopolitans testifying that they were used kindly by them, and that even in the times of their adversity they had treated them with humanity:

31 They gave them thanks exhorting them to be still friendly to their nation, and so they came to Jerusalem, the feast of the weeks being at hand. **32** And after Pentecost they marched against Gorgias the governor of Idumea. **33** And he came out with three thousand footmen, and four hundred horsemen. **34** And when they had joined battle, it happened that a few of the Jews were slain. **35** But Dositheus, a horseman, one of Bacenor's band, a valiant man, took hold of Gorgias: and when he would have taken him alive, a certain horseman of the Thracians came upon him, and cut off his shoulder: and so Gorgias escaped to Maresa.

36 But when they that were with Esdrin had fought long, and were weary, Judas called upon the Lord to be their helper, and leader of the battle: **37** Then beginning in his own language, and singing hymns with a loud voice, he put Gorgias' soldiers to flight. **38** So Judas having gathered together his army, came into the city Odollam: and when the seventh day came, they purified themselves according to the custom, and kept the sabbath in the place. **39** And the day following Judas came with his company, to take away the bodies of them that were slain, and to bury them with their kinsmen, in the sepulchres of their fathers. **40** And they found under the coats of the slain some of the donaries of the idols of Jamnia, which the law forbiddeth to the Jews: so that all plainly saw, that for this cause they were slain.

41 Then they all blessed the just judgment of the Lord, who had discovered the things that were hidden. **42** And so betaking themselves to prayers, they besought him, that the sin which had been committed might be forgotten. But the most valiant Judas exhorted the people to keep themselves from sin, forasmuch as they saw before their eyes what had happened, because of the sins of those that were slain. **43** And making a gathering, he sent twelve thousand drachms of silver to Jerusalem for sacrifice to be offered for the sins of the dead, thinking well and religiously concerning the resurrection, **44** (For if he had not hoped that they that were slain should rise again, it would have seemed superfluous and vain to pray for the dead,) **45** And because he considered that they who had fallen asleep with godliness, had great grace laid up for them.

46 It is therefore a holy and wholesome thought to pray for the dead, that they may be loosed from sins.

Chapter 13

1 In the year one hundred and forty-nine, Judas understood that Antiochus Eupator was coming with a multitude against Judea, **2** And with him Lysias the regent, who had charge over the affairs of the realm, having with him a hundred and ten thousand footmen, five thousand horsemen, twenty-two elephants, and three hundred chariots armed with hooks. **3** Menelaus also joined himself with them: and with great deceitfulness besought Antiochus, not for the welfare of his country, but in hopes that he should be appointed chief ruler. **4** But the King of kings stirred up the mind of Antiochus against the sinner, and upon Lysias suggesting that he was the cause of all the evils, he commanded (as the custom is with them) that he should be apprehended and put to death in the same place. **5** Now there was in that place a tower fifty cubits high, having a heap of ashes on every side: this had a prospect steep down.

6 From thence he commanded the sacrilegious wretch to be thrown down into the ashes, all men thrusting him forward unto death. **7** And by such a law it happened that Menelaus the transgressor of the law was put to death: not having so much as burial in the earth. **8** And indeed very justly, for insomuch as he had committed many sins against the altar of God, the fire and ashes of which were holy: he was condemned to die in ashes. **9** But the king, with his mind full of rage, came on to shew himself worse to the Jews than his father was. **10** Which, when Judas understood, he commanded the people to call upon the Lord day and night, that as he had always done, so now also he would help them:

11 Because they were afraid to be deprived of the law, and of their country, and of the holy temple: and that he would not suffer the people, that had of late taken breath for a little while, to be again in subjection to blasphemous nations. **12** So when they had all done this together, and had craved mercy of the Lord with weeping and fasting, lying prostrate on the ground for three days continually, Judas exhorted them to make themselves ready. **13** But he with the ancients determined, before the king should bring his army into Judea, and make himself master of the city, to go out, and to commit the event of the thing to the judgment of the Lord. **14** So committing all to God, the creator of the world, and having exhorted his people to fight manfully, and to stand up even to death for the laws, the temple, the city, their country, and citizens: he placed his army about Modin. **15** And having given his company for a watchword, The victory of God, with most valiant chosen young men, he set upon the king's quarter by night, and slew four thousand men in the camp, and the greatest of the elephants, with them that had been upon him,

16 And having filled the camp of the enemies with exceeding great fear and tumult, they went off with good success. **17** Now this was done at the break of day, by the protection and help of the Lord. **18** But the king having taken a taste of the hardiness of the Jews, attempted to take the strong places by policy: **19** And he marched with his army to Bethsura, which was a strong hold of the

Jews: but he was repulsed, he failed, he lost his men. **20** Now Judas sent necessaries to them that were within.

21 But Rhodocus, one of the Jews' army, disclosed the secrets to the enemies, so he was sought out, and taken up, and put in prison. **22** Again the king treated with them that were in Bethsura: gave his right hand: took theirs: and went away. **23** He fought with Judas: and was overcome. And when he understood that Philip, who had been left over the affairs, had rebelled at Antioch, he was in a consternation of mind, and entreating the Jews, and yielding to them, he swore to all things that seemed reasonable, and, being reconciled, offered sacrifices, honoured the temple, and left gifts. **24** He embraced Machabeus, and made him governor and prince from Ptolemais unto the Gerrenians. **25** But when he was come to Ptolemais, the men of that city were much displeased with the conditions of the peace, being angry for fear they should break the covenant.

26 Then Lysias went up to the judgment seat, and set forth the reason, and appeased the people, and returned to Antioch: and thus matters went with regard to the king's coming and his return.

Chapter 14

1 But after the space of three years Judas, and they that were with him, understood that Demetrius the son of Seleucus was come up with a great power, and a navy by the haven of Tripolis to places proper for his purpose. **2** And had made himself master of the countries against Antiochus, and his general Lysias. **3** Now one Alcimus, who had been chief priest, but had wilfully defiled himself in the time of mingling with the heathens, seeing that there was no safety for him, nor access to the altar, **4** Came to king Demetrius in the year one hundred and fifty, presenting unto him a crown of gold, and a palm, and besides these, some boughs which seemed to belong to the temple. And that day indeed he held his peace. **5** But having gotten a convenient time to further his madness, being called to counsel by Demetrius, and asked what the Jews relied upon, and what were their counsels,

6 He answered thereunto: They among the Jews that are called Assideans, of whom Judas Machabeus is captain, nourish wars, and raise seditions, and will not suffer the realm to be in peace. **7** For I also being deprived of my ancestors' glory (I mean of the high priesthood) am now come hither: **8** Principally indeed out of fidelity to the king's interests, but in the next place also to provide for the good of my countrymen: for all our nation suffereth much from the evil proceedings of those men. **9** Wherefore, O king, seeing thou knowest all these things, take care, I beseech thee, both

208

of the country, and of our nation, according to thy humanity which is known to all men, **10** For as long as Judas liveth, it is not possible that the state should be quiet.

11 Now when this man had spoken to this effect, the rest also of the king's friends, who were enemies of Judas, incensed Demetrius against him. **12** And forthwith he sent Nicanor, the commander over the elephants, governor into Judea: **13** Giving him in charge, to take Judas himself: and disperse all them that were with him, and to make Alcimus the high priest of the great temple. **14** Then the Gentiles who had fled out of Judea from Judas, came to Nicanor by flocks, thinking the miseries and calamities of the Jews to be the welfare of their affairs. **15** Now when the Jews heard of Nicanor's coming, and that the nations were assembled against them, they cast earth upon their heads, and made supplication to him, who chose his people to keep them for ever, and who protected his portion by evident signs.

16 Then at the commandment of their captain, they forthwith removed from the place where they were, and went to the town of Dessau, to meet them. **17** Now Simon the brother of Judas had joined battle with Nicanor, but was frightened with the sudden coming of the adversaries. **18** Nevertheless Nicanor hearing of the valour of Judas' companions, and the greatness of courage with which they fought for their country, was afraid to try the matter by the sword. **19** Wherefore he sent Posidonius, and Theodotius, and Matthias before to present and receive the right hands. **20** And when there had been a consultation thereupon, and the captain had acquainted the multitude with it, they) were all of one mind to consent to covenants.

21 So they appointed a day upon which they might commune together by themselves: and seats were brought out, and set for each one. **22** But Judas ordered men to be ready in convenient places, lest some mischief might be suddenly practiced by the enemies: so they made an agreeable conference. **23** And Nicanor abode in Jerusalem, and did no wrong, but sent away the flocks of the multitudes that had been gathered together. **24** And Judas was always dear to him from the heart, and he was well affected to the man. **25** And he desired him to marry a wife, and to have children. So he married: he lived quietly, and they lived in common.

26 But Alcimus seeing the love they had one to another, and the covenants, came to Demetrius, and told him that Nicanor assented to the foreign interest, for that he meant to make Judas, who was a traitor to the kingdom, his successor. **27** Then the king being in a rage and provoked with this man's wicked accusations, wrote to Nicanor, signifying, that he was greatly displeased with the covenant of friendship: and that he commanded him nevertheless to send Machabeus prisoner in all haste to Antioch. **28** When this was known, Nicanor was in a consternation, and took it grievously that he should make void the articles that were agreed upon, having received no injury from the man. **29** But because he could not oppose the king, he watched an opportunity to comply with the orders. **30** But when Machabeus perceived that Nicanor was more stern to him, and that when they met together as usual he behaved himself in a rough manner: and was sensible that this rough behaviour came not of good, he gathered together a few of his men, and hid himself from Nicanor.

31 But he finding himself notably prevented by the man, came to the great and holy temple: and commanded the priests that were offering the accustomed sacrifices, to deliver him the man. **32** And when they swore unto him, that they knew not where the man was whom he sought, he stretched out his hand to the temple, **33** And swore, saying: Unless you deliver Judas prisoner to me, I will lay this temple of God even with the ground, and will beat down the altar, and I will dedicate this temple to Bacchus. **34** And when he had spoken thus he departed. But the priests stretching forth their hands to heaven, called upon him that was ever the defender of their nation, saying in this manner: **35** Thou, O Lord of all things, who wantest nothing, wast pleased that the temple of thy habitation should be amongst us.

36 Therefore now, O Lord the holy of all holies, keep this house for ever undefiled which was lately cleansed. **37** Now Razias, one of the ancients of Jerusalem, was accused to Nicanor, a man that was a lover of the city, and of good report, who for his affection was called the father of the Jews. **38** This man, for a long time, had held fast his purpose of keeping himself pure in the Jews' religion, and was ready to expose his body and life, that he might persevere therein. **39** So Nicanor being willing to declare the hatred that he bore the Jews, sent five hundred soldiers to take him. **40** For he thought by insnaring him to hurt the Jews very much.

41 Now as the multitude sought to rush into his house, and to break open the door, and to set fire to it, when he was ready to be taken, he struck himself with his sword: **42** Choosing to die nobly rather than to fall into the hands of the wicked, and to suffer abuses unbecoming his noble birth. **43** But whereas through haste he missed of giving himself a sure wound, and the crowd was breaking into the doors, he ran boldly to the wall, and manfully threw himself down to the crowd: **44** But they quickly making room for his fall, he came upon the midst of the neck. **45** And as he had yet breath in him, being inflamed in mind he arose: and while his blood ran down with a great stream, and he was grievously wounded, he ran through the crowd:

46 And standing upon a steep rock, when he was now almost without blood, grasping his bowels with both hands, he cast them upon the throng, calling upon the Lord of life and spirit, to restore these to him again: and so he departed this life.

Chapter 15

1 But when Nicanor understood that Judas was in the places of Samaria, he purposed to set upon him with all violence on the sabbath day. **2** And when the Jews that were constrained to follow him, said: Do not act so fiercely and barbarously, but give honour to the day that is sanctified: and reverence him that beholdeth all things: **3** That unhappy man asked, if there were a mighty One in heaven, that had commanded the sabbath day to be kept. **4** And when they answered: There is the living Lord himself in heaven, the mighty One, that commanded the seventh day to be kept, **5** Then he said: And I am mighty upon the earth, and I command to take arms, and to do the king's business. Nevertheless he prevailed not to accomplish his design.

6 So Nicanor being puffed up with exceeding great pride, thought to set up a public monument of his victory over Judas. **7** But Machabeus ever trusted with all hope that God would help them. **8** And he exhorted his people not to fear the coming of the nations, but to remember the help they had before received from heaven, and now to hope for victory from the Almighty. **9** And speaking to them out of the law, and the prophets, and withal putting them in mind of the battles they had fought before, he made them more cheerful: **10** Then after he had encouraged them, he shewed withal the falsehood of the Gentiles, and their breach of oaths.

11 So he armed every one of them, not with defence of shield and spear, but with very good speeches and exhortations, and told them a dream worthy to be believed, whereby he rejoiced them all. **12** Now the vision was in this manner: Onias who had been high priest, a good and virtuous man, modest in his looks, gentle in his manners, and graceful in his speech, and who from a child was exercised in virtues, holding up his hands, prayed for all the people of the Jews: **13** After this there appeared also another man, admirable for age, and glory, and environed with great beauty and majesty: **14** Then Onias answering, said: This is a lover of his brethren, and of the people of Israel: this is he that prayeth much for the people, and for all the holy city, Jeremias the prophet of God. **15** Whereupon Jeremias stretched forth his right hand, and gave to Judas a sword of gold, saying:

16 Take this holy sword a gift from God, wherewith thou shalt overthrow the adversaries of my people Israel. **17** Thus being exhorted with the words of Judas, which were very good, and proper to stir up the courage, and strengthen the hearts of the young men, they resolved to fight, and to set upon them manfully: that valour might decide the matter, because the holy city and the temple were in danger. **18** For their concern was less for their wives, and children, and for their brethren, and kinsfolks: but their greatest and principal fear was for the holiness of the temple. **19** And they also that were in the city, had no little concern for them that were to be engaged in battle. **20** And now when all expected what judgment would be given, and the enemies were at hand, and the army was set in array, the beasts and the horsemen ranged in convenient places,

21 Machabeus considering the coming of the multitude, and the divers preparations of armour, and the fierceness of the beasts, stretching out his hands to heaven, called upon the Lord, that worketh wonders, who giveth victory to them that are worthy, not according to the power of their arms, but according as it seemeth good to him. **22** And in his prayer he said after this manner: Thou, O Lord, who didst send thy angel in the time of Ezechias king of Juda, and didst kill a hundred and eighty-five thousand of the army of Sennacherib: **23** Send now also, O Lord of heaven, thy good angel before us, for the fear and dread of the greatness of thy arm, **24** That they may be afraid, who come with blasphemy against thy holy people. And thus he concluded his prayer. **25** But Nicanor, and they that were with him came forward, with trumpets and songs.

26 But Judas, and they that were with him, encountered them, calling upon God by prayers: **27** So fighting with their hands, but praying to the Lord with their hearts, they slew no less than five and thirty thousand, being greatly cheered with the presence of God. **28** And when the battle was over, and they were returning with joy, they understood that Nicanor was slain in his armour. **29** Then making a shout, and a great noise, they blessed the Almighty Lord in their own language. **30** And Judas, who was altogether ready, in body and mind, to die for his countrymen, commanded that Nicanor's head, and his hand with the shoulder should be cut off, and carried to Jerusalem.

31 And when he was come thither, having called together his countrymen, and the priests to the altar, he sent also for them that were in the castle, **32** And shewing them the head of Nicanor, and the wicked hand, which he had stretched out, with proud boasts, against the holy house of the Almighty God, **33** He commanded also, that the tongue of the wicked Nicanor, should be cut out and given by pieces to birds, and the hand of the furious man to be hanged up over against the temple. **34** Then all blessed the Lord of heaven, saying: Blessed be he that hath kept his own place undefiled. **35** And he hung up Nicanor's head in the top of the castle, that it might be an evident and manifest sign of the help of God.

36 And they all ordained by a common decree, by no means to let this day pass without solemnity: **37** But to celebrate the thirteenth day of the month of Adar, called, in the Syrian language, the day before Mardochias' day. **38** So these things being done with relation to Nicanor, and from that time the city being possessed by the Hebrews, I also will here make an end of my narration. **39** Which if I have done well, and as it becometh the history, it is what I desired: but if not so perfectly [not referring to the truth of the story, but to style or manner], it must be pardoned me. **40** For as it is hurtful to drink always wine, or always water, but pleasant to use sometimes the one, and sometimes the other: so if the speech be always nicely framed, it will not be grateful to the readers. But here it shall be ended.